TOLERANCE AND TRUTH
IN RELIGION

Dedicated to the Venerable Theological Faculty
of the University of Marburg/Lahn
as a Sign of Gratitude
for the Bestowal of an Honorary Doctorate
of Religious Sciences

—G. M.

TOLERANCE AND TRUTH IN RELIGION

Gustav Mensching

Translated
by
H.-J. Klimkeit

Augmented
in Collaboration with
the Author

The University of Alabama Press
University, Alabama

Translated into English from
Toleranz und Wahrheit in der Religion
Copyright © 1955 by Quelle & Meyer, Heidelberg, West Germany
English translation Copyright © 1971 by
THE UNIVERSITY OF ALABAMA PRESS
ISBN 0-8173-6701-2
Library of Congress Catalog Card Number 79-169495
Manufactured in the United States of America

Contents

Acknowledgments

This book introduces to the English-speaking world the thinking of one of the leading figures in comparative religion in Germany today. In the course of translation, it became evident that rendering ideas as they are developed here into another language (and a foreign tongue, at that) is necessarily an interpretive attempt. But since the hermeneutical criteria for such an undertaking were gained in years of study under the author, the interpretive venture is, perhaps, legitimate. Yet the translator assumes full responsibility for any errors which may have crept in or been overlooked.

It is the wish of the translator at this point to thank all those who were instrumental in the publication of this English version. First and foremost thanks are due to the University of Alabama Press for their great patience and understanding shown me as my work proceeded in bits of spare time between other obligations. Two American scholars who were most helpful in clearing the way for publication are James Luther Adams, Professor Emeritus of Harvard Divinity School, and Professor William E. Beardslee of Emory University. I am grateful for their advice and encouragement in bringing out this English translation.

H.-J. K.

Translator's Preface

Gustav Mensching has devoted his life work to understanding and interpreting the religious traditions of men of diverse faiths. In a world growing smaller that is becoming aware of its basically pluralistic character, the questions raised by an approach such as his are gaining increasing relevance.

Mensching's thinking has been decisively moulded by his great teacher Rudolf Otto, author of *The Idea of the Holy,* under whom he studied at Marburg in the early 1920s. It was at Marburg that Mensching earned his doctorate in 1924, and it was Marburg University that paid tribute to him as a scholar by bestowing upon him in 1951 the honorary degree of Doctor of Religious Sciences. This book, the first of the author's to be translated into English *in toto,* was dedicated to the Marburg Theological Faculty for that distinction.

Mensching started his career as a lecturer in the History of Religions at the Brunswick Institute of Technology near his native Hanover. A study on *Das Heilige Schweigen* (Sacred Silence) established his reputation as a scholar, and in 1927 he was called to the State University of Latvia to take the chair of Religious History there. After teaching at Riga for eight years, he went to Bonn, where he was to remain until he became emeritus in 1970.*

---

* Mensching took a stand against the race ideology of the Third Reich in the year right after this regime came to power. His major altercation with Nazi ideology could be published only after World War II.

Though outwardly not very eventful, the author's life has been most productive and fruitful in terms of academic and scholarly activity. A long and still growing list of books and essays on various topics of Comparative Religion reveals his wide interest in manifold problems of religious life.[1] His work in phenomenology is summed up most comprehensively in the volume *Die Religion* (1959), and his interest in sociology of religion is best reflected in the two major volumes *Soziologie der Religion* (2nd ed., 1968) and *Soziologie der grossen Religionen* (1966). This book on *Tolerance and Truth in Religion* takes up issues discussed in these and other works, applying the insight gained earlier to the problems addressed here. These are problems with which the author is very personally concerned, as the reader will sense. This study is, so to speak, an applied Comparative Religion. The author starts out as an historian and phenomenologist of religion, but his inquiry is turned toward questions also pertaining to the modern world and the role of religion in a multiform society today.

Though specific in its orientation, this study should yet be seen on the background of the general thinking of the author. Central concepts forcefully championed, like the idea of religious unity in plurality, can only be understood adequately in view of the concept of the holy and the way it is conceived. We shall therefore sketch a few basic ideas of Mensching's approach to Comparative Religion, leaving aside illustrations which will be found very copious in the book itself.

Religion, as Gustav Mensching defines it, "is experiential encounter with the holy and the responsive actions of man who has been determined by the holy." This characterization is a deliberately formal one. It does not specify the contents of the encounter. In historical reality, the author maintains, encounter with the holy

1. Bibliographies are to be found in: R. Thomas (ed.) *Religion und Religionen: Festschrift für Gustav Mensching zu seinem 65. Geburtstag,* Bonn: L. Röhrscheid, 1967 (Bibl.: O.Wenig); and in: G. Mensching, *Topos und Typos: Motive und Strukturen religiösen Lebens* (Essays in Comparative Religion, ed. by H.-J. Klimkeit for the occasion of the author's 70th birthday), Bonn: L. Röhrscheid, 1971 (Bibl.: U. Vollmer).

can take place in many different ways, through many different objects, and at many different times. And the holy, or "numinous" (a term coined by R. Otto), can be sensed or perceived in many different forms as the holy one in a personal sense (*der Heilige*), as the impersonal holy absolute (*das Heilige*), or as multiplicity of holy beings (*die Heiligen*) or things. However conceived, the basic category of religious experience, then, is that of the holy. It is essentially a category which can never be explained in terms foreign to its own modality. In other words, it cannot be reduced to social, psychological, or other anthropological structures.

But the fact that the holy constitutes religion does not mean that one could construe a universal religion fit for all on that basis, as Deism had attempted to do in its own way. Mensching stresses that religion is only real historically in the multiplicity of religions. There is no such thing as a rationally distilled pure essence of religion in historical reality. The Enlightenment, in endeavoring to abstract the basic essence of religion from its historical setting and organic environment and in then proclaiming this as the true religion through its highly sophisticated concept of a "natural religion" (*religio naturalis*), was depriving religion of its vital roots and basic life. For religions are not constructed systems of intellectually comprehensible truths which could be taught and studied as such, Mensching asserts. They are living organisms possessing their own specific "living cores" or "centers of life." And they are only to be comprehended from this central dimension of their pulsing life.

Although *historically* the essence of religion is not objectively graspable, we can, nevertheless, *theoretically* conceptualize the basic essence of religion as the common element in all historical religions. In fact, says Mensching, this is even necessary for a comprehensive study of religion, for only from such a general platform can we proceed in discerning the specific characteristic differences of the various historical religions. From here, also, we can go on to discern common—and distinguishing—structures, forms, and patterns throughout the world of religions.

According to Mensching, both the phenomena common to all

religions as well as the structural relationships connected with these phenomena are the objects of a comparative study of religion. His is therefore not only a phenomenology of religion, but also a typology and sociology, a study of phenomena as well as their basic forms, principles, and patterns in religious history and society.

Now we may ask, how does Mensching suggest we go about such a study of Comparative Religion?

In his introduction to *Die Religion,* the German scholar stresses that he seeks to approach the world of religious phenomena "not from a preconceived theological or confessional position." He therefore does not wish to bring along and apply for this task any criteria with which one could measure the value or truth of religious ideas and practices. "There are no such criteria for the student of Comparative Religion," he emphasizes. "Whence should he derive them and on what should he base them, if he does not wish to presuppose his own faith as the norm?" [2] Mensching, in his approach, then, strives to be independent of any specific faith-oriented position. Yet he is fully aware that that this does not imply the possibility of completely unconditioned understanding. There is no scholarly study of religious history, he emphasizes, which is "without presuppositions." [3] "Every relevant engagement with religion, its essence and phenomena, presupposes inner participation and the capacity for empathy. Whoever lacks these prerequisites and views the often strange world of religious phenomena from a detached rational perspective will soon turn aside unappreciatively and often disapprovingly." [4]

This was precisely the fault of the early nineteenth century school of Comparative Religion, says Mensching. It tended to rationalize all elements of religious history and fell prey to the fallacy that everything in religion could be comprehended intellectually, without developing any sense or understanding for the life pulsing in the phenomenal forms. Hence, for instance, it could not fully appreciate the inner significance and nonrational meaning of myths and

2. *Die Religion.* Stuttgart: C. E. Schwab, 1959, p. 20.
3. *Ibid.*   4. *Ibid.*

symbols. Such an approach rendered a completely false image of religion and religious views and practices, for it failed to see the living reality in the objective historical facts.

"The main thing," says Mensching, "is to seek the *life* that is effective in and behind the perceived phenomena of religious history." [5] And in pointing to the subtitle of R. Otto's *The Idea of the Holy: An Inquiry into the Nonrational Factor in the Idea of the Divine and its Relation to the Rational,* he suggests that it is exactly the nonrational, the intellectually incomprehensible, merely circumscribable, that is the decisive element in religious life.

Since the life in religion, then, is primarily nonrational, it cannot be fully and comprehensively understood from a merely psychological basis, or in terms of sociological functions, or by other rational-reductionist avenues of approach that are bound to miss its decisive dimension. Mensching postulates categories of interpretation that are not derived from any foreign field of inquiry, but from the subject matter of this study. He refers repeatedly to Schleiermacher, who was perhaps the first to express forcefully the notion that "the spirit of religion can only be understood through itself." [6]

The aim of the author's approach to religion, then, is to go beyond the plane of historical data to the dimension of nonrational organic life and meaning. A comparative study of religion in his sense is thus more than just a museum-like perusal of similar outward facts, for it seeks to go behind the facts. It is largely a study of religious phenomena as symbols. Symbols possess an outward empirical dimension pointing to a live inner meaning. "To grasp the meaning," says the author, "through the empirical reality, the concrete symbol, is to understand the symbol." [7] Mensching's approach to Comparative Religion seeks to be such an understanding.

HANS-J. KLIMKEIT

5. *Ibid.,* p. 12.
6. F. Schleiermacher, *Über die Religion,* 1799, p 285f.
7. *Ibid.,* p. 14.

TOLERANCE AND TRUTH
IN RELIGION

Introduction:
The Present Situation

We live in a world which is rent by a deeper schism than hardly any before. This breach is not to be assessed in terms of the contrast between different spheres of life, as in the case of other diversities and distinctions, but pertains to the very existence of men and of nations. It is that division which is constituted politically by the difference between totalitarian states and "free" nations—as the peoples who are not subservient to a totalitarian yoke call themselves. As the term "free" would indicate, the breach dividing the world—whatever its nature may be in particular—ultimately has to do with the liberty of the individual, with the dignity of man, and with human rights.

Totalitarianism can be not only political, but also religious. We shall describe the analogy between the two forms later on. Let it suffice here to point out that any kind of religious totalitarianism necessarily endangers or suppresses the religious freedom of the individual. The problem of tolerance thus requires a solution by religious mankind.

By tolerance we mean—formally speaking—religious freedom granted the individual to choose and to practice as he wishes.

The two types of totalitarianism that deprive the individual of his freedom relate to one another in a particular manner. The totalitarian state, when outspokenly a-religious—or anti-religious, as in the eastern part of Europe—suppresses religious freedom of the individual in the profane sphere of life and consequently also in the religious area; or, at the least, it restricts liberty and prevents the free development of religious life. A state of this type is intolerant toward religion as such. There are, however, totalitarian states, like Spain, which identify with a particular religion. Here, liberty is not only restricted in a general civil sense, but there also prevails a specific religious intolerance—which applies not to religion as such, but to those forms of faith which deviate from the state creed.

In non-totalitarian countries the state does profess to grant religious freedom, but the individual can nevertheless be affected by the rigidity of religious institutions that enjoy liberty yet are quite totalitarian themselves. There are numerous examples for such situations in modern times. Cardinal Segura, of Spain, issued a pastoral letter [1] in which he maintained that an erring conscience should not enjoy lawful protection in the case of a conflict with a "correctly" oriented conscience. Rather, the state is obliged, he said, to promote the "true religion." Hence the Protestants in Spain should not be able to claim the same rights as the Catholics in the public expression and confession of their faith. This attitude corresponds precisely to Article 6 of the Spanish Constitution (*Fuero de los Españoles*) of 1945, which says, "The confession and the exercise of the Catholic faith, which is the religion of the Spanish state, shall enjoy official protection. No person may be molested on account of his religious conviction in the *private* exercise of his worship. Outward acts of worship or religious demonstrations other than those of the Catholic religion shall not be permitted." [2] It goes without saying that as a consequence the church in Spain has surveillance over education. [3] It is not surprising that, due to the dissemination of the principle mentioned above, various instances of violence against adherents of other religions have been reliably reported in recent times. [4]

Since 1962, the world press has often commented on the so-called "Protestant Statute." The Spanish foreign minister Castiella gave the incentive to this bill and announced its drafting. Its intention is to guarantee the complete equality of all citizens before the law. The head of the state is to be Catholic; but, apart from this provision, every person is to have the right to teach his own religion, to wed according to civil marriage statutes, to establish churches, and to edit prayer books.

However, the Spanish government is not free in its religious decisions, but is bound by the Concordat of 1953, which provides (as did the Concordat of 1851): "The Roman Catholic Apostolic religion continues to be the only religion of the Spanish nation, and shall enjoy all rights and privileges which are due to it according to divine law and canonical right." Even the constitution, Article 6 of which was quoted above, would have to be amended, should this bill be passed.

Such tolerant tendencies have, of course, met with vehement opposition by those who would uphold the national and religious unity of Spain, which has been maintained since the Middle Ages, and which in their eyes now seems endangered by the move toward religious freedom. One of the most relentless opponents is Cardinal Ottaviani. On the occasion of the signing of the Concordat, he declared, "It is true that two criteria and two measures should be employed, one for truth and one for error." This dictum implies that only truth—that is, the Catholic Church's doctrine—has a right to freedom. "Error" cannot be granted liberty.

Spanish bishops also fear the disintegration of confessional unity in Spain should this measure be passed. According to the *Rheinische Post* of April 17, 1965, the Jesuit Eustaquio Guerro, one of the strongest opponents of the Protestant Statute, defines what he calls "the natural right to seek the true religion and to confess it publicly when found. . . . It [this right] takes into consideration the appropriate tolerance which true religion authorizes or prescribes for false religions." It is determined, he says, by "the just restrictions which, in a land where Catholic unity prevails, are to be imposed upon false religions according to the Church's teaching and its whole tradition."

Such opinions stand in marked contrast to the "Declarations" of the Second Vatican Council, which based the universal right of religious freedom upon revelation and reason. Authorities in Spain fear the emergence of a pluralistic society, such as exists in other European and democratic countries—for that, of course, would not be compatible with a totalitarian system. It will therefore certainly take time to enact the Protestant Statute.

Not only authoritarian states that acknowledge *one* state religion (like Spain) are intolerant, but also anti-religious totalitarian states like the Soviet Union and the so-called Third Reich, whose racial and religious persecutions surpassed by far the methods employed by the Inquisition in the Middle Ages. (On p. 188, footnote 22, reference is made to the analogy between the intolerance of sacral totalitarian institutions and modern secular totalitarian states.)

The official opinion expressed by the Catholic Church deviates considerably from the practices in Spain and also from the basic rights proclaimed by that country. There is certainly no lack of evidence for radical intolerance in the Catholic Church. As late as 1832, Pope Gregory XVI, in the encyclical *Mirari vos,* condemned the "madness" (*deliramentum*) of freedom of conscience.[5] And Pius IX, in the Syllabus of 1864, denounced the errors of liberalism and declared that a state may adhere to one faith, the Catholic religion, as the state religion, to the exclusion of all other faiths.[6] This syllabus also reprobated what it called "indifferentism"—a term readily used in Catholic circles for tolerance—because it allows every person to embrace the religion which he holds to be the true one.[7] Pope Pius XII, in a 1954 address to a group of lawyers, gave the official view of the Church: that other faiths not in accordance with the Catholic dogma are erroneous and must be rejected. At the same time, however, he also declared it to be the duty of the Christian statesman to provide for formal toleration of "error" as well as of "truth," since God does not grant power to purge out error by violent means.[8] In this connection, the Pope referred to the parable of the tares among the wheat; the Lord of the harvest allows them to grow to the time of reaping without destroying them. Yet even this view reflects basic intolerance, for it readily comprehends other faiths as erroneous; they are to be rejected, although not to be attacked by force.

A certain turning point was the Second Vatican Council. On October 28, 1965 it issued the "Declaration on the Church and the Non-Christian Religions" and on December 7, 1965, the "Declaration on Religious Freedom." Even though a declaration (*declaratio*) has the lowest degree of authority over a decree (*decretum*) and the Constitution (*constitutio*), principles are expressed in both declarations that, when put into action, would mean a decisive withdrawal from past attitudes and practices (as will be described in the historical part of this book). In order to discern what is new in the background of the existing tradition, we shall discuss the basic principles of the Council documents in greater detail in the chapter on "The Intolerance of Sacred Organizations."

Whereas Catholic theology, in its doctrine on general revelation (*revelatio generalis*), has a means of appreciating the highest values in non-Christian religions as references towards the Christian revelation, the one-sided doctrine of Karl Barth in Protestant theology has lead to a radical rejection of even the term "religion" for Christianity. If it were a religion, maintains Barth, it would be placed on the same level as other religions and considered comparable. Such an idea, however, is categorically denied. The religions are, according to Barth, human attempts to approach God from man's level. They all succumb to His judgment; Christianity alone is given from above. Among the historians of religion it was Johannes Witte who adopted this radical view. Influenced by Karl Barth, he concludes in his book, *Offenbarung nur in der Bibel* [Revelation in the Bible alone] (1937), "revelation is given in the Bible alone; it is complete and final, right up to the end of time. Nowhere else has revelation become real for man; nowhere else is it possible" (p. 33).

We need not document this theological opinion further. Our intention is merely to point out that dialectic theology in Protestantism is at present far more intolerant than Catholic theology.[9] This intolerance within Protestant theology pertains not only to non-Christian religions, but also to deviating confessions and church groups within Protestantism itself. During a Bavarian State Synod meeting, for example, in discussing a planned "ecclesiastical order of life," this proposal was made: "Whoever disassociates himself from the Protestant Lutheran Church disregards the gifts which God has given him in the community of His church. He renounces the Lord Jesus Christ by his denial of the church. Futhermore, whoever attaches himself to another Christian church or community abandons the pure doctrine of his own church." [10]

The present situation as we have sketched it is thus dominated by a far-reaching intolerance in Christian churches. It is furthermore a mark of our time that the non-Christian world has come closer to the West than ever before. Buddhism has established congregations in Europe which are constantly on the increase.[11] The message of India has spread throughout the Western world through important publications by prominent personalities like the philosopher and one-time president of India, Radhakrishnan.[12] That message has found many followers. Islam also undertakes missionary work in the West and founds congregations, for instance, through the Ahmadiya mission.[13] Reference must also be made in this connection to the Bahai religion. Springing from Islam, it has developed into an independent religious community and strives for a realization of the truth given in all faiths. All these religions and religious movements have come from the East and confront Western man with an abundance of spiritual thought. Coming to grips with them is therefore the need of the hour.

A prudent confrontation, one that is not determined by an unreflective emotional attitude, will unquestionably require a theoretical consideration of our own faith in relation to other religions. The comparative study of religions is concerned with such relationships as well as with the peculiarities of particular religions, with the laws of their development, their social structures, etc.[14] Pondering questions of this kind will lead us to practical attitudes—both positive and negative ones. And tolerance and intolerance are the terms which reflect such a basic confrontation.

In order to characterize the religious situation today, it is necessary to refer at least briefly to the various movements that strive for religious cooperation or, sometimes, for a standard religion. Of the supra-confessional communities, we should first mention the Bahai movement, which originated in Islam. It goes back to Bahā-Ullāh (1817–1892), who in turn developed his religion from Babism, a creed formulated by Mizra Ali Mohammed of Shiraz, or Bāb ("the gate to that which is concealed"), as he was called. Then there is the Sufi Society, a religious community that acknowledges all faiths and places all holy scriptures on its altars for readings; it was founded by Inayat Khan (died 1929) and has its center near Paris. A third attempt to synthesize religions is the Cao-Dai church in Vietnam; it seeks to unite the faiths of that country—namely, ancestor worship, Confucianism, Taoism, Buddhism, and Christianity.

Beside these syncretistic attempts to establish a unity of religions by integration, there are endeavors to bring about an exchange of religious impulses and to further fraternal cooperation among adherents of different faiths without abolishing the independence of the respective religions. Here reference must first be made to the *Religiöse Menschheitsbund* [Religious League of Man], which was founded by Rudolf Otto in 1922. Its main aim was to bring about religious cooperation on the ethical level. Furthermore, there is the World Congress of Faiths, which was started by Sir Francis Younghusband and dates back to the year 1938. The *Religiöse Menschheitsbund* was prohibited and ceased to exist in Nazi Germany, but was revived in 1956 and was incorporated into the World Congress of Faiths, as the German Branch of the World Alliance of Religions. The World Parliament of Religions, the Universal Religious Alliance, and the *Vishva Dharma Sammelan* [Union of All Religions], which originated in India, pursue similar goals.

In this book we shall discuss the problem of tolerance and intolerance in their manifold aspects on the basis of a comprehensive comparative study of religions. Needless to say, our study will be carried on academically, as objectively as possible. However, I think the problem of tolerance is not only an interesting academic question but also a matter of human concern affecting man's life most profoundly today. Considering the facts that are to be presented, I would like to say at this point that I believe this question to be one of the greatest and most urgent challenges now confronting our world. The reader need not fear that what is presented here is biased by a basic preconceived purpose to prove that tolerance is the demand of the hour. Conducting research objectively means remaining open for every result the inquiry may yield; in other words, one should not have a result in mind at the outset, for it would determine one's considerations as well as the selection of the material one wishes to analyze. The inquiry would then no longer be objective and would only serve as an ensuing proof for what the author thought in the first place and had apprehended on other than scholarly grounds. Therefore I wish to emphasize again that in this case the problem was studied first, and that the practical goals expressed here in the beginning are the result of that study. The only effect the results do have relates to the way the material is presented; but that, I believe, is justified.

For the sake of the problem at stake we would like this study on tolerance to be accessible to those who have not received academic training in the field. Therefore the material documenting the study will, to the greatest extent, not be presented within the text but in more copious notes at the back.

I. *Tolerance and Intolerance in Religious History*

In this part we shall present the historical data that will form the basis for our considerations. Let us start with a short clarification of the terms tolerance and intolerance. As religious history reveals, these concepts are by no means unequivocal. Obviously, a fruitful discussion will demand that we first determine in all clarity what these terms are to mean.

First we shall have to consider the fact that tolerance and intolerance can be attitudes pertaining either to the *form* or to the *content* of a religion. Formal tolerance is mere noninterference with another faith. Viewing the matter from the perspective of the object tolerated, we speak in this case of religious liberty. When we say a country grants religious liberty, we mean formal tolerance alone. Different faiths and religions are allowed to exist beside each other —for whatever reasons—and the state does not interfere with their free practice. The corresponding negative attitude is formal intolerance. Here the state does not refrain from encroaching upon foreign religions, but rather forces its members to subject themselves to a sacred state or church institution, the formal *unity* of which would be upset if deviating forms of religiousness and cult were to be permitted.

Apart from this formal attitude of tolerance or intolerance there is another position with which we shall be concerned; it relates to the contents of other faiths. Tolerance in this sense is not only noninterference with other religions, but also positive acknowledgment of a foreign religion as a genuine and legitimate religious possibility of encounter with the sacred. This type of tolerance, which I would like to designate actual positive tolerance, is not indifferentism—a tolerance based on unconcern—but rather an attitude of utmost sympathy. The recognition of other religions as genuine possibilities of encounter with the sacred is not rooted in indifference but presupposes critical encounter and insight. Tolerance with regard to content, or intrinsic tolerance (as we shall call it here), does not imply the surrender of one's own religious convictions. At a later stage, when we deal with the nature of truth in religion, we shall see how one can hold a religous position and yet at the same time be intrinsically tolerant.

The negative attitude corresponding to intrinsic tolerance is, of course, intrinsic intolerance, or intolerance with regard to content. It is marked by opposition to other faiths and religions, not on formal grounds, but on the basis of what is regarded as truth. On account of this attitude, other religions are repudiated or even attacked and persecuted because they are regarded as untrue and misleading in content.

It is quite readily clear that these two types of tolerance—with regard to form and to content—can combine in various ways and actually do so in religious history. Without illustrating our issue in detail we want to point out that essentially three combinations do occur: formal intolerance together with intrinsic intolerance; formal tolerance in connection with intrinsic intolerance; and formal intolerance bound up with intrinsic tolerance.

The matter gets even more involved when we consider the different objects to which such attitudes can pertain. These objects can lie either within or without the accepted religion. In such cases we shall speak of inner or outer tolerance, or intolerance, respectively; according to whether the attitude pertains either to the accepted religion, its phenomena and teachings, or to another religion.

In the sense of the distinction made above between formal and intrinsic tolerance, inner tolerance can be either formal toleration or positive acknowledgment of differences—in teaching or in cult—within the religion or religious community. The corresponding negative attitude is inner intolerance towards opinions diverging from the one official religion. All other views are then termed heresies. Formal and intrinsic inner intolerance appear in history in the garb of persecutions and inquisitions.

Outward tolerance and intolerance pertain to foreign religions. They can also be formal or intrinsic in nature, or both.

Finally, we can distinguish a few more elements if we consider who assumes these attitudes. Of course the individual can do so, but we need not deal with the practical consequences of his intolerant outlook, since he lacks the outward power to make such feelings effective (but the inner attitudes are, of course, in his case all possible). In general, the position of the individual will depend upon the attitude of the group—that is, of the religious community or organization to which he belongs. For such groups demand of their members that they share the general convictions and propensities of the whole; they are necessarily concerned about their religious unity, which would be upset by deviating views and beliefs of individual members. In a certain sense, this requirement—that the individual be in accord with the community—implies subordination to the community and means that individual religious independence is suspended or at least imperiled.[1]

Which communities come into question as exponents of tolerance or intolerance? Historically, there is first the sacred community of the ethnic and state religion. As a sacred primeval institution it assumes a very particular attitude to other faiths, requiring its members to share its own way of thinking. It is in a position to evoke this compliance by outward means of force, as we shall see later. The second type of collective group to be referred to here is the church, the organization of a developed or universal religion. Finally, there is of course the secular state, which can assume an attitude of tolerance or intolerance. It always has played and still does play a decisive role in the struggle for religious freedom.

I. TOLERANCE AND INTOLERANCE IN THE ETHNIC RELIGIONS

Having clarified our terminology, we shall now turn to religious history in order to discover what the positions of particular religions have been with regard to the question of tolerance.

We distinguish two major basic types of religions, ethnic and universal religions. The difference between the two types lies not only in the fact that the first type is limited to ethnic groups, or tribes—or at least to natural communities (whereas the other is not), but in a basic structural dissimilarity.[2] Ethnic religions are always maintained by communities, not by individuals—although individuals, of course, form these communities. The ethnic-religious community is a people, an ethnic group (*Volk*). In the world of early man this is the only religious community that existed. The ethnic-religious community is the setting within which human life in all its functions takes place. Finally, it is characteristic of ethnic religions that salvation or weal (*Heil*), is bestowed within them, or within the ethnic community that maintains them. It is met with by those who are born into the community. Salvation is positive contact with the world of the holy; and in ethnic religions, this contact exists between the people and their respective deities. Everyone who does not sever connections with the ethnic community—as the *niding* (outlaw) does in the Teutonic tradition—partakes of that communion.

This basic structure of ethnic religion[3] has important consequences for the problem of tolerance. The religions of primeval peoples exercise outward tolerance with regard to content, for they readily acknowledge the existence of foreign gods among foreign peoples. Let us cite a few illustrations from history in order to make the fundamental issue clear. The religion of the Romans is a classical example for the outward tolerance of an ethnic religion. Its tolerance was based on the recognition of foreign gods as existing among alien peoples. This view becomes apparent in a Roman custom, the so-called *evocatio* of foreign gods from a city being besieged by the Roman army. The local deities were called out of the city by a definite solemn formula,[4] and they were promised cultic veneration in return for their help. With the increasing expansion of the Roman empire, the Roman pantheon grew in this way by the incorporation of foreign deities (*sacra peregrina*) and by other types of borrowings from non-Roman cults.

Quite similar concepts lie at the base of an incident in the Old Testament.[5] After the cities of Samaria had been depopulated by the deportation, the king of Assyria made foreign peoples from Babylon and other parts of his empire settle there; "and at the beginning of their dwelling there, they did not fear the Lord; therefore the Lord sent lions amongst them." This was reported to the king, and he was told in explanation, "They do not know the law of the God of the land [i.e., Yahweh]." Thereupon, he sent an Israelite priest to the country to teach the foreigners the worship of Yahweh. The text continues, "But every nation still made gods of its own. . . . They also feared the Lord."

This is exactly what we call the outward tolerance of an ethnic religion. At this time and in this world, there were no scruples about acknowledging other deities. People did not have any reservations about foreign gods on the grounds of belief in the exclusive reality of their own god or gods, for such a belief and such a sense of truth had not arisen before the appearance of the Israelite prophets upon the scene. In the book of Judges (11:24), a clear distinction is made between Yahweh's claim to certain lands and that of the Amorite god Chemosh, whose claim was equally acknowledged.

We said that those who maintained the ethnic religion had no scruples about acknowledging foreign deities on the grounds of their own god and faith being exclusive. But that tolerant attitude could suddenly turn into intolerance for quite different reasons. As we noted above, the deities in ethnic religions relate to the nation, the state, or the land; they are national, state, or territorial deities. This means they must be acknowledged by the respective ethnic religion or its organization. The veneration of foreign gods who are not accepted is, therefore, not permitted. Let us call the intolerant, rejective attitude which appears here formal inner intolerance.

The Greeks were a people who were inclined religiously to a

broad outlook and to outward tolerance, as their syncretism reveals. But it was not permissible to subject their state gods to any criticism whatsoever, for the sacred unity of the state had to be preserved. Socrates had to drink the cup of poison because he undermined the old state-protected belief in gods; by his teachings, he was jeopardizing the state unity. For this very reason, even Plato wrote,[6] "No one shall possess shrines of the gods in private houses, and he who is found to possess them and to perform any sacred rights not publicly authorized . . . shall be informed against . . . to the guardians of the law. . . . And if a person be proven guilty of impiety, not merely from childish levity, but such as grown-up men may be guilty of, . . . let him be punished with death."

The official religion of the Roman state exercised formal inner intolerance in exactly the same way. The persecution of Christians was based not on the rejection of the Christian religion as such on account of its lacking truth, but merely on an attempt to maintain the unity of the state, which was being endangered by the Christians because they refused to honor the cult of the emperor. That cult was the bond holding together the Roman Empire, an empire that comprised within its sacred institution, the *Imperium Romanum,* the most different peoples.[7]

We saw that Israelite religion in the pre-prophetic period exercised intrinsic tolerance insofar as other religions were concerned. Here the situation differed somewhat from the polytheistic religions which could broaden their pantheon. Since the time of Moses, Israel had a monotheistic religion that knew of a covenant between Yahweh and his chosen people. This connection was exclusive in nature and it therefore definitely prohibited the people of that nation to worship other gods. Exodus 20:2 says, "I am the Lord your [the people of Israel's] God, who brought you [the people] out of the land of Egypt, out of the house of bondage. You shall have no other [actually existing] gods before me."

The worship of other gods in Israel meant turning away from Yahweh. Judges 10:6 and 7 expresses this notion when it says, "And the people of Israel again did what is evil in the sight of the Lord and served the Baals and the Ashtaroth. . . . And the anger of the Lord was kindled against Israel." [8] Here we come upon a claim to absoluteness which is peculiar to ethnic religions. It evolves from the close relationship between the people and their god. Whoever turns against the god of the people, or nation, is subject to intolerant rejection and punishment by him. This is how the sacred institution of the ethnic-religious community protects itself against infringement upon its unity and sacrosanctity.

The inner intolerance of ethnic religions can be traced throughout religious history. In the Teutonic culture, for instance, religious faith was part of the integrated life within the sacred tribal community. To relinquish that faith was condemned and punished as blasphemous. The Kristni-Saga, the account of the Christianization of Iceland, tells us,[9] "During that summer the law was passed on the Alt-thing that Christians should be persecuted for blasphemy by their relatives if the relationship was such that they were closer than of the fifth and further than of the third grade." And at another point, the same text records, "During this summer Stefnir was accused of being a Christian. The accusation was put forth by his relatives because turning to Christianity was at that time regarded as desecrating the tribe." [10]

2. THE FOUNDERS OF THE WORLD RELIGIONS

The ethnic religions which we have examined in respect to their attitudes of tolerance or intolerance were characterized by a peculiar ambiguity; they revealed outward tolerance and at the same time inner intolerance. This fact is connected with the structure of ethnic religions, but it also has to do with the peculiarity of the claim to absoluteness; we shall deal with this question at a later point in our inquiry. Let us first turn to universal religions and begin with a short summary of the elements that characterize them.

Whereas ethnic religions are maintained by the natural community into which one is born—the individual being of quite secondary importance—the universal religions are maintained by individuals.[11]

Unlike ethnic religions, where the single member participates in a collective weal or salvation, man in universal religion finds himself in a state of individual doom; he is isolated from basic sacred powers. In this condition, a salvation (*Heil*) is offered to him, to everyone, and hence to all men. It must either be earned by the individual or be granted to him by grace.

A religion of this type is universal because the plightful condition from which it offers redemption is a universal category and because the salvation it offers is also universal. In both respects, then, the universal religion is independent of ethnic peculiarities; it transcends ethnic and territorial boundaries and spreads into the world. Naturally, the gods of universal religions are also universal in nature; they are not limited to specific peoples and lands. We usually speak of three religions as being world religions—Christianity, Islam, and Buddhism. They were all founded by historical personalities. We shall now be concerned with these founders and with their attitude toward tolerance.

Buddha   Buddhism, whose doctrines we need not discuss at this point,[12] is in structure a mystic religion. As we shall see later, this fact is of decisive importance for our problem. The mystical character of Buddhism lies in the fact that it connects the idea of the holy with the concept of an impersonal *Nirvāna*. The Buddhist strives to enter *Nirvāna* and thereby to gain redemption from the plightful cycle of rebirth and hence from individual existence. Entering into the Absolute and annulling the personality with its self-centered desires is a typically mystical goal. It can be traced in other mystical religions in a similar form.[13]

Buddha himself was outspokenly tolerant. Intolerance is usually expressed first and foremost in doctrinal disputes. Concerning this matter, Buddha says:

> The opinion to which one adheres as the best
> Is praised in the world above all else.
> Whosoever does not teach the same
> Is decried as a fool. Thus there is no end to strife.[14]

Buddha sees this conflict of diverging opinions as a symptom that men lack redemption from vanity and egoistic desire. He says of himself in this connection: "Therefore I say that the perfect one is redeemed beyond desire . . . by the elimination, rejection, and disavowment of all self-centeredness, vanity and conceit." [15]

Buddha indicated his tolerant attitude very impressively by a parable, which puts across his main point quite plainly, and which also makes clear the basis of his intrinsic tolerance: the parable of the blind men and the elephant. Buddha narrates this story when he is told about certain ascetics and Brahmans who argue quite narrow-mindedly about theological and metaphysical questions pertaining to the eternity of the world and to Buddha's post-mortal existence. He sees the root of the quarrel in the fact that these people fail to realize what is really decisive. It says in the text, "Not knowing what matters and what does not, and unaware of truth and error, these contentious, quarrelsome, arguing people attack and injure each other with these words: 'Truth is like this, not like that; it is so, not otherwise.'" Buddha then tells of a king who called together all the blind men in Sāvatthī and had them assembled around an elephant. Every one of them touched one part of the elephant's body, then they were asked about the animal's appearance. The king received various answers: "Those among the blind men who had felt the head of the elephant said, 'Your Majesty, the elephant is like a cauldron.' Those who had touched its ear said, 'Your Majesty, the elephant is like a shovel.' Those who had felt its trunk said, 'Your Majesty, it is like the shaft of a plough.'" This continued until finally "they attacked each other with their firsts, crying, 'An elephant is like this, not like that. . . .'" [16]

This parable has a deep significance; it reveals the innermost reasons for Buddha's attitude. Every one of the blind men really does have contact with a part of the true elephant. Transposed into religious terms, the implication is that different religious views are all based on true contact with the sacred. The concrete expressions referring to the object of contact are figurative statements, in the sense of the blind men's claim when they say the elephant is *like*

this or that worldly phenomenon. The error and the reason for engaging in strife is the fact that every one of these blind men holds
his partial insight to be universally valid. Yet, in fact, none of their
perceptions does full justice to the complete nature of the real object.
The same applies to the realm of religion: no one statement can
fully encompass and express the whole truth.

There is yet another motive for Buddha's tolerance, and we can
find it in his teachings. As in the case of other religious masters,
his teachings, too, pertain to salvation. But he never holds his doctrines to be decisive and significant in themselves. He emphasizes,
"The doctrine is like a raft which is used to ford a stream [the
fleeting world], and to reach the other side [*Nirvāna*]. When it has
fulfilled its use it is no longer carried along." [17] We may infer that
for Buddha the doctrine possesses but relative significance. It should
therefore not be an object of dispute stirring up passions and causing
schisms.

It is precisely this insight that the great Indian king Ashoka expressed (ca. 250 B.C.) when he inscribed these words of intrinsic
tolerance into one of his Rock Edicts: "King Piyadasi, dear to the
gods, honors *all* sects; the ascetics [hermits] or those who dwell at
home he honors with charity and in other ways. But the king, dear
to the gods, attributes less importance to this charity and these honors than to the vow of seeing the reign of virtue, *which constitutes
the essential part of them*." [18] Promoting that "which constitutes the
essential part" presupposes a distinction between that which truly
matters and that which does not. And the question of what the main
thing is always leads to such doctrinal disputes, as we shall see.

There is a third motive for tolerance in Buddha's teaching: the
definite renunciation of every kind of belief in authority. Emphasis
on authority is very often the reason for an intolerant attitude, whatever form it may take. In Indian Brahmanism, for instance, the
Brahmans often debated the truth of their doctrines—which were
based on the authority of the Vedas, or the holy tradition. When
a disciple in doubt asked Buddha about his opinion concerning the

matter, he remarked, "Don't rely on rumors, on traditions, on mere statements, on the information of sacred scriptures, on pure intellectual reasoning and logical inference, on conformity with your own opinions and contemplations, on the sole appearance of reality. . . . Rather, *when you yourself realize* this or that to be evil and reprehensible, oh Kālāma, when you see that the wise reproach it, and that it leads to harm and suffering when undertaken or commenced, reject it" (Ang.-Nik. 888, 65).

This opinion corresponds exactly to the view that Jesus adopted when he taught his disciples, not on the basis of outward authority, but on the living and personal experience of those who would endeavor to do the will of God. Thus would they comprehend the inner justification of his message and mission (John 7:17).

In later Mahāyāna-Buddhism we come upon an opinion which had already appeared in the Upanishads and which can also be regarded as a basis for intrinsic tolerance. In the Mundaka-Upanishad (1, 4ff) it says, "Two kinds of knowledge must be known . . . the higher and the lower knowledge. The lower knowledge is the Rig-veda [etc.] . . . , but the higher knowledge is that by which the Indestructible [Brahman] is apprehended. That which cannot be seen, nor seized, . . . that which is imperishable, that it is which the wise regard as the source of all being."

There is, then, a twofold knowledge or truth: the lower—which is to be found in popular sacred books of folk-religion, and the higher—which is actually decisive and through which man attains salvation. Similarly, Mahāyāna-Buddhism also distinguishes between the truth which is geared to meet the requirements of the world, the "[veiled] truth of existence" (*samvriti-satya*), and the "highest truth" (*paramātha-satya*).[19] It is in this sense that Nāgārjuna (ca. 200 A.D.) points out, "There are two truths according to Buddha's opinion: the highest truth and the truth of the appearance."[20]

The later Mahāyāna-Buddhism is more tolerant than Hīnayāna because it incorporates this earlier form of Buddhism into its own tradition in a characteristically mystic fashion, regarding it to be a sub-structure and preliminary stage of its own religious system. The gods become incarnations of the one primeval Buddha, and even the real, historical Buddha is considered to be his manifestation.

At the time of Ashoka, Buddhism was said to have eighteen sects. Their number was constantly on the increase, a sign that there were disputes about the doctrine even in Buddha's congregation. But these doctrinal differences were not taken to be decisive; they never led to oppressions and persecutions. Followers of different sects could readily receive the monastic ordination in monasteries other than their own.[21]

Buddhism was and is, on the whole, an outspokenly tolerant religion; this is documented by the fact that wherever it has spread it has never tried to annihilate the foreign, or original religion, but rather has existed beside it, often borrowing from it doctrines and customs. This is what happened in China and Japan, for instance, where the indigenous religions, Confucianism, Taoism, and Shinto (in Japan), could continue to thrive unimpeded. Buddhism has tolerance in its blood, one might say. Therefore, it lacks doctrines determining a political or social order in the world, for originally it was not interested in these spheres of life. Thus it retained the possibility of associating itself with the most varied political systems.[21a]

At the end of the nineteenth century, various circumstances led to the decline of Buddhism. The reasons were the activity of Christian missions and the expansion of colonialism. Unfortunately, both were closely connected. On account of this alliance, through which missions either prepared the way for colonial conquest or were themselves furthered by attempts on the part of the colonial powers, Christianity became the "religion of the conqueror" in Asia and many other parts of the world.

The reaction to the encounter with the aggressive forms of Western religious and political life has led to the rise of a Buddhist modernism which adopts the methods employed by the European opponents in their intellectual challenge. It stresses the rational elements in Buddhism and emphasizes the harmony of its teachings with

Western scientific insights. It founds lay organizations and cultivates new national feelings.

The representatives of Buddhist modernism recognize the demand to change and improve the world that is inherent in their religion's original teachings and ethical precepts. But that idea stands in contrast to the doctrine of *karma,* according to which outward conditions of life necessarily spring from deeds committed in a former life. In modification of the old teaching, it is now claimed that *karma* (the past deed) is not the cause for *all* conditions of an individual's existence.[21b] An attempt is thus made to adapt Buddhism to the conditions of the present.

Especially in Vietnam—where Buddhism has never existed in its pure form but has always been mingled with Confucianism and animistic elements—the confrontation with the aggressive Catholicism of a former regime, which had practically ignored and discriminated against this religion of the majority, led to the emergence of a politically-oriented Buddhism. Thus Buddha's teachings on self-renunciation and tolerance were shaken, and were revised considerably. With regard to this change, H. von Stockhausen observed, "Vietnamese Buddhists want to lead their adherents into the modern age and to make them members of the modern economic society. This is an enormous process, it is a revolutionary reinterpretation of the great world religion." [21c]

Jesus   Although Jesus' basic religious attitude was quite different from that of Buddha so far as the type of religiosity which he represented is concerned, he, too, was tolerant in various ways. We will have to consider the motives for his attitude in greater detail.

The Israelite church was outspokenly intolerant toward those who did not conform to certain of its precepts regarding general conduct and professional activity. It declared tax collectors and sinners impure, for example; these people were to be avoided. But the regulations about cleanliness did not prevent Jesus from turning to those who were despised and ostracized, thus arousing the indignation of the Scribes and Pharisees, who rigorously adhered to the Law. They said of him, "This man receives sinners and eats with them" (Luke 15:2). Jesus' attitude sprang from his searching love, which transcended the boundaries established by the organized religion. Of course it must be pointed out that this attitude is not actually religious tolerance, for that term should be limited to the relationship toward people with a specific religion or religious attitude (not to people in a certain profession as in the case of the tax collector). But in this instance, as well as in others, Jesus does oppose the religious intolerance of the Israelite church representatives. That is why we can cite this example here. Jesus opposes the intolerant, law-oriented attitude of his home church, and he does so here as well as at other points.[22]

Jesus advocates genuine religious tolerance when he reproaches the disciples who want to call down fire from heaven on the Samaritans who refuse to accept him. He says, "You do not know what manner of spirit you are of" (Luke 9:55). This is formal tolerance in the sense of our definition. But Jesus' attitude is also one of intrinsic tolerance. This becomes clear in his relationship to people outside the Israelite fold. The two accounts upon which we want to base our claim are, characteristically enough, both to be found in the Gospel of Saint John. The influence of mystic trends from the environment of early Christianity are especially pronounced in this book; indeed, it has always been the favorite writing of Christian mystics. This attitude of Jesus can also be understood on the basis of his teachings in the Synoptic Gospels (Matthew, Mark, Luke). However, let us turn first to the account of the official at Capernaum (John 4:46ff), and then to Jesus' discussion with the Samaritan woman (John 4:7ff).

In the first narrative we are told that an official who stood outside the Israelite community and religion requested Jesus to heal his son. Jesus fulfilled the plea because of the official's faith. Matthew 8:5ff probably narrates the same story as the account of the centurion's servant; and, in this narrative, Jesus adds the words, "not even in Israel have I found such faith." Jesus thus holds faith—in the sense of trust, devotion, and openness to God—to be the decisive factor for gaining salvation. It was not membership in an organized community nor, as was the accepted view in Israel's religious society, in an ethnically limited or restricted society. Jesus' teaching makes clear that he reduces religion to personal decision in matters of faith and that he holds peripheral rules and regulations to be inessential.

The same attitude is at the base of his discussion with the Samaritan woman. She had asked him about the right way to worship God. Should such worship take place on the holy mountain, as the Samaritans believed, or in Jerusalem alone, as the Jews claimed? Jesus' answer is, "The hour is coming when neither on this mountain nor in Jerusalem will you worship the Father. . . . God is Spirit, and those who worship Him must worship Him in spirit and in truth" (John 4:21, 24). "Right" worship depends not on the locality, nor on any outer form whatsoever, but on the "right" attitude alone, and this can be present anywhere. This is intrinsic tolerance.

Another example of such tolerance in Jesus' thinking is the parable of the Good Samaritan (Luke 10:30ff). Two representatives of the Israelite church, a priest and a Levite, pass by the man who has fallen among robbers, but a Samaritan, a member of a non-Jewish religious community, grants aid to the wounded man. It follows that Jesus deems it possible that the attitude of neighborly love, which he demands be realized, can exist outside his own home church rather than within it.

Finally, we could also point to Jesus' cleansing of the temple (Matthew 21), or to Jesus' attitude toward the Pharisees and Scribes. Reference is made to this relationship over and over again, most basically in the great dispute recorded in Matthew 23. One could see intolerance here, but this attitude is not an intolerant one—rather, a radical one. Jesus' religiousness is of the prophetic type; it demands radical obedience to God if a man has made an unconditional decision for Him. For Jesus there can be no compromise in this matter.[23] But one aspect does become apparent, and we shall have occasion to deal with it in greater detail later: tolerance as indifference and as failure to react has a limit. For the religious person, this limit is the a-religious, intolerant attitude of others.

ıed Mohammed is another one of the prophets of re-
_ _ _istory, and the religion he founded is, in structure, prophetic. In his case the issue of tolerance is more involved than it is
with Jesus, one of the reasons being that the prophet did not hold
the same opinion on the matter throughout his life. There can be no
question that Mohammed was deeply convinced about the exclusive
truth of his message. He attributed it to divine revelation. He
thought it was the religion of Abraham that he was proclaiming at
Allah's command, a religion restored to its original form and purged
of Jewish and Christian distortions.[24] Since his mission was not
only to present a teaching objectively but also to subject people to
Allah's rule, nothing but an intolerant attitude is to be expected of
him. Nevertheless, some Koranic suras of the Medina period [25] reveal
an outspokenly tolerant attitude. Thus, for instance, sura 2:258 says,
"There is no compulsion in religion."

At first, the tolerance the prophet proclaimed had as its object the
so-called "peoples of the book"—that is, members of religions which,
according to Mohammed's opinion, possessed in their sacred scriptures the same revelation that the Arabic people had in their Koran.
Later Mohammed realized that this idea was erroneous. But in the
beginning, he counted the Jews and Christians to be "peoples of the
book" in this sense, and afterwards he added adherents to Zoroastrianism.[26] The concept is that Islam is the only true religion and
that Allah originally gave this religion to all peoples in their holy
scriptures. The idea is clearly expressed in sura 3:20, which says,
"Verily, [the true] religion in God's [Allah's] sight is Islam [com-
plete submission], and those to whom the Book was given disagreed
not until afterwards that there was given to them knowledge,
through mutual envy." Because of disunity, then, the one true religion of Islam was obscured and distorted by the possessors of
scripture. Since the revelation given to the non-Moslems is the same
as the one contained in the Koran, the faithful are exhorted: "And
do not wrangle about what is better with the people of the Book
(save with those who have been unjust among them) who say,
'We believe in what is sent down to us, and what has been sent

Surahs — (chapters of the Koran)

down to you; our God and your God is one, and we are unto him resigned' " (29:45).

To Mohammed, Moses and Jesus were also Allah's prophets.[27] It is thus understandable that Mohammed ordered even intrinsic tolerance to prevail toward "the peoples of the Book" (since he regarded their religion to be identical in content with his). In a well-known sura (2:258) the prophet even prohibits conversion by force: "There is no compulsion in religion." The reason for this attitude is indicated in sura 10:98ff: "But had the Lord pleased, all who are in the earth would have believed all together; as for thee, wilt thou force men to become believers? It is not for any person to believe save by the permission of God."

Since everything in the world depends upon Allah and His almighty and exclusively determining Will, man should not interfere with His intentions by wanting to convert others by force, for they evidently became or remained unbelievers by His Will.

[The attitude of tolerance toward the "peoples of the Book" was not kept up. Furthermore, in the following period the prophet himself commanded the waging of holy war against infidels.] Such people were "idolaters"—people who were not the possessors of scripture. [Therefore there arose strict and radical outward intolerance, springing from the exclusive Islamic claim to revelation, and from the revealed command to conquer world empires and to place them under Allah's dominion. Sura 8:40 says, "Fight them [the infidels] then, that there should be no sedition, and that the religion may be wholly God's." The Koran even orders the slaying of idolaters: "But when the sacred months are passed away, kill the idolaters wherever ye may find them, and besiege them, and lie in wait for them in every place of observation." [28]]

Increasingly, Islam became a belligerent religious organization, waging war for Allah's sake. "Fight in God's [Allah's] way with those who fight with you. . . . Kill them wherever you find them . . . but fight them that there may be no sedition and that the religion may be Allah's" (sura 2:186ff). The fight is, hence, to continue until all empires are subject to Allah's rule. For this reason

Islam divides the world into two realms, one of Islam and one of holy war. The theological implication is that holy war should in fact be conducted in those parts of the world where Islam does not prevail.[29]

Islam practices particular inward intolerance[30] against those who have turned away from the Islamic faith. An Islamic law-book contains this provision for such cases, "As for Apostates, it is permitted to kill them by facing them or coming upon them from behind, just as in the case of Polytheists. Secondly, their blood, if shed, brings no vengeance. Thirdly, their property is the spoil of true believers. Fourthly, their marriage ties become null and void."[31]

Islam has, indeed, often acted according to these ordinances. Abu Hanifah (died 767), head of one of the orthodox schools, laid down the death penalty for apostasy.[32] And various mystics were tortured and put to death for heresy—for instance, al-Hallāj in 932.

The political character that marked Islam from the very beginning led to the fact that various ordinances regarding tolerance were not always observed in the case of the "peoples of the book." One of the first caliphs who ordered churches to be destroyed was Walīd (705–715). Forced conversions of Christian Arabs and persecutions of Jews and Parsees are also reported.[33]

Under certain circumstance, formal tolerance could be granted within an Islamic state or a state that had become Islamic (by conquest). One of these conditions was that nonbelievers had to pay a poll tax, but there were also other provisions. It was not permitted to bring the sacred book into discredit, to accuse the Prophet of falsehood, or to speak critically of Islam. According to the statement of al-Mawardi in the eleventh century, these requirements are—beside some others—"the indispensable conditions" of tolerance. There were, in addition, a few more "commendable" restrictions—having to wear distinctive marks, being prohibited from erecting buildings higher than the mosque and from offending the ears of Mohammedans by the sounding of church bells and the reading of scriptures of other faiths.[34]

Blaise Pascal once formulated the difference between Mohammed and Christ: "Mohammed established a dominion by slaying, Christ by being slain." [35] Over and beyond specific differences, the two men doubtlessly lived in completely different atmospheres, and this becomes clear in their attitudes toward tolerance.

An example of quite unchristian intolerance, finally, is F. Blank's verdict on Islam. He writes in his book, *Der Islam als missionarisches Problem* [Islam as a Missionary Problem] (1936), "One thing is for sure, in Islam we have to do with an especially dangerous product of Satan's power" (p. 375).

3. PROPHETIC INTOLERANCE

After considering the founders of world religions and their attitudes toward tolerance, let us now turn to some prophets to see if there is any specific type of intolerance necessarily connected with the pattern of religiosity they represent—as in the case of Mohammed.[36]

Zarathustra   The religion of the Iranian prophet Zarathustra (or Zoroaster) is basically a religion of struggle or conflict.[37] This is because of its dualism; this religion recognizes a good spiritual and a good physical world existing beside a bad spiritual and a bad physical world. The prophet Zarathustra, who proclaimed the one God to be Ahura Mazda, felt called "to awaken the soul in agreement with the good spirit." [38] He summoned people to decide "man for man" for Ahura Mazda and to participate in the struggle against the powers of Satan, who has intruded into the good world of creation. Men who obey demonic powers directed against God are termed "false believers," and Zarathustra repeatedly calls his followers to a passionate struggle against them: "May no one of you listen to the solemn words and teachings of the false believer, for he brings discord and destruction to the home, the clan, the province, and the land. Therefore chastise him with the force of arms. . . . And whosoever does evil to the false believers with words or thoughts or hands, or whoever converts his followers to the good, does so according to the wish of the Wise Lord [Ahura Mazda] and to His satisfaction." [39]

In a more recent part of the Avesta, in Vendīdād 19:26, we read that the Prophet puts this question to his God: "O thou all-knowing Ahura Mazda: Should I urge upon the godly man, should I urge upon the godly woman, should I urge upon the wicked Daêva-worshipper who lives in sin, that they have once to leave behind them the earth made by Ahura, that they have to leave the water that runs, the corn that grows, and all the rest of their wealth?" The question is answered affirmatively by Ahura Mazda, "Thou shouldst, O holy Zarathustra."

After the Prophet's death, a significant development occurred that was most consequential so far as the matter of tolerance is concerned. For his whole life Zarathustra had fought against the powerful representatives of the old ethnic religion, against kings and priests. He stood up against the polytheism of his people and replaced that form of faith by a strictly exclusive monotheism, but after his death the old ethnic-religious views and practices started creeping up again. Mazdaism became a sacerdotal religion with many gods and numinous powers. In the seventh century B.C. it became the state religion of Media and thus entered into a new stage. Whereas Zarathustra, at the demand of Ahura Mazda, had striven for piety based on *personal* decision, an organized state religion gradually emerged, unifying a whole society. Mazdaism, with its heightened religious sensitivity, could only fulfill this role by making concessions to the requirements of the masses and to the old ethnic-religious practices, and this was done by a polytheism. This meant that an intrinsically tolerant ethnic religion replaced the original intrinsically intolerant prophetic monotheism. But as in other cases we have been discussing, the new ethnic religion became intolerant again when the unity of the state was at stake. This was the situation that arose in Persia.

Rather than adhere to the religious exclusiveness preached by Zarathustra, King Cyrus, for instance, permitted shrines to be erected in Asia Minor. Furthermore, he presented himself to the Babylonians as the chosen one of God Marduk and allowed the Jews to build a new temple in Jerusalem.[40] This attitude reflects typical ethnic-religious tolerance with regard to content.

When Zoroastrianism flowered again as a state religion under the Sassanides (226–651 A.D.), it adopted formal tolerance toward Buddhism and Jainism because these religions, being typically mystical, had no aggressive designs. This formal tolerance, however, became formal intolerance when Christianity appeared upon the scene as a missionary religion. Marcion's church in Persia, for instance, and the gnosticism of Basilides and Valentinian developed such a missionary activity. Thus the Christians in Persia, as in Rome, were oppressed by force because they were endangering the unity of the state.

At the beginning of the Sassanide period, another prophetic movement appeared which the state-recognized Mazda cult had to resist; it was Manichaeism. Mani, who was born in Babylon around 215 or 216, first presented his teachings in 242. At first he was successful at the court of the emperor, but later he was unable to prevail against the intolerant Mazdaistic priesthood. He was finally crucified publicly (273 or 274 A.D.).[41]

The Prophets of Israel   We have already noted that Israel's ethnic religion in the pre-prophetic period was inwardly intolerant, but tolerant so far as acknowledging the existence of foreign gods and their territorially limited claims was concerned. At the time of the prophets this picture changed, in that the great personalities of this period decried the manifold polytheistic tendencies of the people with exceeding passion. They uncovered apostasy from Yahweh by looking right into the concealed depths of men's hearts. On the other hand they resolutely denied the existence of other gods. We read in Jeremiah 2:11, "Has a nation changed its gods, even though they are no gods? But my people have changed their glory for that which does not profit." And, in Isaiah 2:8, "Their land is filled with idols; they bow down to the work of their hands, to what their own fingers have made." In the ever more universally oriented message of the prophets, the foreign gods appear as unreal creations of man. Yahweh alone is the Lord of nations. This religious view is expressed in all clarity in Psalm 96:4ff. "For great is the Lord and greatly to be praised; he is to be feared above all gods. For all the gods of the peoples are idols; but the Lord made the heavens. . . . Ascribe to the Lord, O families of the peoples, ascribe to the Lord glory and strength! Ascribe to the Lord the glory due his name; bring an offering and come into his courts! . . . Say among the nations, 'The Lord reigns!' "

The Israelite prophets not only denounced apostasy to foreign gods—who they did not believe even existed—as sinful, but they also branded bustling religiosity itself as inner defection from God. Hosea 7:14, for example, says in the name of Yahweh, "They do not cry to me from the heart, but they wail upon their beds." And Amos (5:21ff) as well as Isaiah (1:11ff) turn against the multitude of sacrifices and burnt offerings, against the "noise" of the cult songs, and against pilgrimages and feasts. Isaiah 29:13ff indicates the reason for this attitude, thereby revealing the deepest meaning of prophetic intolerance: "Because this people draw near with their mouth and honor me with their lips, while their hearts are far from me, and their fear of me is a commandment of men learned by rote; therefore, behold, I will again do marvelous things among this people. . . ."

As we saw above, Jesus, too, fought against the complicated and superficial cultic religious practices of his own Jewish church on these grounds. This is not intolerance, however, but rather radicalism springing from a prophetic imbuing with an ideal infused by God. Thus the Israelite prophets preach to the people calamity and judgment, and later some proclaim the advent of a time of salvation for those who truly repent.[42]

Paul   The overpowering personality of Paul—we shall not sketch his religious and theological significance here [43]—is a classical example for different types of intolerance. This applies both to the pre-Christian as well as to the Christian stage of his life. Born in Tarsus, the capital of the Roman province of Cilicia, Paul came from a

Jewish family connected with the sect of the Pharisees. Thus he grew up in the strictly law-oriented tradition of the Pharisees, and he went to Jerusalem as a young man to take up their scriptural studies. On account of his background in a city populated by Orientals and Greeks, he had from youth a close connection to Hellenism, and this evidently strongly influenced his thinking and his terminology. Of course, his thinking was also determined by his study of rabbinic theology.

It was in Jerusalem that Paul first came into contact with the Christian church and began persecuting the young Christian congregation. He did so in the spirit of his home church. According to Acts, Paul was present when Stephen was stoned: "And Saul was consenting to his death" (8:1). In several places (e.g., 1 Corinthians 15:9; Philippians 3:6), Paul himself remarks that he was "zealous" in the persecution of the Christian church "for the tradition of my fathers" (Galatians 1:14). In Acts 26:9ff, he describes his activity more closely with these words: "I myself was convinced that I ought to do many things in opposing the name of Jesus of Nazareth. And I did so in Jerusalem; I not only shut up many of the saints in prison, by authority from the chief priests, but when they were put to death, I cast my vote against them. And I punished them often in all the synagogues and tried to make them blaspheme; and in raging fury against them, I persecuted them even to foreign cities."

As M. Dibelius points out,[44] it was not the belief of the Christians in Jesus the Messiah that caused Paul to persecute them, it was their claim that the Messiah was sent to those who lived on the fringe of law-abiding Judaism and who thus stood outside the actual Jewish church. Because Paul represented a rigid and aristocratic Pharisaic ideal, he felt the Christian claim to be an insult to God. It had to be countered by force according to Old Testament patterns.[45] This attitude is formal intolerance, deriving from the ideal of a community that is sacred and religious, and that is at the same time an ethnic community. It is the same type of intolerance Paul himself experienced later at the hands of the Jewish church, right after his conversion on the way to Damascus—where he himself had wanted to initiate new persecutions of the Christians (Acts 9:1; 2 Corinthians 11:12ff).

Paul felt that his experience near Damascus was a prophetic summons to spread the gospel, especially to the so-called heathen. Thus he became the apostle to the nations, and to them he proclaimed his view of the person of Jesus. He did so in a manner that was marked by his detachment from the law and determined by specific factors —his understanding of the incarnation, the sacrificial death, and the resurrection of God's Son.[46] As is well known, this liberal type of preaching brought him into conflict with the Jewish-Christian congregations and their representatives who continued to adhere to their fathers' law, demanding that the heathen, too, should keep Israel's law. Acts 21:20 tells us that the Jewish Christians remained under the law a generation after Jesus: "You see, brother, how many thousands there are among the Jews of those who have believed; they are all zealous for the law [zelotai tou nomou]."

Here two streams clash: the law-oriented church tradtion, to which the Jewish Christians cleaved in the beginning, and the liberal tendency that freed itself from the tradition and from the encumbering laws of the sacred organization, just as Jesus had done himself.

We found that Paul represented a rigid form of inward intolerance toward those who stood within the church. He could say (Galatians 1:8), "But even if we, or an angel from heaven, should preach to you a gospel contrary to that which we preached to you, let him be accursed." [47] And in Romans 16:17 he warns of teachings that create "dissentions and difficulties, in opposition to the doctrine that you have been taught." These words presuppose an idea of religious unity, a theory that sees danger for the church in deviating teachings.

Quite opposed to Jesus' teaching, Paul strongly emphasizes the doctrinal aspects of the message. Later, doctrinal correctness and deviation therefrom even turn out to be the main reason for intolerant persecution, strife, and countless divisions. But something of that later spirit is already present in the New Testament writings. It gains expression in the so-called pastoral epistles—which were actually not written by Paul—for we find here this warning, "As for a man who is factitious, . . . have nothing more to do with him." (Titus 3:10). That attitude is also alive in the matters to which 1 Timothy 1:20 makes reference, for there apostates are spoken of who were delivered to Satan.

Luther   Many have thought that the Reformation, kindled by Luther and the other reformers with their protest against the authority of the Catholic Church (and this question of authority is a matter we shall deal with separately), championed the idea of tolerance and religious liberty. But that is certainly *not* the case. The idea of tolerance was quite foreign to Luther and the other reformers. The "liberty of a Christian," for which Luther stood, can easily be and has often been misunderstood as tolerance in the modern sense. What it meant was the liberty of the conscience bound to God. In negative terms, it meant freedom from the surveillance of the church as an institution, for in the reformer's view that institution infringed upon the rights of the conscience. In positive terms, however, the "liberty of a Christian" implies that the conscience is bound to the word of God and that it is true, or right, only if it accepts this obligation. "A true conscience does and wants nothing more than to hear the teaching of the Scripture." [48] Now this is something quite different from tolerance. There can be no doubt, however, that the principle Luther represented—the principle of personal religious decision independent of an institution's demands—has, nevertheless, indirectly led to the emergence of the modern concept of tolerance.

Luther did not hold the same attitude toward the matter of tolerance throughout his life. Basically, he was intolerant, but it must be noted that he changed his mind; at first he advocated less intolerance than he later did, and in the beginning he also limited it to the intellectual realm, whereas afterwards it also involved the use of force. This change of mind had to do with factors that we shall discuss shortly.

For Luther, the concept of the heretic related to faith alone; heresy was not a juridical matter, as the Catholics viewed it. Said the young Luther, "A heretic is a person who does not believe the articles [of faith] which ought to be and must be believed," [49] and this idea is still quite juridically Roman. In his earlier years, Luther also said on several occasions, "I am a heretic only if I violate an explicit Council resolution, but I can utter what the Council has not condemned." [50] Gradually, however, Luther's idea of the church changed and so did his concept of the heretic. For him, the church was to become the community of believers, visible in word and sacrament, free of hierarchic bonds. [51] It is on the basis of this notion that he found the Catholic concept of the heretic to be false. For him, faith is decisive, and faith is not a juridical matter. The sole criterion for heresy is faith bound to the word of God, and to His word alone. One must bear in mind that Luther considered only one interpretation of the Holy Scripture to be true, the interpretation wrought by the Holy Spirit. A heretic interprets the Bible in quite a different way. This assumption, which seemed self-evident to Luther, was the basis for his intolerance. He was of the opinion that his interpretation was the one wrought by the Holy Spirit itself.

Since we do not wish to voice criticism in this chapter, but only to present the data and to try to understand the historical situation, we shall let the question of whether this view is legitimate or not rest upon itself. In any case, there is a shift of accent in the concept of the heretic from juridical aspect to the realm of faith—to the heart—as that which is decisive, and this shift implies that the use of force is essentially inappropriate in matters of faith. "Another handhold is necessary, . . . the use of force will not achieve it, for there is something free about faith and nobody can be forced to accept it." [52] In the case of the heretic who continues to adhere to error in spite of spiritual admonition one thing can be done, however, and that is to debar him from the congregation. [53] It is on this basis that we can understand Luther's indicating outspoken tolerance when he wrote to the Elector [The Elector was a German prince entitled

to participate in the electing of the Holy Roman Emperor] concerning the Anabaptists: "Let them preach in good cheer and in
good courage whatever they can and against whomever they want.
. . . They are necessarily sects. . . . Let the opinions meet upon
each other and clash." [54] This does not mean that Luther recognizes
the sects as legitimate possibilities of religious life. Rather, he views
them as being instrumental in awakening the congregation and
admonishing it to vigilance.

It was the Anabaptist movement, with its elementary impact,
which caused Luther to change his mind about the interpretation of
the Scriptures and made him realize that his assumptions turned out
to be wrong in practice. He had thought, first of all, that there
could be but *one* interpretation of the biblical word, the one wrought
by the Spirit. But it was the Anabaptists who referred to the Spirit
when they interpreted the Word. Also, Luther had believed that
only the Word, when preached, vanquishes every heresy. But he
observed that obviously this was not its effect. Therefore, he was
compelled to revise his view; and he did so, in fact, to the extent
that he then thought the state should intervene against heretics to
protect its subjects. Luther saw no contradiction between this opinion and what he maintained otherwise, for he kept on believing
that faith was an inner quality which could not be forced upon man,
but only granted by God. In his eyes, the use of force is justified
only in the public, political sphere of life. Thus he can say, "If anyone wants to teach anything contradicting a common article of faith
which is clearly grounded in the Scriptures and believed in the
whole world by all of Christendom . . . he should not be tolerated
but punished as a *public slanderer*." [55] Here Luther adopts a view
that stems from the Middle Ages, which he never abandoned: the
idea that the body of Christ has two sides, a spiritual and a worldly
one. Worldly power and church both stand in the service of Christendom. The worldly authorities have the right and the duty to
force individuals to conform to a general pattern, which, of course,
is necessarily Christian. The heretic who is active in public upsets
this pattern. So far as the juridical sphere is concerned, which is

a matter of the state, heresy appears as a public crime which the state must punish. Says Luther, "A worldly ruler should not tolerate his subjects being led into disunity and discord by loathsome preachers; for that will ultimately lead to uprising and the assembly of mobs. There should be but one message [or way to preach] at one place." [56] At this point we come upon typical formal intolerance in Luther's thinking. It is based upon the concept of unity, first the unity of the state; but Luther also went on to defend intolerantly the unity of the church, as we shall see shortly. We must first consider the consequences of this basic attitude allowing the use of public force. In 1525 Luther had stated, "The authorities should not resist anyone teaching or believing whatever he wills, be it the gospel or an untruth; it is sufficient if they arrest the preaching of uprising and discord." [57] But in 1532 he wrote to Duke Albrecht of Prussia regarding the Zwinglians: "It is both dangerous and terrible to believe something against the unanimous witness, faith, and teaching of the entire holy Christian Church. . . . Therefore I exhort and beg Your Princely Majesty to avoid such people and *not to tolerate them in the country.*" [58] What is more, the hearing of the Ten Commandments is to be enforced by the authorities. "Even if the people do not believe, they should be driven to church for the sake of the Ten Commandments so that they may at least learn outward acts of obedience." [59]

For Luther, the Catholic cultus also belonged to those things which were public and therefore seditious heresy. Hence he also demanded of the authorities that this "public blasphemy," as he called it, be abolished. "Therefore, dear Christians, let us flee from such abomination and be united in this one cause to remove by proper force that slander (the ritual of the mass). . . . The authorities are obliged to ward off and to punish such blasphemy." [60]

Luther is similarly intolerant toward the Jews and their public worship. His advice is "that their synagogues and schools be set on fire, and that those portions which will not burn be overheaped and covered up with earth. . . . And this should be done to the honor of our Lord and of Christendom, so that God may see that we are

Christians and have not knowingly tolerated nor willed such public lies, maledictions, and blasphemies against His Son and His Christians." [61]

As for Luther's later attitude in matters of faith, the same formal intolerance appears in his thinking which he upheld in connection with public, juridical matters. This became especially true as the Protestant faith was increasingly organized into a church. Here again, "ramparts" were erected against possible heresy. The Apostles' Creed is such a rampart. In the Ecclesiastical Order of Goslar in 1531, Amsdorf had considered it to require a general commitment of all preachers to the "clear and pure Gospel of Jesus Christ without additions and without enthusiasm" [The ecstatic rapture of the Enthusiasts (*Schwärmer*) is referred to here].[62] After 1533, however, the Creed took the place of the Gospel. From this time on, preachers were bound to the Apostles' Creed, the Nicene Creed, the Athanasian Creed, and the Augsburg Confession. They thus became guardians of the pure doctrine. Heresy was no longer dealt with according to Matthew 18 alone but was to be punished by death, reference being made to Deuteronomy 13:7ff as scriptural justification.[63]

Luther's thoughts had initially revolved around the personal salvation of the individual. It was on this basis that he had laid claim to the freedom of conscience for the individual. Now it is quite clear that, as matters were brought under ecclesiastical control, such freedom was increasingly limited and finally even displaced by the very formal and intrinsic intolerance he had opposed in the Catholic Church. The endeavor to enforce unity outwardly in the state and inwardly in the church makes it clear that there was an effort again to establish, on the basis of a prophetic universal religion, a religious community of the ethnic type, exhibiting the same symptoms of intolerance as do all ethnic religions. This is apparent in the fact that the intolerance of the Israelite religion, an ethnic one, was set as an example for the Christian church.

The other reformers adopted the same view in this matter as did Luther. We will mention a few examples. In 1530, Melanchthon demanded that the Anabaptists be punished by the authorities; [64] and when Servetus was burned at Calvin's instigation in 1553, he called this execution a pious example, memorable to all following generations" (*pium et memorabile ad omnem posteritatem exemplum*).[65]

Zwingli hoped to establish a total state church in Zurich; state and church were to be united in a theocracy, and the design was to bring all subjects into uniformity. Thus the state church would have the power to impose censorship and penalties.

The best known similar example is the church rule established by Calvin at Geneva. His aim was to build a sacred church without heretical and immoral members. Thus the church-directed state began persecutions, which were carried out not only against those who deviated from the official faith, but also against those who infringed upon the very narrow-minded moral regulations which were enforced here. When Servetus was burned, Calvin wrote a paper of defense in 1554. (A refutation by the humanist Castellio was not published until 1612.) In his paper, Calvin tried to prove that heretics are justly attacked by force. This religious and ethical intolerance can only be understood on the basis of his theology, wherein law and grace are intimately connected.[66]

We have hitherto dealt essentially with the question of *inner* tolerance or intolerance in the case of Luther and the other reformers. As for *outward* tolerance (i.e., tolerance toward other religions) or intolerance, a remark of Luther's in his *Great Catechism* is striking. It shows that other religions and their adherents are rejected in an exclusivist manner that is typical of prophetic religiosity: ". . . These articles of faith divide and separate us Christians from all other people on earth; for none of those who stand outside of Christendom—be they heathens, Turks, Jews, or false Christians and hypocrites—know how the one and only true God is disposed toward them, even if they believe in Him and pray to Him. They are unable to bring forth any love or goodness toward Him, wherefore *they will remain in eternal wrath and damnation,* for they do not have Christ the Lord, nor have they received enlightenment and favor by any gift of the Holy Spirit." [67]

Nichiren   In the tolerant religious world of the Far East, and even within Buddhism, which is known for its tolerance, there lived in the thirteenth century an exceptional man. He revealed all qualities typical of a prophet, hence also the intolerance which is always connected with such a one. Nichiren was born in 1222 in a Japanese port city, and he entered a Shingon monastery at the age of twelve. Through a detailed study of the holy scriptures and extensive observations of contemporary Buddhism, he realized that the religion of his day and age had departed far from the creed taught by Buddha. For Nichiren, the existence of the various sects was but an indication that they had abandoned truth, which could only be *one*.

We can note here again that prophetic reformers are always inspired by a certain one-sidedness. It makes them hold *one* truth alone to be possible in religion. Then they regard their own insight as the only binding truth and proclaim it quite aggressively. It should also be observed that such prophetic reformers always single out specific motifs in their religious traditions, motifs that have stirred them particularly and which they regard as the sole criteria for judging all other views and practices in their respective religions. This is true, for instance, of Luther as well as of Nichiren. As Luther was moved by Romans 3:24, considering the Pauline doctrine of justification by faith alone to be the central message of Christianity and criticizing all other contemporary forms thereof on that basis; so Nichiren, too, selected one scripture from the abundance of Buddhist texts, the *Saddharma-pundarīka Sūtra* [The Lotus Sutra of the True Law], considering it and propagating it to be Buddha's only true teaching, quite contrary to historical matters of fact.[68] On the background of this sutra, all other sects, especially the widespread "Pure Land School" (of Amida Buddhism) appeared to Nichiren as defection from the historical Buddha's original teaching. He fought against the conditions in the country in caustic and most intolerant writings and sermons, calling the Amida School a pathway to hell, since it moved the historical Buddha into the background and replaced him by Amida Buddha. Nichiren claimed that

Amida's Paradise was nothing but imagination, and he called Zen Buddhism—which has many followers in Japan even in the present —a doctrine of demons and hell-spirits. The adherents of other Buddhist sects were termed robbers and treasoners. In a way that is typical of the prophet, he called upon people to "realize the time" and to turn to the Lotus Sutra right away. "Listen to the cuckoo above the clouds. He knows the time and knows that you must plant now. Therefore plant so that you will not have to repent when the time of harvest comes. Now is the time to plant the Lotus Sutra, and I am the messenger whom the venerable one has sent for this purpose." [69]

We have met with exactly the same attitude in the case of other prophetic personalities. There is the exclusive sense of being called to preach the truth, and the pressing for a decision right away. It is just this reference to the present as the right moment of conversion that is quite foreign to the historical Buddha's way of thinking. When *he* presented his teachings, he emphasized that he was unable to do anything about its acceptance, for that depends upon the inner maturity acquired by a person in the long course of his previous existences.

Considering this religious pattern, it is quite understandable that Nichiren represented the spirit of ruthless intolerance throughout his life. He even bequeathed that spirit to his disciples right up to the present.[70] He advised his government to suppress by force all heretics deviating from his own teaching, and to do so in order to ensure peace and prosperity throughout the land.

4. THE INTOLERANCE OF SACRED ORGANIZATIONS

Before we deal with the nature and historical forms of mystic tolerance let us turn to the intolerance of sacred organizations, which is, essentially, to be found outside mysticism.

When we speak of sacred organizations we mean communities that are distinct from the natural religious communities of ethnic or national groups; that is, they are constituted by religiously patterned social structures other than those of natural societies. These sociological systems are usually called churches. Sociologically speaking, such church organizations exist not only in Christianity but also in other religions, although Christianity has doubtless created the most marked and differentiated church forms in religious history. We shall therefore deal with the Christian church in particular detail first, but we can limit our scope to the Catholic Church and its attitude toward the question of tolerance, for we have already discussed the problem in reference to Protestantism in dealing with Luther and other reformers.

The Catholic Church   The Catholic Church—we need not trace it historical development here—understands itself as the Kingdom of God, as Saint Augustine put it.[71] Cyprian had already maintained that there is no salvation outside the Church.[72] Boniface VIII confirmed the same rigid view in the Bull *Unam sanctam* (1302),[73] and the *Catechismus Romanus* defined the Catholic Church's exclusive claim to salvation by maintaining that the Church was infallible in matters of faith and ethics. Now this notion is based upon the idea that the Church is guided by the Holy Spirit. Consequently all other churches that presume to such a claim—this is the teaching of the Bull—are led by Satan's spirit and must needs have fallen prey to most pernicious error in regard to doctrine and ethics.[74]

Let us now briefly trace the stages by which the Catholic—the early Christian—Church proceeded in doctrine and in practice, until it arrived at the ultimate consequences of the dogmatic self-understanding whereby it is the sole salvation-granting institution.

The Roman Empire's struggle against Christianity and its increasingly organized church—which was endangering the unity of the state—commenced when Christians were first persecuted under Nero. The struggle continued with changing vehemence in the course of the following centuries, reaching its climax under Decius (249–251) and Diocletian (283–305). Decius' predecessor, Philip the Arabian, had festively celebrated the thousandth anniversary of the Roman Empire, but its existence was even then already greatly threatened. In order to preserve it, Decius turned back to the old state religion. In attempting to enforce its general recognition, he ordered sacrifices to be made to the gods, and many Christians who disobeyed were put to death.

Under Diocletian, the battle against the Christian church flared up again and turned out to be a decisive struggle between the Roman state and the steadily growing church. In accordance with an edict by Diocletian in the year 303, churches were destroyed, the Holy Scriptures burned, and Christians holding public offices degraded. A decree in 304 ushered in the last bloody persecutions, which continued under Diocletian's successors.[75] This period ended with the Edict of Milan under Constantine in 313.

The Edict of Milan, a classical document of formal religious liberty granted to the individual by the state, contains this sentence, "It seemed to us . . . that it was proper that we should give to the Christians, as well as to all others, the right to follow that religion which to each of them appeared best." [76] Thus the liberty granted here to choose in matters of faith was in accordance with the spirit of ancient Rome. But just as that ancient ethnic religious state had been interested in religion for mainly formal reasons, wanting to employ it as a means of unifying the peoples of the Empire, so this also turned out to be the case with the new state (now Christian). Therefore, the same situation necessarily arose that had existed under non-Christian rulers. Thus Theodosius (378-395), in his edict of 378, issued an order compelling all people under his rule to embrace the Catholic faith.[77] Any doctrines deviating from the Church's teachings were declared criminal, those responsible for such doctrines deserving punishment.

During Theodosius' reign, a most significant offer was made to the ruler by Nestor, the bishop of Constantinople. The bishop wrote to the emperor, "Give me, my Prince, the earth purged of heretics, and I will give you heaven as a recompense. Assist me in destroying the heretics and I will assist you in vanquishing the Persians." [78] This is where the cooperation between state and church began so far as the fight against heretics is concerned. Later this led to the most disastrous consequences. In any event, a principle is visible here which is attested in the heresy laws of the time.[79] Later it even formed the legal basis for the state's inquisitorial practice of persecuting heretics. It implies that heresy, beyond being an offense subject to the most severe condemnation by the Church and the religious authorities, is also a public crime (*crimen publicum*) infringing upon that sphere of order which is maintained by the state and guarded by its interests according to its own regulations.

Before we inquire into the basic principles and practices of the Inquisition, which was the most extreme form of intolerance practiced by the Catholic Church in the Middle Ages, we want to refer to an episode which makes the peculiar, inevitable dialectic of tolerance and intolerance in organizations quite strikingly clear. In 361 Julian was proclaimed emperor. Although he was brought up in a Christian spirit, he relinquished the Christian faith and deprived Christianity of all the privileges that had been granted to it. He reintroduced the mystery religions and reestablished their legal status, thereby attempting to restore the worship of ancient gods. But such worship was not to take place in the naive manner relating to ancient mythology, but rather in an allegorical sense, in a sense developed by the Neoplatonic philosopher Iamblichus. Originally, Julian the Apostate, as he is called, thus championed tolerance of a mystic type, but later he endeavored to establish a kind of polytheistic, theocratic church, observing formal tolerance, for in his view there is but one universal God, above the national or ethnic gods who are subordinate to Him as provincial deities. But this tolerance also turned into intolerance, for, as Christians would not subject themselves to the theocracy, they were excluded from certain offices. Julian also turned against every kind of free thinking,[80] which makes it obvious once again that a sacred institution necessarily has intolerance in its wake.

Julian's attempt to restore the old religion was unsuccessful. For the sake of historical truth it should be noted that the epithet "the Apostate," which was given to him by history, is expressive of a negative assessment that is understandable from the viewpoint of the Christian church, but which does not do justice to Julian's high—though often unclear—religious motives.

There is a second episode in this period to which we want to refer here. In 382, Emperor Gratian, the fourth emperor after Julian, had the altar of the goddess Victoria removed from the session hall of the Roman Senate. The heathen senate party still existing at this time requested that it be rebuilt, and sent a delegation under Q. Aurelius Symmachus as speaker to the Emperor. At the instigation of Bishop Ambrose of Milan, however, the delegation was not permitted to present its cause. Gratian died soon after this, and then the same attempt was made again and a petition was handed over to Emperor Valentinian II. It said, "All people have their own customs and their own cult, and Fate has assigned different watchmen to different cities. . . . If venerable age can grant esteem to a religion, one must remain true to all the preceding centuries and follow the ancestors who in prosperity followed theirs. Consider that Rome is standing beside me now; this is what it says, 'Most benign sovereigns, fathers of the home land, have respect for the many years which I have experienced by adhering to pious customs. I wish to keep the rites of the ancestors. . . . I wish to live in my own way, I am free! This my religion has brought the whole orb under its law. These my sacrifices have driven Hannibal back from my walls, the Gauls from the Capitol.' . . . We beg for grace for the paternal, the native gods. Every person should justly have the same right, whomever he may worship. We [all] look up to the same stars, we all have the same heavens [above us], we are all surrounded by the same world. What does it matter according to which path of knowledge a person seeks truth? *It is not possible to arrive at such a great mystery on one path alone.*" [81]

Here representatives of a former state and its religion, which had persecuted Christians in its own name, beg for tolerance of those who had once requested the state for toleration themselves—and who had urged its rulers to grant such toleration not only because of the misery of persecution but also because they, according to their own words, held it to be the right attitude in matters of faith. Tertullian, for instance, wrote to Emperor Septimius Severus, who had issued a decree prohibiting conversion to Christianity in 202, "It is a fundamental right, a privilege of nature, that every man should worship according to his own conviction." [82] And Athanasius declared, "For it is not with the sword and spear, nor with soldiers and armed force that truth is to be propagated, but by counsel and sweet persuasion." [83] Lactantius, the Christian tutor of Emperor Constantine's son, also gave reasons why tolerance should be required. He did so most emphatically in his *Institutiones divinae,* by pointing out, "It is only in religion that liberty has chosen to dwell. For nothing is so much a matter of free will as religion, and no one can be required to worship what he does not will to worship."

As a successor to the old Roman state, the new Christian state and the church connected with it adopted the same intolerant attitude against which Christians had, for good reason, protested. This is another example of the dialectic of organizational tolerance.

Before we turn to the Inquisition in the Middle Ages, to its basic principles and practices, let us first discuss briefly the attitude of the Church to Judaism; for the practices which were employed against the Jews in the Middle Ages had their roots in the early church, just as did the Inquisition of heretics.

In the beginning, Judaism was a permitted religion enjoying toleration. But even in the Theodosian Code it is characterized as "abominable superstition" and Jews are referred to as "sacrilegious assemblies." The presence of Christians in a synagogue was regarded as *lèse-majesté* liable to persecution. From 423 on, no new synagogue could be erected without the permission of the Church.[84] Similar restrictions applied to Jews throughout the Middle Ages. A Christian who converted to the Jewish faith lost his property and his right of bequest. In the fifth century, capital punishment was imposed upon Jews who solicited new adherents for their faith. In the seventh century, the Jews in Spain, Italy, and France were ordered to chose between baptism and expulsion. Saint Isidore of

Seville (ca. 560–636) summoned a persecution of Jews, and there-upon King Sisebut ordered their forcible conversion. Although the Church did not endorse this procedure officially, it did subject the Jews to all penalties for heresy if they could be accused of in-clinations to their former faith, from which they had been averted by force. The reason given was that baptism once performed is indelible, even if it is performed by coercion. In 694, the Council of Toledo decreed perpetual servitude for Jews. The Fourth Lateran Council of 1215, which had particular significance for the treatment of heretics, as we shall have occasion to see, determined that Jews should wear a distinctive dress or particular badge, putting these regulations into Canon Law.

The Inquisition commenced with the establishment of bishops' courts during the Carolingian period. In the course of the following centuries it adopted ever more rigorous methods, letting the Chris-tian church betray its most holy ideals. These ideals and the obligation to them had been quite alive in the early Church; they were testified to repeatedly in warnings of important personalities. Lactantius, for example, wrote, "We must defend our religion, even by dying for it, but not by putting others to death; not by cruelty, but by patience alone. . . . If you believe you can defend your faith with blood, murder, and evil, you are really not defending it any more, for such practices stain and injure it." [85] The church father Chrysostom also warns of shedding blood: "Our master certainly does not prohibit us from restraining the false believers, from closing their mouths and rejecting their oaths; but he does prohibit us from shedding their blood and slaying them." [86] And Saint Augustine took the same view when he said, "The Church's love is directed toward rescuing the false believers from their eternal ruin without any of them having to die thereby." [87]

Such arguments against the violent persecution of dissenters were disregarded more and more in the course of time, especially by the end of the twelfth century. We do not intend to write a history of the Inquisition here; we only want to consider the Church's main proclamations with regard to the Inquisition's treatment of heretics, for this data is to form the basis for our reflection upon the intrinsic nature of this dreadful phenomenon and of the views conditioning it.

Innocent III is the first one we have to mention in this connection. In various documents he expressed the claim of the Church (or of the Pope), to worldly jurisdiction,[88] demanding that the state be subordinate to the Church.[89] During his papacy, the Fourth Lateran Council took place, which laid down regulations concerning the treatment of heretics and the Inquisition (*De haereticis, ch. 3*). Innocent also sent approximately twelve hundred Cistercian monks as Papal representatives to southern France to suppress the movement of the Albigensians. For this purpose, the worldly authorities were to grant every aid, and they actually did so.

Gradually there thus emerged, besides the Bishops' Inquisition, the Papal Inquisition—which was later called the "Holy Office" (*Sanctum Officium*), a term belying all this office ever did in the following period.

Around 1200, death by fire was the usual form of punishment for heretics. The *Sachsenspiegel* [Old Saxon Code] (1215–1235) contains this provision: "If a Christian, be he a man or a woman, is unbelieving, or if he deals with sorcery or poisoning or is proved guilty thereof, he should be burned on the pyre." [90] In 1252, Innocent IV (in the Bull *Ad Extirpanda*) permitted the moderate use of torture to compel heretics to make confessions.

As the church endeavored to uphold the principle *ecclesia non sitit sanguinem* ("the church does not shed blood") at least formally, Pope Alexander IV (1245–1261) granted absolution privileges to such priests as *had* shed blood by the use of torture during the Inquisition, thus annulling the disorder caused thereby. Innocent IV and Alexander IV together issued over one hundred heresy bulls, which were followed by further decrees demanding the persecution and extirpation of dissidents in ever more severe terms. In his *Summa theologica,* Thomas Aquinas spoke in favor of exterminat-

ing heretics when he wrote, "The Church hands the obstinate heretics over the worldly court. . . . It does not save those who relapse
from the peril of death." [91]

State laws also legalized the Inquisition. Beyond the regulations
we have already referred to, such was especially the case with the
Heretic Law of Ravenna of 1232, which was later (in 1238 and 1239)
formulated in even stricter terms. It demanded of every believer
that he report heretics known to him. [92] The heretic was not permitted to argue his cause and prove the truth of his view, for not
primarily truth but the unity of the institution was at stake. The
accused was convicted when he himself confessed or when two wit-
nesses agreed in statements against him. All methods of cunning
and fraud were expressly permitted. Eymericus writes, in his *Directorium inquisitorium* (1587), that everything done to convert a
heretic is laudable. [93] The height of hypocrisy was the church's re-
quest to the state, to whom the persistent heretic was handed over
for the execution of the verdict, to spare his "life and limbs." [94]

This, then, was the procedure the church observed: it established
the guilt of the accused and then handed him over to the worldly
arm of the state to execute sentence. The climax of the procedure
was the proclamation of the sentence. It is clear that the main thing
for the Inquisition was the effect upon the masses. They were to be
kept in the unity of faith, for when the sentence was proclaimed—
and this happened in public with great pomp—the purpose was to
point out the vileness of the persecuted sect and the propriety of
the church's teaching, and at the same time to demonstrate strikingly the power of the church.

Penitent sinners usually had to wear the sign of the cross for
several years. In this case, a cross was sewn to the clothes of the
remorseful heretic so that everyone could discern him as such.
Furthermore, the church ordered fasting, alms-giving, and pilgrimages as penal measures. If the dissident continued to adhere to his
belief, the worldly arm of the state was called upon, as we have
already pointed out, to execute the death penalty, and usually this
meant death by burning. The remains of the body were not buried

by the Church, the possessions of the executed were confiscated, and the descendants of the heretic were regarded as unfit for taking a public office unless specifically rehabilitated.[95]

Hitherto we have spoken mainly of the Roman Catholic Inquisition. Let us now turn to the Orthodox Church of Russia. The Russian Church had a form of rule called Caesaro-Papism where the absolute sovereign of the state also wielded the highest power in religious and church matters, thus ensuring the unity of state and church. The spirit of the Inquisition that prevailed here is best characterized by a malediction which was proclaimed in every Orthodox Church once a year ever since the seventh century. It reads: "To those who do not believe that the Orthodox monarchs have been raised to the throne by virtue of a special grace of God and that, at the moment the sacred oil is laid on them, the gifts of the Holy Ghost are infused into them anent the accomplishment of their exalted mission . . . Anathema! Anathema! Anathema!" [96] The Church Council of 1666 decided to lay upon the dissidents not only ecclesiastical but also "imperial" penalties.[97] And Nicholas I continued to place dissenters under special severe laws.

The unity defended in this manner was commented upon by Tolstoi, who said, "The interference of government in the sphere of faith produces the . . . worst of vices, hypocrisy. . . . Union is no wise attained by the compulsory . . . retention of all men in the external profession of one bond of religious teaching . . . but only by the free advance of the comunity towards truth." [98]

After reviewing the institutional intolerance of the Christian Church in the Inquisition, let us now search for the ideas that preconditioned this fatal development. This leads us, once again, to the idea of unity. The fact that the institution strives to preserve its unity is the root of every kind of formal intolerance. The Inquisition with all its bloodshed is a result of the close connection between the *sacerdotium,* the priesthood, and the *imperium,* the imperial power. Both were united in the idea of the *Corpus Christianum,* the body of Christ, state and church being regarded as its limbs.[99] The Christian claim to absoluteness—we shall discuss its inner significance at another point—was derived from the ancient concept of the state; for when Theodosius made the Christian faith the exclusive state religion in 380, he took up the idea of the Roman state and connected it in the manner of Jewish theocracy with the concept of the visible Kingdom of God in the Church.[100] Such a notion of the *Corpus Christianum* led to various consequences in the relationship between church and state in the Middle Ages. In the first place, it was believed that the Church as the visible Kingdom of God possesses powers derived from the Otherworld. They are, however, lawfully wielded in this world by the authorities of the church organization(the bishops etc.). The Church alone has absolute truth, and this truth is binding unto salvation. It is the duty of those who possess such truth to ward off ruin from others by subjugating them to this truth, even if it be against their will. Hence the Church also has the right to subject individuals to its law by force. The state is lawful only as a Christian state; that is, in being connected to the Church. The Christian state and church overlap, and the people of Christ in the spiritual and the physical sense are subject to a worldly and a spiritual authority. But the spiritual authority is superior to the worldly power. Salvation can only be acquired by subjection to the Church, and obedience to the state power has its limits when the state no longer carries out the Church's orders. The separation between faith and order in the Church thus appears as a rending apart of its salvation assuring unity. This unity gained its outward expression in the uniform culture of the Middle Ages. It was the purpose of the Inquisition to defend such unity.[101]

It should be noted at this point that the Catholic Church has been formally intolerant ever since the time of Gregory the Great in the sixth century. However, the Church does actually exercise tolerance with regard to content, not expressedly but implicitly. Since Gregory, the Church has assimilated an abundance of pre- and sub-Christian folk-religious elements, which should have been warded off if the ideal of Christian faith were to be upheld. Friedrich Heiler says of Gregory: "He reduced the great and pure thoughts of Saint

Augustine to the level of mass Christianity; he is the theological representative of average Catholicism."[102] Ancient fear of demons and a craze for miracles, a vulger concept of the sacraments, and the veneration of saints—all were tolerantly sanctioned by Gregory. Whatever did not oppose the unity of the Church but rather adapted itself to it and enhanced its power, especially over the broad masses, was permitted and tolerated. It is a peculiar type of intrinsic tolerance we come upon here. It was not at all consciously exercised; for, according to dogma, non-Christian cult practices were of course rejected. But in practice they *were* taken up, and were given Christian designations and retained. This syncretism within the Church is the result of an unconsciously exercised intrinsic tolerance. Its limit was the feasibility of assimilation within the ecclesiastical system.

Let us now turn to the "Declarations" of the Church and expound the principles which were expressed by the Second Vatican Council. We shall take two Declarations as the basis for our considerations, the one on "Religious Liberty" (RL) of December 7, 1965, and the other on the "Relationship of the Church to Non-Christian Religions" (NCR) of October, 1965.[103]

First to the former: assuming that the "only true religion has its concrete form of existence in the Catholic and Apostolic Church" (RL 1), the Council nevertheless advocates that every person has a right to religious liberty. It defines that liberty as implying "that all people should be free of every constraint by individuals or by groups in the society, as well as of every form of human power." "No one shall ever be compelled to act against his conscience in religious matters, and within due limits no one shall be prevented from acting according to his conscience, either privately or openly, as an individual or together with others" (RL 2). This right to religious liberty is based upon "the dignity of the human being, as it is perceived in the revealed word of God and also by reason itself." (RL 2). The denial of "free practice of religion in society" is considered to be "injustice against the human being and against the order into which man has been placed by God." (RL 3).

The limit of religious freedom is determined by the ethnical law which demands of people and groups that they "observe the rights of others as well as their own obligations toward others and the public weal. It is furthermore determined by considerations of public order" (RL 7). This is quite clearly what we have described as "formal tolerance."

The Declaration attempts to prove that this doctrine of religious liberty is founded upon revelation; Jesus himself as well as the apostles, so it says, called for freedom and the absence of constraint in decisions regarding matters of faith (RL 10).

The spirit of the Declaration stands in marked contrast to the many practices which had been common, especially in the Inquisition, ever since the Theodosian Edict on Religion in 380. That edict had declared adherence to the Christian faith to be the state duty and had demanded such adherence of every subject. Now it is noteworthy that the Declaration specifically points out this departure from the spirit of the gospel. It says (RL 12), "Certainly the people of God, in their pilgrimage through changing human history, have acted in ways that hardly correspond to the spirit of the Gospel, aye, that even contradict it. Yet the teaching of the Church, that no one should be forced to accept its faith, has been retained throughout the ages." [104]

The second Declaration we want to discuss here (NCR) is especially important for our study, because it adopts an attitude that is very similar to the one we have termed "intrinsic tolerance." It acknowledges that there is something true and holy in non-Christian religions (NCR 2): "Nothing of all that is true and sacred in these religions is discarded by the Catholic Church. She takes all those actions and patterns of life, those principles and teachings, most sincerely, which not seldom reflect a ray of the truth enlightening all men, even though they deviate in many points from what she herself holds and teaches to be true." The Declaration recognizes that there is in non-Christian religions the "perception of the hidden power—and often even of the knowledge—of a highest God, or even of a Father" (NCR 2). This is even established in detail by short, pertinent characterizations of what we term the "living core" of these religions.

Of *Hinduism,* the Declaration says, "Men in Hinduism search for the mystery of the Divine in its depths and express it with an overwhelming wealth of myths and philosophical endeavors; they seek delivery from our confined and limited situation by following ascetic life, or by deep contemplation, and also by taking refuge with God in love and confidence." (NCR 2). Concerning *Buddhism,* the Declaration says that this religion "in its various forms realizes the radical insufficiency of this fleeting world and teaches a path by which men of devout and faithful heart can acquire the state of complete liberation or reach the highest stage of enlightenment, either by their own actions or by help from above" (NCR 2). The verdict of the Declaration on *Islam* which, as a religion, was radically condemned by Christian theologians for centuries—as was the prophet Mohammed himself [105]—is also most positive. It declares that "the Church also looks with high regard upon the Moslems, for they worship the one and only, the living and self-existing God, the Merciful and Almighty, the maker of heaven and earth, who has spoken to men. They attempt to submit themselves with all their soul to even his hidden ways" (NSR 3).

A lengthier portion of the Declaration, finally, is devoted to the *Jewish religion.* The Church is aware of common bonds with this religion, bonds that reach back to Moses and the prophets, for in them lie "the beginnings of her faith and her being elect" (NCR 4). The Declaration hence points out that there is a common spiritual heritage uniting Christians and Jews. The Church expressly disavows the idea that Jews are rejected and condemned by God, and it deplores "emphatically all outbreaks of hatred and persecution, all manifestations of anti-Semitism" that have been directed against the Jews.

It is especially what this second Declaration has to say about the relationship of the Church to non-Christian religions that is expressive of a basically new attitude, one we have called "intrinsic tolerance." It is to be hoped that these principles will also be applied in practice. The present struggle in Spain about the so-called "Protestant Statute" is still far from the spirit of the Council.

The Jewish Church   We have already discussed the outward and inward tolerance of the Israelite religion. This was a genuine ethnic religion maintained by an independent national Jewish state. A decisive point in the development of the Jewish religion was the Babylonian Exile in the sixth century; it brought about a basic change in the structure of the religious community. Disregarding the short period of the Maccabean rule, post-Exilic Judaism no longer maintained an independent state of its own. What emerged in Palestine after the Exile was in structure not a politico-religious community but a cultural alliance, a sort of church. The old Israel was a genuine ethnic-religious community, determined and ordered by the law of Yahweh in all areas of life, in the profane sphere of everyday duties, in politics, and in cultic matters. After the Exile, politics became a sector of life determined by reference to the Holy. Under Ezra, an allegedly old law book (which was, however, actually new), the so-called Priestly Code, was made to form the basis of community life (Nehemiah 8–10). Judaism was marked off from all pagan and semi-Jewish forms of worship by the introduction of a specific cult that was laid down in the most minute detail.[106] What was gradually established here was in structure a church, a hierarchic theocracy.

The most diverse elements coalesced in the Jewish church: age-old Semitic folk-belief, facets of a strictly law-oriented faith, and features of a pronounced book-religion. Ethics were casuistic, moral precepts pertaining to particular cases precisely laid down by the law. Temple worship was, essentially, sacrificial cult carried out by priests and Levites and involving complicated rituals. The priesthood was set up hierarchically, and it wielded administrative power. (The Sanhedrin was the legislative assembly at Jerusalem.) [107]

It was this church that asked Jesus about his authority (Mark 11:28) and took penal measures against the young Christian congregation (Acts 4:1ff; 6:12). According to Acts 24:5, the accusation brought forward against Paul was this: "We have found this man a pestilent fellow, an agitator among all the Jews throughout the world, and a ringleader of the sect of the Nazarenes. He even tried to profane the temple, but we seized him and would have judged him according to our law."

Here again it was the unity and integrity of the institution that seemed threatened by Jesus' and the apostles' prophetic preaching. Their spontaneous and dynamic activity could not be contained within the rigid structure of the sacred Jewish church, which was determined by innumerable intricately connected rules and regulations. Jesus' great discussion with the Pharisees and Scribes (Matthew 23), the representatives of this church, brings out the protest of one who possesses direct religious apprehension against those of the organized religion whose spiritual apprehension is mediated by the law. This is an ever-recurring dialectic: first the attitude of a consolidated religious institution with its inevitable intolerance of independent prophetic personalities, and later its tolerant incorporation of such prophets into the church system. Jesus points out that dialectic with these words, "Woe to you, Scribes and Pharisees, hypocrites! For you build the tombs of the prophets and adorn the monuments of the righteous, saying, 'If we had lived in the days of our fathers, we would not have taken part with them, in shedding the blood of the prophets'" (Matthew 23:29f). The constantly recurring situation which Jesus points out here is this: the prophets of the past who turned against the superficial cult activity of their religious community were persecuted by that community, and even put to death. Now, however, the church was rebuilding the tombs of these prophets and worshipping them as saints. Turning back to the past, it was including them into its worship system, although they were once persecuted as unbearable to the community of their time. The representatives of the church even assert that if those prophets lived today they would not persecute them. And here Jesus stands before them with an even greater authority, but again they fail to recognize or acknowledge it. They will rather slay him soon, just as they eliminated the prophets before him.

We know how things developed later. After Jesus' life and death, a new religious community was established, which inevitably became another organized church, persecuting the prophets who would not integrate into its ecclesiastical system, stamping them out, or at least excommunicating and condemning them.

The Confucian Church　　The term "church" is also applied to the Confucian state system in China. Only in a very limited sense can Confucius himself be regarded as the founder of this later state religion. What interests us here is how this Confucian state related to other religions.

The Confucian church persecuted heretics too. In the year 845, the Chinese Emperor We-tsung abolished Buddhism in his realm, destroying 4600 Buddhist monasteries and forcing 265,000 monks and nuns to turn to worldly professions.[108] The founder of the Ming Dynasty, T'ai-tsu (1368–96), resumed these persecutions and issued an order that no woman under forty years of age (later over twenty years of age) may become a Buddhist nun. Shih-tsung (1521–66) commanded all temples in his empire to be destroyed, and no young man was permitted to renounce the world. Punishment for violation was directed against family members too.

The Codes of the Manchu Dynasty (1644–1911) also included a great many restrictive and penal measures pertaining to Buddhism. One such law was directed "Against Heresies of Religious Leaders or Instructors, and of Priests." The Sacred Edict of 1724, in its seventh homily, contained this admonition: "Exclude heterodoxy in order to exalt orthodoxy."

In a decree of 1784 against the Mohammedans, the extermination of the Wahabi sect was demanded. In the same year ordinates were issued against Christians. In one of them it says: "Europeans propagating their religion here, and thereby leading the people into error, are extremely fatal to the manners and customs and to the human heart. . . . And as for natives who keep the Christian commandments and profess that religion . . . they shall, of course, be forced to conversion; and so their books, writings, and other things brought to light must be melted or burned, and they shall be tried to the supplementary articles [of the Law Against Heresy]." [109]

The ideology of uniform state pattern, finally, led to the issuing of imperial orders in 1811 and 1812 which contain these sentences: "Let us remember that this religion [Christianity] does not profess the worship of any gods, nor the veneration of ancestors or the dead, and therefore overtly opposes the orthodox Tao [principle or teaching]; so, when the natives listen to it and follow it, spread and observe it, accept its falsehoods, and use its insignia, is this anything short of opposition and rebellion?" [110]

It was only after the Chinese Revolution of 1911 that formal intolerance which was determined by the interests of the Confucian state gave way to formal tolerance, for in 1923 the second Chinese constitution ("Constitution of the Republic of China") declared (in Article 12): "Citizens of the Republic of China shall have the liberty to honor Confucius and to profess any religion, on which no restraint shall be imposed except in accordance with the law." [111] This provision dissolved the Confucian state church.

The Japanese State Organization   Shinto, the ethnic or national religion of Japan, is still alive today. It was the state religion for centuries, and in this role it defended the sacred unity of the state against disordering influences. In fact it did so in a most intolerant manner in spite of all its intrinsic tolerance toward Buddhism. That religion was introduced in Japan in 552 A.D. and became the state creed under Shotoku Taishi in 593. As long as Buddhism had decisive influence on public life, there was complete tolerance. In the Great Reform of 645, the impulses coming from the various religious creeds in Japan (Confucianism, Buddhism, Shinto) were intentionally integrated to serve the common welfare of the state. Thus a far-reaching fusion of the three religions took place.

After the Edict of Hideyoshi (1587), however, this period of tolerance was replaced by one of formal intolerance on the part of the sacred institution, for now every religion was prohibited that did not recognize the special deities of Shinto. Consequently there were persecutions, closure of the country to all contact with Christianity, censorship of books, and the death penalty for those who promoted Christianity. During this so-called Tokugawa Period (1600–1868), Buddhism, too, was pushed into the background. Religious propagation as well as conversion from one sect to another were prohibited.[112]

The Great Restoration of the Imperial House of Japan in 1868, which ushered in the country's rise to a world power, was also connected with a renewal of state Shinto. As in ancient times, the cult of the innumerable Shinto deities, the Kami, was henceforth to be sponsored by and related to the state government. This implied a sharp turn toward intolerance, especially as regards Buddhism, which was now accused of having falsified Shinto for centuries. Thus in 1871 an order was issued to differentiate strictly between Kami cult and Buddhism.[113] Buddhism was banned from the court of the Emperor and honors which had been bestowed upon Buddhist priests by the state were withdrawn.

But this period of typically institutional intolerance soon passed; for, when the country opened to Western influence, the Western idea of religious liberty gained ground in Japan. We cannot trace the changes that took place regarding the attitude toward Shinto, but they amounted to the fact that this religion was deprived of its true religious character by the state and reduced to a purely national matter.[114] Of course Shinto sects continued to exist beside the official shrine cult, and they retained their religious nature.

In 1867 the penal laws against Christians were officially renounced, so that practically all creeds now enjoy religious liberty. It was first guaranteed by Article 28 of the Japanese Constitution of 1889.

The Lamaistic Church   In the eighth century A.D., Padmasambhava introduced into Tibet a particular type of Mahāyāna Buddhism that coalesced with the indigenous Bon faith, a religion characterized by belief in demonic powers. In the course of time and after a reformation lead by Tsong-kha-pa in the fourteenth century, there emerged a regular ecclesiastical system with an hierarchically organized clergy, an actual church, and a complicated ritual. Now Tibet is the only land where Buddhism ever established a real church organization that grew to be a true Pontifical state. In fact a kind of double papacy developed: the Dalai Lama mainly determined worldly affairs, and the Panchen Lama was responsible for spiritual matters.

As Lamaism is a mystic religion, which can integrate the most differing religious views and doctrines into its religious system and render mystic significance to the most peculiar cult practices, there are no evidences of intolerance here. This is probably because in the main Lamaism is a cult religion that interprets its doctrines and practices in mystic terms. Hence it lacks the element of exclusively rationalistic obligation to a tradition which, in other cases, has always led to intolerant practices.

The Indian Caste System   India is usually called the land of tolerance, and rightly so. But there is also in Hinduism an institutionally determined intolerance; this leads us to consider the Indian caste system, for it is within this order that we encounter religiously motivated intolerance, even though there is no mention of such within the actual religions of India. Those who do display intolerance, however, are not individuals, but rather sociological groups within the religiously motivated social pattern of Hinduism.

Before we go on, we must further specify the meaning of religious tolerance in this study. By religious tolerance or intolerance we always mean attitudes pertaining to religious views or practices, or to religions themselves.

If we take the term in this sense, we shall encounter mainly genuine tolerance in India. In the caste system there is an exclusiveness which is upheld by certain groups and is directed against other groups and their patterns of life. These groups themselves do not form religious communities possessing their own forms of faith; rather, they are social structures determined in some way or other by religion. Certain groups and their members are regarded as being pure or impure—this is also religiously motivated—and that determines the relationship among the groups. For this reason we believe we should deal with this particular hybrid form of institutional intolerance in a religious connection.

In India, human existence is existence within the caste system. According to the Indian view, human existence is more than biological life in time and space. Hence the caste, too, is more than a this-worldly pattern; it has a metaphysical basis, it is the manifestation of an invisible, eternal cosmic order.

In trying to comprehend and express the concept lying at the base of Indian religious systems, we may say that the decisive motif here is a twofold movement of life: a movement from original unity to plurality in the phenomenal world, and a return from segmented plurality back to unity. In its deepest sense, human life participates in eternal unity, but it is actualized in plurality. The movement from unity to plurality, which leads to individual being, creates great differences within the world of men, differences that cannot be eradicated or obliterated. They constitute the various castes—of which there are four basic ones (the Brahmans, the martial nobility, the people of the middle class, and the laborers).

Because of the growing differentiation of life, these castes have been split into 2000 to 3000 subcastes in the course of time. Like all these subcastes, the four original castes are genuine "birth communities" (communities into which one is born), not "optional communities" (communities which one chooses to join). Being born into a caste is not a matter of contingency but is determined by the law which ensures that all deeds receive their recompense, the law of *karma*. Therefore the caste is the lot man creates for himself by his own deeds, by his inner attitude, and hence by his whole personal life. The sequence of rebirths (*samsāra*), which leads all beings to a new existence after death, is governed by this universal karmic law. Hence wherever the order or the caste system is observed in India, it is seen not as a hierarchical structure created by the demands of society, but rather as a series of patterns within which men can live. Heinrich Zimmer expresses this thought aptly when he says, "There are born men of the spirit [priests and keepers of knowledge], born men of deeds [warriors and rulers], born citizens who live by commerce, craftsmanship, and trade of every kind, and born disinherited." [115]

According to the basic religious view in India, an eternal law called *dharma* rules the world of nature and of men. It is expressed in human society as the caste law and it prescribes for every caste its particular functions and duties. [116]

We are interested here only in the relationship between the castes. It is marked by the "caste spirit," a term we have adopted in our language to indicate narrow-minded segregation. The idea is that every mingling of castes must be avoided. A word in the Bhagavadgītā points out how disastrous the results are in the opinion of the ancient Indians:

> On the extinction of a family, the eternal rites of families are destroyed. Those rites being destroyed, impiety predominates over the whole family. In consequence of the predominance of impiety, O Krishna! the women of the family become corrupt; and the women being corrupt, O descendant of Vrishni! intermingling of castes results; that intermingling necessarily leads the family and the destroyers of the family to hell. . . . By these transgressions of the destroyers of families, which occasion intermingling of castes, the eternal rites of castes and rites of families are subverted. And O Ganārdana! we have heard that men whose family rites are subverted must necessarily live in hell. [117]

The main thing is to do one's duty as prescribed by one's own caste. Hence the Bhagavadgītā points out, "One's own duty, though defective, is better than another's duty well performed. Death in [performing] one's own duty is preferable; the [performance of the] duty of others is dangerous." [118] As a consequence of this view, one caste separates itself quite exclusively from another; if a man from a higher caste deals with one of a lower he immediately defiles himself. Even the shadow of a *Shudra* falling on a member of a higher caste pollutes him.

We need not describe the negative and often cruel effects of the caste system in detail. What we have here is quite clearly intolerance in the sense characterized above, as it is basically determined by religious views and motives. This is why it is so difficult to abolish the caste system—although such endeavors have been made repeatedly in Indian religious history.

Many representatives of modern Hinduism, like Radhakrishnan, attempt to prove the legitimacy of the caste system and to confirm its positive values.[119] Others, like Rabindranath Tagore, realize that the harm it has done far outweighs its benefits. Tagore writes, "The regeneration of the Indian people, to my mind, directly and perhaps solely depends upon the removal of this condition of caste."[120] Gandhi regarded the treatment of the outcastes as a disgrace to India and he worked for its abolition as long as he lived. But he himself became a victim to fanaticism because of his relationship to the Mohammedans, for according to the caste order all who do not belong to Hinduism—and hence also all members of other religious communities—are *pariahs* (outcastes), with whom the caste Hindu should have just as little contact as with the Indian outcaste.

5. Mystic Tolerance

Hinduism   Whereas tolerance has to be fought for in prophetic religions, mystic faiths have tolerance "in their blood." And it is not only formal, but primarily even intrinsic tolerance that we find here. Because of the character of their religious experience and their understanding of that experience, the mystics adopt an attitude that prophetic religions and religious organizations assume only after engaging in great struggles and undergoing various inner changes —if they ever acquire it at all.

Let us now turn to religious history to gain a sound basis for our later considerations. We shall begin with Hinduism.

The different forms of mysticism within the setting of the Indian caste system[121] all have one common basis: they start with the experience of the divine Absolute being in and beyond the world of plurality. The ancient Vedic gods were considered to belong to this plurality, for the religion of the Vedas was, on the whole, polytheistic, world-affirming, and oriented toward this life. In the more recent sections of the Rigveda as well as in the Atharvaveda, there are initial forms of the mystical experience of unity which also forms the basis of mystic tolerance. In a famous hymn in the Rigveda we find these words:

> There was not non-being, nor was there being
> at that time,[122]
> There was no air, no firmament above,
> What moved at that time? Where? Under whose protection?
> Was mist the unfathomable depth?
> Nor death nor life was there,
> No discerning mark between night and day.
> *The One* breathed, but in its own manner, breathlessly,
> *the One*.[123]

Such is the language and the creed of mysticism. This passage dismisses the idea that anything tangible or this-worldly could have existed in the beginning, and then it goes on to say—although nothing has been spoken of conceptually—*"the One* breathed." Obviously, this means that the Absolute cannot be expressed in worldly, human terms; it does not exist in the same way other things in this world of plurality do. "The One" is the true numinous Being which existed in the beginning of this temporal world, not only in a chronological sense in the beginning, but also in a basic sense, as that which was there "in principle" (*in principio*), as that which is actual beyond all plurality.

This experience of envisioned unity is the key to the understanding of a word in the Rigveda, a scripture which actually contains hymns addressed to particular gods considered as quite independent beings. Here the plurality of gods is absorbed into the numinous One. It says: "They [the pious seers and sages in the holy scriptures] call him Indra, Mitra, Varuna, Agni. . . . Sages name variously him who is but one." [124] What are the old gods of the ethnic religion, then? Nothing but names for the eternal One, different names and therefore different aspects of the same One.

This basic mystic attitude even becomes dominant in the course of India's later religious history.

Whereas the divine One is the numinous reality acknowledged by impersonal mysticism, the God Vishnu appears as the divine Reality in the personal mysticism of Vishnu devotion; *all* particular deities relate to him. [The author distinguishes between *impersonal* and *personal mysticism*—the former acknowledges an *impersonal* sacred, or numinous, absolute as the highest Being, the latter a *personal* God.] Thus it says in the Bhagavadgītā (X, 20ff):

> I am the self . . . seated in the hearts of all beings . . . I am Vishnu among the Ādityas, the beaming sun among the shining [bodies].[125]

The passage continues by enumerating all important phenomena in the world of gods and of men, and by relating them to Vishnu as the one who constitutes their nature. Then it concludes with this summary (X, 39ff):

> There is nothing movable or immovable which cannot exist without me. O terror of your foes! there is no end to my divine emanations. Here I have declared the extent of [those] emanations only in part. Whatever thing [there is] or power, or glorious, or splendid, know all that to be produced from portions of my energy.

The basic attitude expressed here necessarily leads to intrinsic tolerance. Quite in contrast to the prophetic religions' exclusive rejection of other gods, we come upon a verse in the Bhagavadgītā which says (IX, 23): "Even those . . . who being devotees of other divinities worship with faith, worship me only."

This is especially instructive. It is expressive of an attitude which I call "inclusive absoluteness." The Vishnu devotee is quite convinced that his God is the only true one, but he implicates other religious cults and views in his faith by assuming that they all refer to Vishnu, without the respective worshippers knowing it themselves. Vishnu is for them a kind of "unknown God" whom they "worship as unknown" (Acts 17:23). Hence Vishnu regards faith as decisive, not the idea of God a man of other faith may have.

Whichever form [of deity] any worshipper wishes to worship with faith, to that form I render his faith steady. Possessed of that faith he seeks to propitiate [the deity in] that [form], and obtains from it those beneficial things which he desires, [though they are] really given by me [Gītā VII, 21f].

This is the basic structure of what we have called intrinsic tolerance: the acknowledgment of other forms of worship as genuine possibilities of encounter with the divine. It is in this sense that the celebrated North Indian Brahman poet Tulsī Dās (1552–1623) speaks; his continuing popularity in India is certainly due, among other factors, to this tolerance.[126]

In the Telugu country the poet Vēmana—we do not know for certain when he lived—had great influence on the people for centuries. For him, too, the main thing in religion, in every religion, was love of God. All outward forms of worship and ideas about God are inessential and unimportant compared to this relationship. Vēmana says:

> . . .
> Religions counted by the score
> There are. But yet not one is good
> If faith be lacking in its lore.
> Faith makes our worship please our God.[127]

The spirit of this venerable tradition has remained alive right into contemporary Hinduism. Its most noted representative is Radhakrishnan, whose works are also known in the West.[128] Radhakrishnan's deep sense of the oneness of the Holy and Eternal leads him not to neglect the many diverse opinions about God, but rather to uphold their due significance and full legitimacy—while discarding their exclusiveness and segregative character:

If the Hindu chants the Vedas on the banks of the Ganges, if the Chinese meditates on the Analects, if the Japanese worships the image of Buddha, if the European is convinced of Christ's mediatorship, if the Arab reads the Qu'rān in his mosque, and if the African bows down to a fetish, each one of them has exactly the same reason for his particular confidence. Each form of faith appeals in precisely the same way to the inner certitude and devotion of its followers. It is their deepest apprehension of God and God's fullest revelation to them. The claim of any religion to validity is the fact that only through it have its followers become what they are.[129]

The two basic ways of conceiving of the divine in religion, as personal and impersonal, both appear to the Hindu as being determined by man and his capacity to understand, and they are therefore quite compatible. This is because of the Hindu idea of numinous reality. Says Radhakrishnan, "The supra-personal and the personal representations of the real are the absolute and the relative ways of expressing the one reality. When we emphasize the nature of reality in itself we get the absolute Brahman; when we emphasize its relation to us we get the personal Bhagavan."[130] In content, too, the various terms applying to God comprehend but partial truth: "These different representations do not tell us about what God is in himself, but only what he is to us."[131]

It is most important, furthermore, that Hinduism, because of its attitude regarding different concepts of God (as we have traced them), never declared a particular view to be the only true and binding one. Hence it never regarded conversion to its own concepts as its duty. For Hinduism, religious life was always more important than dogmatic preaching. "Truth for the Hindu does not mean dogmatism. He does not smell heresy in those who are not entirely of his mind. It is not devotion that leads to the assertive temper, but limitation of outlook, hardness, and uncharity."[132]

The basic tolerant character of Hinduism cannot be summed up more aptly than with these words of Radhakrishnan: "As a result of this tolerant attitude, Hinduism itself has become a mosaic of almost all the types and stages of religious aspiration and endeavor. It has adapted itself with infinite grace to every human need and it has not shrunk from the acceptance of every aspect of God conceived by man, and yet reserved its unity by interpreting the different historical forms as modes, emanations, or aspects of the Supreme."[133]

Paul Hacker, in *Religiöse Toleranz und Intoleranz im Hinduismus* [Religious Tolerance and Intolerance in Hinduism] (*Saeculum* VIII, 1957), an essay written not without a certain bias, has adopted a critical attitude towards Hindu tolerance. He shows up many instances of intolerance within the caste system. We have also pointed out its institutionally determined intolerance; but Hacker fails to see that tolerance dominates among the religious leaders of India, quite in contrast to the situation in the Christian church, where the idea of tolerance has had to maintain itself against the opposition of Christian leaders and institutions, if it has been able to do so at all. This fact is also emphasized by H. von Glasenapp in his article, *Toleranz und Fanatismus in Indien* [Tolerance and Fanaticism in India] (*Schopenhauer-Jahrbuch*, 1960). He writes, "The tolerant spirit of religious Indians who are desirous of hearing about other faiths, and the irenic attitude they adopt in life towards such religions is, indeed, quite different from the manner in which Christianity and Islam deal with the teachings of other religions. Of course passages in authoritative [Hindu] scriptures can be quoted which do not display such a liberal attitude, and in the age-old history of Hinduism there are cases where adherents of one particular faith have fought against those who were of different opinion, not only with peaceful means, but also by the use of force. But these are exceptions in the general conciliatory mentality of the Indian. We find exactly the opposite in Christianity."

Sufism   On the ground of Islam with its prophetic exclusivism and manifold intolerance there sprang up, as a reaction against these qualities, a mystic movement which was called Sufism because of the clothes its adherents wore. (*Sūfi* means a person clothed in wool, a wearer of a monk's garb.) There are records of this mysticism dating back to the second century after the Prophet Mohammed's *hegira* (622). Of course the movement met with the passionate opposition of Islamic orthodoxy because of its liberal interpretation of the Koran [134] and its indifference toward cultic obligations. Thus the great mystic al-Hallāj was put to death in Bagdad in 921 A.D. because of his genuinely mystic confession, "My Self is God." The greatest representatives of this mysticism are to be found in Persia. The most important of them lived in the thirteenth century: Ferīdu-d-Dīn Attār (died 1230), Jalālu-d-Dīn Rūmi (died 1273) and Muslihu-d-Dīn Sca'di (died 1292). In the fourteenth century there lived the lyric poet Hāfiz (died 1388).

The "living core" of Sufi mysticism lies, negatively speaking, in the renunciation of all outward cult formalities and in the discarding of binding theological doctrines. In positive terms, it lies in the reduction of all forms of religious life to the love of God, the friend and beloved:

> Should the trumpet sound tomorrow for the Judgment Day, men and women would stand before Him with countenance pale. But I would approach thee with love in my hands, saying, "Consider all my deeds, O Lord, naught do I fear." [135]

For the Sufi mystics, union with God in love is the only standard for judging a religion and its worship practices. This is the basis of the Sufis' truly intrinsic tolerance. For them, the mystical union with God alone is decisive for the acceptance or rejection of a religion. This is expressed by the beautiful words of Jalālu-d-Dīn Rūmi, who was probably the most significant of the Sufi mystics:

> Perceivest thou God's image in the idol's shrine,
> Worship him there, and abandon your journey around the Kaaba.
> For is it not filled with the scent of the union with God,
> And do you find this scent clinging to the Jewish temple,
>   enter there. [136]

This word is a classical example of intrinsic tolerance, for it purports that the reality of God can also be encountered in worship halls other than one's own. But it also suggests that one's own cult may lack the "scent of union with God." In such a case, it is better to take avail of the possibility to worship where it arises.

We defined intrinsic tolerance as the recognition of other religions as genuine possibilities of encounter with the divine. This thought cannot be indicated more accurately and beautifully than by a verse of another Sufi mystic, Omar Khayyam (died 1123):

> Pagoda and Kaaba are the place of the pious,
> The music of the bells their melody;
> The Parsee's girdle, church, rosary, and cross
> Are all, forsooth, the tokens of the pious.[137]

He who is filled with love of God sees no separating differences in confessions and religions. That idea is expressed by Ibn al-'Arabī (died 1240):

> There was a time when I would take it amiss if my companion's religion was other than mine. But now my heart accepts every form [of worship]; it is a pasture for gazelles, a cloister for monks, a temple for graven images and a Kaaba for pilgrims; it is the table of the Torah and the holy book of the Koran. Love alone is my religion, and my creed and my faith are wherever its horses draw me.[138]

For the Sufi, the Absolute is like a book, the letters of which reveal its meaning. The Hurūfis ("Letter Expounders"), members of a certain Sufi sect, compare the twenty-eight Arabic and thirty-two Persian letters to God's countenance shining forth from behind all that is written. To them the Koran is His face because it consists of the sum of all these letters. This understanding leads to a positive attitude toward non-Islamic holy writ: other books are also regarded as representing God's face, for they, too, consist of the sum of all letters. A Turkish mystic, Niyazi al Misri, who lived in the seventeenth century, once said with reference to this idea, "You have realized that thirty-two letters are the basis of the four books [Koran, Gospel, Psalms, Torah]. They are all written on the sheet of His countenance."

Christian Mysticism   In our earlier considerations regarding Christianity and its attitude to tolerance, it became clear that Jesus' radicalism, which was based on the substance of his message, turned into formal and intrinsic intolerance as the church assumed the garb of an organization. As we saw, there were those in the early church who opposed coercion in matters of faith, but this protest arose from the pressure of the situation; the Christians, who desired religious liberty, had to suffer the intolerance of others. The Swiss political scientist Bluntschli has characterized this attitude quite pertinently in a way which is still valid today. He says, "When error prevails, it is right to invoke liberty of conscience; but when, on the contrary, the truth predominates, it is just to use coercion." [139] This remark refers particularly to Saint Augustine's attitude. As long as heretics held power in North Africa, he advocated freedom of conscience, but later he called upon the civil power to direct itself against the dissident Donatists.

On the one hand, we can find this tolerant remark in Saint Augustine's writings: "That which is called the Christian religion existed under the ancients and has always existed from the beginning of human history right up to Christ's incarnation. From this time on the true religion which had already existed started to be called Christianity." [140] These are ideas coming from the world of mysticism. But on the other hand they hardly correspond to Augustine's explication of the words in the parable of the great feast (Luke 14:23), "Compel them to come in." For he applied this verse to heretics and the way they should be treated: "For many it is good that they first be compelled by fear and pain, so that they can be taught later." [141]

We have already sketched the main stages of the intolerant persecutions which began at that time. We must now show that in Christian mysticism true tolerance was also preached as a high ideal by various of its best known representatives.

It must be noted that the mystics in Catholicism always remained loyal sons of the Church. Their basic views correspond to those of mystics in other religions. [142] But for them the Church remained the sphere of encounter with God, for it was comprehensive enough, as they thought; else they broadened it (in latent antithesis to the official Church). Thus the possibility of encounter with the divine outside the Church was to them no matter of discussion. One hardly finds a word of outward tolerance in the writings of the great Christian mystics. The tolerance of the Catholic mystics is of the type we have termed "inner tolerance."

An impressive example of this fact is Meister Eckhart (1260–1329). In his *Talks of Instruction* he makes this statement: "Now consider: Our Lord was to them [to the saints with their particular ways of life] a pattern and also the strength to follow it as they understood it and therefore that was the way they could do their best; *but God never* tied man's salvation to any pattern. Whatever possibilities inhere in any pattern of life inhere in all, because God has given it so and denied it to none. *One good way does not conflict with another* and people should know that they are wrong; seeing or hearing of some good man that his way is not like their own, they say that his is just so much labor lost. Because that person's life pattern does not please them, they decry it, together with his good intentions. That is not right! *We ought rather to observe the ways of other good people and despise none of them.*" [143]

Clearly, this is inner tolerance, directed towards the accepted religion and its possible differentiations. The non-Christian religions, which were in neither Eckhart's nor other Christian mystics' field of vision, are not reflected upon. This was done by other men of those centuries.

The Crusades brought about an encounter of the Christian Occident with Islam and Judaism. This encounter led to the necessity of Western Christianity's coming to terms with these religions. So far as Christianity is concerned this was done, among others, by Peter the Venerable, Abbot of Cluny (died 1156), and Bishop Odo of Cambrai (died 1113). But it is especially Abelard (died 1142) who has to be mentioned in this connection. In the last months of his life he wrote his *Dialogus inter Philosophum, Judaeum et Christianum.* The basic thought of this book is that all religions have a natural and common basis. Starting here, the Christian in the dialog shows that Jesus in his teaching wanted to renew and deepen the eternal moral law by relating ethics to the salvation granted by God. The discussion with the representatives of the other religions takes place on the basis of the acceptance of the Holy Scripture as a book for the people; it is adapted to their capacity of understanding. Beyond the tangible and limited views expressed in the Bible, the educated person has to acquire a higher insight, says Abelard. This thought is reminiscent of the idea of a twofold truth, as is found in Indian mysticism and Mahāyāna Buddhism.

In the thirteenth century, Abelard's ideas gained prominence again in the thinking of Roger Bacon, who, in his *Opus tertium* (1267), propounds a universal religion. For him, too, the ecclesiastical tradition stands beyond doubt, but he also strives for a higher understanding of Christianity as a natural religion.

Whereas Abelard and Bacon attempt to make Christian truths credible and generally binding by transforming them into rational truths, the matter is the other way around with the Spanish scholastic Raymond Lully (Raymundus Lullus). In his *Liber de gentili et tribus sapientibus* (1277), he attempts to prove that Christian truth is true enlightenment. Lully's goals are conciliation, concord, and finally agreement upon one universal religion—which, again, is the Christian one.

Similar in his thinking to the personalities we have mentioned is the ingenious Nicholas of Cusa (1401–1464). His *Pace seu concordantia fide,* a book written in dialog form, sets forth the idea of a meeting of representatives of different faiths; their goal is to create a uniform religion. In this work the idea of religious unity is expressed in the form of a prayer, from which we quote these lines: "It is Thou who art sought in various ways in the different religions [*ritibus*] and art called with diverse names. . . . Be merciful and reveal Thy countenance, and salvation will come to all peoples. . . . When Thou doest so by mercy, the [use of the] sword and envious hatred and all [manner of] evil shall end, and all will see that there is only *one* religion in the manifold religious customs [*una religio in rituum varietate*]."

Although the medieval theologians referred to above were undoubtedly influenced by the spirit of mysticism, one gets the feeling that their motives spring, rather, from a kind of rationalistic attitude, and that they anticipate ideas expressed later by the European Enlightenment.

The Protestant mystic Jakob Boehme (1575–1624) drew full consequences out of his mystic experience. In his writings we find all the forms of tolerance we have discerned above; in fact they are quite clearly and consciously expressed. He demands formal tolerance—that is, the absence of every kind of coercion in matters of faith: "In the image of God there is no coercion, but rather free, eager service of love, just as a limb of the body or a branch of the tree gladly serves the other members." [144] Boehme goes even further: "Faith is a longing for God," [145] and the conclusion he draws is that religious doctrines can only be regarded as "opinions"; one should not fight about them in an intolerant manner. "Why do we continue to quarrel about knowledge? Knowledge is not the only way to salvation. The devil knows more than we do. . . . It is not vast knowledge that gives me joy, but the longing for God. For desiring is taking." [146] This is genuine mystical reduction of religion to inner life, to an existential attitude of contact with God; everything else is peripheral and mere "opinion." It may be quite necessary but it is not universally binding. "You want to seek God by this or that opinion: one is of the Pope's opinion, the other of Luther's opinion, the third of Calvin's, the fourth of Schwenckfeld's, and so forth. There is no end to opinions. . . . Oh, leave off from all opinions, whatever they may be; all this is nothing but intellectual contention. You will not find rebirth and the precious stone [of salvation] in strife or any great wisdom. You must relinquish everything in this world, be it as high-sounding as it is, and must go into yourself." [147] The religiousness the mystic Boehme represents is undogmatic. "It weaves in God . . . it is free and bound to no article [of faith] but right love." [148]

For Boehme, inner tolerance leads to outward tolerance of other religions. The mystics of the Middle Ages did not draw this consequence, as we have noted; but Boehme says, "Thus speaketh the spirit: many heathen who do not possess your knowledge and yet fight against the wrath [of God] shall have the Kingdom of Heaven before you do. Who will judge them if their heart is at peace with God? Though they do not know Him [the Christian God], they work in His spirit." [149] Boehme thus claims, "A heathen can attain salvation if he turns to the living God and resigns to His will." [150] This is "inclusive absoluteness"; it includes the other religions—if they be living creeds—into the scope of one's own faith. We have already observed such an attitude in the case of other mystical religions.

Hence it is not surprising that Boehme broadens the concepts "revelation" and "word" [of God] in the Christian sense, making them cover more than the biblical word of revelation: "The word has become flesh everywhere; it is revealed everywhere in God's being, wherein our eternal humanity rests." [151] For the mystic, even the Bible is present in the depth of his own being. "Had I no other book than my own book, which is my self, I would have books enough, for is not the whole Bible in me?" [152]

In the year Jakob Boehme died (1626), Johann Scheffler was born. He, too, was one of the few great mystics coming from Protestantism and not from the Catholic Church. Thus the idea of man standing alone before God and not the Catholic doctrine of Grace (being bestowed in the Church) was his point of departure. Johann Scheffler had studied medicine and was the physician of the Duke Sylvius of Württemberg. It was here in Württemberg that he became familiar with German mysticism. As Protestantism was in opposition to mysticism, Scheffler experienced difficulties because of his mystic ideas, and he turned to the Catholic Church, calling himself Angelus Silesius ("the Silesian Angel"). In 1657 he wrote his most famous work, *The Cherubinic Wanderer*. There are no direct statements concerning tolerance here, but Scheffler expresses ideas about God and man's relationship to Him that are of the type the mystics uttered when they reflected upon the question of tolerance.

Angelus Silesius developed his thoughts in a peculiar manner. He either expressed general mystic insights, quite independent of Christian ideas, or else started out with Christian concepts and then proceeded to explain their general mystical meaning. Here are some illustrations for the first type of thought pattern:

God is in me the fire, and I in Him the light,
Do we not with each other in deepest bonds unite?
(*The Cherubinic Wanderer I,* 15).

Enough is not, I deem, what men of God do speak:
The Super-Godhead is the life and light I seek (I, 15).

The Godhead is a Naught, and Over-Naught, indeed,
Who seeth naught in all, he truly God can heed (I, 111).

God is, and that is all: He does not live and love
In ways that we do speak of that which men does move (II, 55).

These are examples of mystical theology; they have many parallels in nonchristian mysticism. They imply that God and the Divinity—the deity conceived of in personal and in impersonal terms —are experienced in all realms of reality, in the depth of human personality itself as well as in the extensive exterior world. However, that experience is inexpressible in words derived from this world of appearance.[153]

Whenever Angelus Silesius employs the religious ideas and images of Christianity, he makes them transparent for the universal numinous reality and for man's primal relationship to that reality, the *unio mystica:*

Halt, whither dost thou run, for heaven is in thee,
Seekest thou God elsewhere, ne'er willst thou Him then see (I, 82).

Were Christ in Bethl'em born a thousand times anew,
In vain such birth would be, were he not born in you (I, 61).

What am I then to be? God's priest, the church, the rock,
The sacrifice, all these, while I on earth do walk (I, 180).

The Christian Middle Ages knew another specific form of tolerance, which does not spring from mysticism but is similar to it in that it, too, is derived from an idea of universal unity. It is the tolerance we encounter in the poetry of the Hohenstaufen period (1138–1254) and it is, as it were, independent of the confessional status. The common basis of this poetry is the sense of being the Father's creation. Quite in contrast to the Church's teaching at the time, Wolfram of Eschenbach, in his *Willehalm,* lets Gyburg speak of tolerance and express in all boldness that pagans, too, are created by God and that hence they will not be condemned, for they can also experience God's grace. The whole universe reveals His love.[154] Walther von der Vogelweide expresses this thought too, when he says, "If someone wants to recite Your Ten Commandments without servile fear, Lord God, but does not keep the one he is about to utter, this is not true love. Many call you Father, but he who does not take me for a brother speaks the stern words with a weak spirit. We are all made of the same substance; food nourishes us, it becomes worthless when it enters into the mouth. If someone found naked bones from which worms had devoured the flesh, who could then discern the servant from the master? Not even having known them well in life would help. *Christians, Jews, and heathens all serve Him who upholds every living wondrous thing.*"[155]

SPIRITUALISM ON THE FRINGE OF THE REFORMATION

It was not the Reformation which gave birth to the idea of formal or even intrinsic tolerance in Europe, but rather the so-called side streams of the Reformation. There were the many different and often conflicting movements of the Anabaptists and Spiritualists. Common to them all was their opposition to the confessional churches and their religious individualism, which emphasized the individual's religious liberty and independence. The demand for man's right to free self-determination, especially in matters of faith, is one of the roots of formal tolerance.[156]

The Anabaptist movement, with its ideas about placidity and

inner enlightenment, also had its origin in mysticism. At first this movement aimed at establishing a community of real saints and believers who had received supernatural enlightenment, but of course that led to bitter conflict with the confessional churches of Christianity. Thomas Münzer in his rising fanaticism preached insurrection and associated himself with the Peasant Revolution until he experienced its catastrophe.

Before this happened, the Anabaptists in Münster succeeded in establishing what they called the "Kingdom of Zion" (1534). They persecuted adherents of other faiths in a most brutal manner. Now they, too, had been persecuted and had begged for tolerance, but upon coming to power became ruthlessly intolerant rulers themselves. When Münster was assaulted in 1535 and the Anabaptist rule put to an end, Catholicism was re-established in that city and cruel punishment was inflicted upon the sectarians. Those who had participated in the revolutionary movement as well as those who had lived in quiet Anabaptist congregations (having establishing themselves there after the Catastrophe of Münster) were mercilessly persecuted.

The mysticism of the Middle Ages continued to thrive in the so-called Spiritualist circles. The Spiritualists also stood aloof from the great churches as well as from Anabaptism, although they outwardly belonged to Anabaptist congregations. The term "Spiritualism" indicates the basic factor that is of importance to both this movement and early European mysticism: the "spirit." Spiritualism seeks the union of God and man in a truly mystical fashion, by direct contact through the spirit. Spiritualists therefore discard all outward institutions and their objective means of bestowing grace, they disregard the church and the sacraments, and they have no concern for the biblical "word" and the historical events of salvation. Instead of objective, institutional authority they acknowledge the "inner light" as the only way to enlightenment and revelation, and this is their basis for intrinsic tolerance over against others.

Modern Spiritualism starts with Sebastian Franck, Castellio, and Schwenckfeld, all of whom lived at the time of the Reformation.[157]

In the following generations, personalities like Valentin Weigel, Giordano Bruno, and Jakob Boehme (of whom we have already spoken) furthered the movement.

In England, significant changes in matters regarding tolerance took place at Cromwell's time (1599–1657). We shall have occasion to deal with Cromwell and political tolerance at a later point. Let us be on the lookout here for religious movements which were important and influential in England at Cromwell's time and which raised the demand for tolerance of their own accord, even if what they meant was still very limited. Indeed, after studying the intrinsic tolerance of pure mysticism in India and Persia, the toleration postulated and laboriously struggled for here seems very modest. But one must keep in mind that the religious situation was quite different in the Orient from in England with its stern Established Church, against which even Puritans had to assert themselves.[158]

Alongside the State Church and Puritanism there sprang up at Cromwell's time a new movement rejecting every form of established church and requiring that all congregations be autonomous and that every person enjoy religious freedom. These were the Congregationalists, or Independents.[159] A passionate zealousness stirred their circles, reviving the spiritualism and ecstasy of the "Enthusiast" sects (*Schwärmer*) of the Reformation period. The Independents firmly believed in direct enlightenment and this belief led them to demand free expression of their basic religious principles and complete liberty of conscience for the individual. However, that postulate was still a far cry from the ideal of general religious liberty, for only the most radical of these Independents either demanded religious liberty for non-Protestants as well or required that the state strip off its Christian character. In the established Anglican Church of the time, Protestantism was thus just as rigorous and exclusive as Catholicism in the uniform culture of the Middle Ages, and it was just as intolerant, too.

Cromwell belonged to the Independents even though he had to turn against extreme forms of over-enthusiastic Independentism when he came to power. Such were the radical resolutions of the so-called "Parliament of Saints" (1653). Under Cromwell's rule, some Protestant denominations (but only they!) experienced religious liberty for the first time in Europe, even though it was limited by certain restrictions.[160]

John Milton (1608–1674) also belonged to the Independents. In addition to *Paradise Lost* he published polemical church-political writings in which he raised a demand for tolerance.

The mystic and sectarian sidelines of the Reformation reached their climax at this time, too. This is highlighted by a fact we have just mentioned: the endeavor of the Independents in the "Parliament of Saints" to establish a kingdom of those who were truly holy.[161] But when this last attempt to place all of cultural life under a purely religious principle failed, a new movement sprang up among the "Enthusiast" sectarians, although they withdrew from the political sphere. This movement, perhaps the ripest fruit of Puritanism, was Quakerism.[162]

The founder of the Quaker congregation was George Fox (1624–1691), a markedly religious man, whose religiousness was a blending of the mystic and the prophetic, dynamic type. In early years he discovered anticipatory silence as the appropriate way to God. William Penn (1644–1718), the second founder of Quakerism, in his preface to Fox's *Journal,* writes: "When at the age of twenty he left his home and friends, he sought for light in solitude and silence, and often walked in the chase to wait upon the Lord." [163] Fox's later desire to lead others to divine experience on this path led to the development of those peculiar Quaker services which are marked by expectant silence.[164] It is such divine experience which also determines the Quakers' attitude to other historical religions. God is experienced as Spirit, and this implies that he cannot be perceived graphically in any way whatsoever. He is not a god of intimate mystical relationship either, but rather a mighty, enrapturing, fiery energy. This view of the divine leads to the idea that God has unrestrained liberty, that he is independent of space, time, and the hour of his revelation.[165] This concept, in turn, which is often stressed by mystics as well, implies that the believer can go beyond the facts of salvation and history and their demands. God, say the Quakers, keeps on revealing himself repeatedly whenever and wherever and to whomever he wills. His freedom to act as he wishes is manifest in his sovereign lordship over space and time and in his independence of people. There are no specific persons who are predestined to receive his revelation, say the Quakers, and there are no particular messengers of revelation. Everyone is capable and worthy of innerly becoming aware of God's will. "The Spirit must speak through them [the believers] so that it is not they who speak but their Father's Spirit. Hence they should tarry until they are incited; they should not be hasty but appear before the Lord with patience, taking care not to follow their own inspirations or to mingle them with the inspirations of the Spirit." [166]

The Quakers conduct their services in silence because they believe that God can reveal himself at any time. On the part of man there is, correspondingly, a constant ability to perceive such revelation. Quaker Theology speaks of the "Inward Light." Edward Grubb, a Quaker author, describes it like this, "It is by the 'Inward Light' that we have the knowledge of God. This knowledge does not come to us by observation of the things about us, like our knowledge of the world of nature, . . . nor by the testimony of others. . . . All these are invaluable aids to, and preparations for, the true knowledge of God, but they cannot give it us until we come to the point of 'seeing' with our own inward eyes." [167] These are mystical sounds. But since anticipatory silence leads to prophetic, pneumatic speech and creative action, this reflects the sort of religious immediacy reported of the spirit-inspired congregations of early Christianity. Such religious ideas allow us to understand why the Quakers have always passionately advocated intrinsic tolerance and still do so.

The spirit of Quakerism was instrumental in the establishment of a state in North America. Pennsylvania was founded by William Penn, and it granted full religious liberty to Christians of all denominations including Catholicism. Pennsylvania prospered well outwardly, but the fundamental principles of Quakerism could not assert themselves within the state setup itself. [168]

6. RATIONALISTIC TOLERANCE

The roots of the great intellectual movement of Rationalism go back beyond the Renaissance to antiquity. Mysticism always postulated religious tolerance on emotional grounds, its motives being bound up with the intrinsic nature of the mystics' religious life and experience. Rationalism, however, in keeping with its own principle, which is reason, put forward intellectual arguments for tolerance. As the Enlightenment often misunderstood the nature of living religion, no one of its arguments for religious tolerance is convincing to us. Nevertheless, it was not mysticism that gave rise to formal tolerance in Europe, at least in the political sphere, but rather the Enlightenment.

Tendencies toward the Enlightenment can be traced back to antiquity. There, the fixed religious patterns and myths were at times called into question for rational reasons by men standing aloof from the religious tradition. Such was the case in sixth century Greece, when the Homeric religion was losing its significance in leading circles. The question was raised, for example by Theognis (ca. 546 B.C.), whether the gods were just. Because of a heightened ethical sensitivity, man's traditional image of the deities was considered inadequate and unworthy of the gods. In one famous fragment, Xenophanes (ca. 500 B.C.) expresses this criticism aptly: "Homer and Hesiod have ascribed to the gods all things that among men are a shame and a reproach—theft and adultery and deceiving one another." [169]

Another matter of criticism for rationalistic thinkers was the traditional cult. Heraclitus censured the outward practices of purification and ridiculed the fact that men were holding conversations with dead images, supposing them to be gods.[170] So far as Roman religion is concerned, which really only copies the spirit of Greek religion, we refer but to Seneca (died 65 A.D.), whose religious criticism stems from Greek Stoicism. He comments upon the lack of spirituality in the traditional image of the gods when he says, "You like to imagine God as being great and merciful. . . . Then why do you deem it mandatory to worship Him with bloody sacrifices? What delight should He have in the death of innocent beings? Worship Him rather with pure hearts and with good moral intentions. It is not necessary to build temples of highly erected stone blocks for Him; everyone should rather dedicate to Him his heart." [171]

Alongside the more or less negative assessment of religion, there is in Greece also a positive attempt to reinterpret religious myth. Apparently Heraclitus realized that religious concepts are not to be understood in their superficial, rational sense. One of his mysterious sayings is: "One, the All Wise, wills and yet wills not to be named after Zeus." [172] Obviously this utterance implies that the names of the gods do not fully express their unfathomable and irrational nature. The names are, as we would say today, symbols, means by which allusion is made to the sacred.[173]

There were also other rather rationalistic approaches to the interpretation of myth in antiquity. Myths would be regarded as containing rational truths or as being allegories pertaining to personified natural phenomena. They would also be looked upon as means of expressing an ethical message.[174]

All these conceptions gained importance again in the European Enlightenment of the seventeenth and eighteenth centuries. Combined with other ideas, they led to a relativizing of religious and specifically dogmatic concepts, and this intellectual process is one of the most important stages on the way to the emergence of a rationalistic idea of tolerance.

We said that the roots of the Enlightenment go back beyond the Renaissance to antiquity. The intellectual current that paved the way for the Enlightenment was the Renaissance, the "Rebirth" of antiquity, a movement affecting all realms of intellectual life. It already bore distinctive traits of a rational understanding of religion, although it essentially did not break out of the sphere of the Christian Church, but rather continued to uphold the sacrosanctity of the truths termed "fundamental." The—still moderate and limited —criticism of dogma that arose at the time of the Renaissance was linked to a differentiation between the "fundamentals" and the adjunctive "nonessentials." The fundamental truths, so it was said, can be apprehended by reason. This idea is quite typically rationalistic. It establishes natural reason as a new epistemological principle, valid in addition to revelation—which is, of course, still acknowledged. Beyond basic truths, there are hence religiously unimportant ones. When the Renaissance strove for freedom, it meant liberty in this more or less broad area of matters that do relate to church dogma but are not of basic religious importance. Such were especially concerns of social life, which had previously been determined by religion—by the Church—and which were now to be independent of ecclesiastical control. The state itself was involved here.

The new liberty, however, infringed upon the Church's claim to absoluteness and upon its unchallenged sovereignty. It made religious persecution of dissidents meaningless because differences in the nonessentials of religion were now no longer reason for punishment.

Different thinkers in the Renaissance of course had differing opinions about particular matters, but the common basic ideas sketched above led many to assume an attitude of relative tolerance. Petrarch (1304–1374), for instance, the first typical representative of the Renaissance, held Christianity to be "the best and most perfect religion," [175] but he acknowledged that partial truths had already been perceived in antiquity. And Marsilius Ficinus (1433–1499), one of the most renowned Neoplatonists and a member of the Academy of Florence, expressed the view that there is such a thing as a common religion (*religio communis*) prevalent in all historical faiths, for these all issue from the one Divine Spirit, participating in its truth in varying degrees.[176] Pico della Mirandola (1463–1494), seeking to integrate Neoplatonist, Kabbalistic, and Christian elements into one harmonized system, considered the core of Christianity—quite typically rationalistically—to be salvation wrought by ethical insight and corresponding moral deed. Within this scope, the Church, of course, is of no great importance. The humanist Mutianus Rufus (1471–1526), finally, who had thoroughly imbibed the Ancients' view of life, dared to declare: "There are many gods, rather many names, but one God." This utterance reminds us strongly of the mystical passages cited above; but the ideas expressed here are based on a rationalistic foundation.[177]

German Humanism felt the influence of the Italian Renaissance, although it had quite different characteristics. It paved the way for intellectual liberty and freedom from the patronage of the Church, as actuated in the Enlightenment. Especially Erasmus of Rotterdam (1466–1536), the head of the German Humanist movement, must be named in this connection. He made a distinction between the true Church of old and the Church of a later period, which, to him, was marred by pagan superstition. Taking up the *logos*-doctrine of the old Church, Erasmus identified the center of Christianity with the truths of pre-Christian antiquity. The core of the Christian religion was for him the Sermon on the Mount; here he saw the truths of antiquity confirmed. It is quite understandable that Erasmus therefore opposed the punishment of heretics. He drew up thirty-two articles against such penalization, on account of which he was condemned by the Theological Faculty of Paris in 1527.[178]

In England, the ideas of the Renaissance as we sketched them above fell on especially fruitful soil. Many significant personalities championed the idea of tolerance on the basis and in the spirit of the fundamental principles developed in the Renaissance. We shall name only a few. First, Sir Thomas More (1478–1535), in his *Utopia*, ascribes value to all religions because they, to him, are different garbs for the worship of God: "For every one of them, whatsoever that is which he taketh to be the chief god, thinketh it to be the very same nature to whose only divine might and majesty the sum and sovereignty of all things by the consent of all people is attributed and given." [179] Only those things are seen and heard in the temples of this land of Utopia that are fitting for all religions.[180] But tolerance has a limit with those who deny the immortality of the soul.

Francis Bacon of Verulam (1561–1626), also advocating the ideal of an encompassing Church, pleaded for toleration and mildness within it. He strove for unity, but not uniformity.[181] But he, too, demanded ruthless persecution of those who doubted the fundamental truths, thus shaking the integratedness of the Church. His basic attitude is hence the same as More's, except that for Bacon Church rule, rites, and cult are inessential.

The distinction between fundamental and nonessential truths was also upheld by William Chillingworth (1602–1644), one of the first to strive for tolerance in England.[182] He refrained from determining the contents of faith exactly and propounded the view, "it is sufficient for a man's Salvation that he believe the Scripture: that he endeavor to believe it in the true sense of it, as far as concerns his duty: And that he conform his life unto it either by Obedience or Repentance." [183]

Finally we may refer to Jeremy Taylor (1613–1667), whose writings reflect typically rationalistic aims. Taylor points out the many contradictions in the resolutions of the Church councils and demands that reason be the sole criterion for ascertaining the validity of the Bible's contents. The standard for the acceptance of truth is ethics. Tolerance has a limit when basic truths are disavowed, when views are propounded and propagated that are immoral and that threaten the state.[184]

The movement outlined above flows into the broad current of the Enlightenment, which became the decisive intellectual force in England, France, and Germany in the eighteenth century. On its soil, a much more radical and comprehensive idea of tolerance sprang up than had been possible within the setting or in the wake of the Renaissance. The broadening of the European horizon prior to the actual Enlightenment, occasioned by the extensive sea voyages in the fifteenth and sixteenth centuries, brought to light hitherto unknown and unthought of religious worlds outside Christendom. At this time of travel and discovery, people in Europe started to become aware of the fact that there is a deep piety and a sublime sense of the Divine outside the Christian Church, comparable to Christian religiousness and to the Christian understanding of God. This awareness effected basic changes in man's thinking, especially since many parallels between Christian and non-Christian religions were now being discovered for the first time.

The intellectual process constituting the Enlightenment can best be understood and described (briefly) as a development espousing the individual's independence and self-consciousness. Whereas organic ties had originally bound the individual to the Church with its set of views and experiential patterns, a situation arises here which is marked by the individual's increasing detachment from the sphere of religious affiliation determining his world view. Unquestionably Luther was partly instrumental in ushering in this general process of man's coming of age; he declared that the individual is mature religiously, or at least in respect to the Church as an institution. In growing measure, reason became the standard for judging and understanding all human situations, institutions and opinions. Thus the intellect became the organ employed to comprehend the world, irrespective of any traditional or ecclesiastical claims. This is the basis for the eminently one-sided attitude assumed in the Enlightenment.

The—really unfounded—unrestricted belief in reason led to the depreciation of everything emotional, non-rational, intellectually incomprehensible in religion. On the other hand, however—and this is the creative effect of the Enlightenment on the study of religions— inquiry could turn to the empirical reality of religion and religions, unimpeded by sacred or ecclesiastical taboos.

In the wake of this development, two general tendencies can be discerned. The focusing on the rational subject of religion, characteristic as it is of the Enlightenment, led to the propounding of subjectivistic theories that sought to understand religion by concentrating on man, his desires, patterns of thinking, and creative intellectual abilities. On the other hand, there was also a tendency to apply the mind to this world and to comprehend it in all its aspects. So far as the study of religious history is concerned, the effect was to direct inquiry toward the outward phenomena of historical religions.[185]

According to W. Dilthey, Herbert of Cherbury (1582–1648) was the first thinker in Europe to establish the autonomy of religious consciousness by analyzing the faculty of religious perception.[186] This was, as we have just pointed out, one of the two basic trends in the Enlightenment (and its study of religions). Beyond the endeavor to gain insight into the nature of the religious subject, there was the other tendency to investigate the objective side of religion, the data presented to us by religious history. Berkeley (1685-1753) was a case in point. He compared the Chinese concept of God (*tien*) with the Zoroastrian doctrine of the Divine in the fire, and the Chinese notion of custom (*li*) with the teaching of the Greek Peripatetics about form.[187] These are still all very bold comparisons, but the main thing is the principle at base, which implies that there are analogies in the wide world of religious forms and ideas. This principle was gradually acknowledged in increasing measure.

The Enlightenment rationally deduced what is common to all religions and thus arrived at its favorite idea: the concept of a "natural religion" (*religio naturalis*). This is rather decisive. By abstracting from the historical phenomena of religions, certain *general truths* were discerned concerning God, immortality, virtue and piety. The sum of these was then regarded as the actual, the "natural religion," which is either at the base of all historical religions or at the end of a development to which all of religious history leads. The idea of "natural religion" is the foundation-stone for the Enlightenment's concept of tolerance; for to the extent that natural religion, born of the natural (that is, reasonable) perception of God, is present in the historical religions, they are to be tolerated. So far as they deviate from the *religio naturalis,* they obscure the one true and natural faith. John Locke (1632–1704) expresses the idea at stake quite clearly:

> Reason is natural revelation, whereby the eternal Father of Light and foundation of all knowledge, communicates to mankind that portion of truth which he has laid within the reach of their natural faculties: revelation is natural reason enlarged by a new set of discoveries communicated by God immediately; which reason vouches the truth of, by the testimony and proofs it gives that they come from God.[188]

This attitude makes Locke an apostle of tolerance, at least in its formal garb. In 1689–92 he wrote his *Letters on Toleration,* in which he denies that the Christian Church has any right to persecute dissidents: "... but that the church of Christ should persecute others, and force others by fire and sword to embrace her faith and doctrine, I could never yet find in any of the books of the New Testament." [189] Christianity is not a form of rule like the worldly state, Locke emphasizes, but something in principle different: " 'The kings of the Gentiles exercise lordship over them,' said our Saviour to his disciples, 'but ye shall not be so.' This business of true religion is quite another thing. It is not instituted in order to the erecting an external pomp, not to the obtaining of ecclesiastical dominion, not to the exercising of compulsive force, but to the regulating of men's lives according to rules of virtue and piety." [190]

For the same reason, the church in sociological perspective is not a community which one joins by birth, but is rather a voluntary association: "I say it [the church] is a free and voluntary society. Nobody is born a member of any church; otherwise the religion of parents would be descended into children, by the same right of inheritance as their temporal estates, and everyone would hold his faith by the same tenure he does his lands." [191]

But also the worldly authority, which, as we saw, often claimed the right to assume responsibility in religious matters, does so unjustly, says Locke: "The care of souls cannot belong to the civil magistrate, because his power consists only in the outward force: but true and saving religion consists in the inward persuasion of the mind, without which nothing can be acceptable to God. And such is the nature of the understanding, that it cannot be compelled to the belief of anything by outward force." [192]

It should not be overlooked that for Locke, too, tolerance has a limit for political and social reasons. The limit is atheism. Locke gives this reason: "Those are not at all to be tolerated who deny the being of God. Promises, covenants, and oaths, which are the bonds of human society, can have no hold upon an atheist. The taking away of God ... dissolves all." [193]

From England, the Enlightenment spread to France, where Voltaire (1694–1778) was one of the chief figures in popularizing its ideas. In a manner quite typical of the Enlightenment, Voltaire, with his deistic views, fought passionately against all positive (that is, historical) religions, especially against the Catholic Church and its intolerance ("écrasez l'infâme!"). His *Traité sur la Tolérance* (1763) was written after the execution of an innocent Huguenot, Jean Calas, in Toulouse. Untiringly, Voltaire urged a review of the trial, which finally did lead to the subsequent acquittal of the accused. It will be fair to say that it was especially because of Voltaire that a change took place in the direction of formal tolerance in France.[104] No new thoughts were expressed, however, in the French Enlightenment so far as tolerance and its motivation are concerned.

The Enlightenment spread to Holland at an early stage. A practical kind of toleration was exercised here, for in addition to the Calvinist state church, Catholics, Lutherans, and various other sects were permitted to practice their religion.

Representatives of the Enlightenment who should be named are René Descartes (1596-1650), Pierre Bayle (1647-1706), and especially Baruch Spinoza (1632-1677). Spinoza saw the essence of religion as lying in love and devotion. With an air of sovereignty over the authority of the synagogue and the church, he advocated the detachment of scientific thinking from religious dogma.

While the Enlightenment had its origin and roots in England, it was deepened in Germany. Here Leibniz (1646-1716), the philosopher, championed tolerance on the grounds of the differentiation between essential and contingent truths. The distinction is reminiscent of ideas expressed in the Renaissance; it was taken up again by Lessing.

The Enlightenment attempted to determine the relationship between reason and revelation, natural religion and historical religion, by explaining historical religion in terms of allegory or as intentional fraud. History and its variegated patterns of religion thus have no positive meaning for it. Only what is universal, what can be comprehended by reason, has value. For the Enlightenment, generalizaton is the chief perceptive function of the intellect. It thus tended to eliminate the historical and particular, and that accounts for its view of religious history, according to which historical religions are "contingent," and natural religon is "essential"—since it is constituted by that which all faiths have in common. This is the root of the particular idea of tolerance the Enlightenment propounded. But this concept is also the point at which the Enlightenment is later surpassed.

We shall not trace the stages that led to the overcoming of the Enlightenment so far as the study of religions is concerned. We merely wish to stress at this point that a change did gradually take place and that the unhistorical approach of rationalism was replaced by one which aspired to appreciate the non-rational historical element in religion as well. Unlike the Enlightenment's inquiry into the nature of religion, the new approach is marked by the endeavor to comprehend historical particulars, to be sensitive to the nonrational dimensions of such historical particulars, and to seek the essence of religious phenomena in the non-rational field.

The first name that comes to mind in this connection is that of Gotthold Ephraim Lessing (1729–1781). He is usually regarded as a son of the Enlightenment, but he actually surpasses it. In the first place, he turns against its lack of understanding for history and for its particular and non-recurring events. Lessing attacks the Enlightenment's disregard for historical religions as well as its urge to abstract. This method can never grasp the non-rational factor which gives to a phenomenon in religion all its life. Lessing realized that there were two forms of rationalism so far as the study of religion is concerned. Both share the same principle, and yet they strive against each other passionately. On the one hand there is the rationalistic criticism of religious traditions, and on the other the orthodox preservation and anxious vindication of that tradition. Both types of rationalism, in defending their respective positions and attacking each other, misjudge the historical character of religions. Lessing, in employing Leibnizian ideas, pointed out that God does not reveal perfect truths, but "contingent" ones. But these latently contain eternal, "essential" truths in a manner relating to man's ability to understand them. Historical religions develop; they embody contingent and hence changing truths, but they are not to be despised for this reason. They are inadequate vessels containing eternal truths. In response to advocates of Orthodoxy, Lessing emphasizes that the idea of the changelessness of a religion and its doctrines has to be surrendered if the spirit and life of the religion is not to be jeopardized. The main thing in a religion, says that poet, is not its doctrine, but its life. For Lessing this means that in the religion of Christ—which he distinguishes from the Christian religion—love demanding tolerance is the essential core. "What is the use of having the right faith," says Lessing in an essay on the Moravians, "if a person lives improperly."

There is yet another idea of Lessing's which entails the demand for tolerance: his concept of development. With this notion he opens up a historical view of religions which the Enlightenment was essentially incapable of conceiving. Lessing's view of development in religion implies that what is rational—and this is still the universal —is present in particular manifestations. But there is no degeneration of an initial rational faith into particular non-rational historical religions, as the Enlightenment had purported, but rather a general maturative process leading toward a rational religion lying in the future, at the end of an historical development. This process serves the *Education of the Human Race,* as one of Lessing's important writings of 1780 is entitled. Hence the particular historical forms of religion are necessary, but they are only of limited duration and relative importance. This, then, is also the basis for Lessing's idea of tolerance. For him, Christianity is not the final stage in the religious development of mankind.

We do not wish to criticize the idea of development propounded by Lessing. It had a far-reaching effect upon evolutionism in scientific thinking as well as in the study of religions.[195] We only want to make clear what the basis is for his demand for tolerance. That demand is championed most forcibly in his *Nathan the Wise* (1779). In this drama there is the famous parable of the three rings, referring to Judaism, Christianity, and Islam. Its message is summed up in these words:

Let each one follow zealously his uncorrupted, unprejudiced love!
Let each one of you vie in competition to bring to the daylight the

power of the stone in his ring! Assist that power by gentleness, by
heartfelt peaceability, by charity, by fervent devotion to God.

7. POLITICAL TOLERANCE

We turn now to a last form of tolerance that we want to trace
historically, the tolerance granted by the state. In structure, such
tolerance is always of the formal type. The state that does not persecute or restrict religion or particular religions can only be tolerant
in a formal manner, by not violating religious rights. More cannot
be expected and was never expected of the state in struggles for
tolerance and religious liberty.

The motives that make a state grant tolerance lie either in its
own interests—it may want to enhance harmony and prosperity in
the land—or in those of its citizens, whose rights are officially
acknowledged. In order to make the matter at stake clear, let us consider some prominent examples of how political tolerance was
granted.

On of the earliest illustrations for state-bestowed tolerance is the
liberty granted by the Buddhist king Ashoka (250 B.C.). In his
Twelfth Rock Edict, we read:

> King Piyadasi [Ashoka], dear to the gods, honors all sects; the
> ascetics, or those who dwell at home, he honors them with charity
> and in other ways. But the king, dear to the gods, attributes less
> importance to this charity and these honors than to the vow of
> seeing the reign of virtue, *which constitutes the essential part of
> them.* . . .
>   Acting thus, we contribute to the progress of our sect by serving
> the others . . . and for this reason concord is good only so far as
> all listen to each other's creed and love to listen to them. It is the
> desire of the king, dear to the gods, that all creeds be illumined
> and that they profess pure doctrines.[196]

Ashoka has been called the Constantine of Buddhism, for he, too,
practiced a policy of religious toleration. The Rock Edict quoted
above is noteworthy in that the king distinguishes between the es-
sentials in religion and that which is not essential. He expects the

various sects to hear others in a tolerant spirit and to learn from one another.

Centuries later, in 607 A.D., Prince Shōtoku Taishi, of Japan, who was the reigning crown prince at the time of the imperial rule of his aunt, and who had imbibed the tolerant spirit of Buddhism, issued a decree which is expressive of the true Japanese attitude toward a multiplicity of religions. It states that all religions are acknowledged, but they are all made to serve the state.[197] The three religions coming into question were Shinto, Buddhism, and Confucianism. The laws of 701 in the era of Taihō, by virtue of which Japan received a constitution which it retained in form until the nineteenth century, reveal how the state intended to utilize these creeds for its own interests. Confucianism was regarded as a guiding principle for civil authority since it advocates such virtues as loyalty, order, justice, and good conduct in public life. It was also seen as enhancing piety and understanding in the private sphere. Shinto was to form the basis for political and social life, as it cultivates a sense of family community and maintains the divine status of the emperor. Buddhism, finally, being a religion of metaphysical depth and universal comprehensiveness, was to serve the personal religious needs of the individual.[198]

In the religious world of the East there were, on the whole, no struggles for tolerance. As we said earlier, these mostly mystical religions have tolerance in their blood, as it were. In Europe, or at least in most European states, on the other hand, a lengthy, passionate, and often even bloody fight had to be waged before the idea of the state granting formal tolerance could emerge. Let us now briefly consider the main stages of this development.

The history of the Christian state and church in Europe begins with the edict on tolerance proclaimed by Constantine and Licinius in Milan in 313 A.D. By virtue of this decree, Christians and non-Christians received the liberty to follow the religion they held to be appropriate for themselves.[199] Christianity became a *religio licita,* a religion permitted by the law, and it received equal status with non-Christian religions. When the first Christian state emerged, there thus prevailed a situation of tolerance which had to be restored again later, in fact centuries later after long struggles, because it was soon abolished again on behalf of Christianity. Hence the idea of various religions existing tolerantly beside each other in one and the same state was actually put into practice at an early stage in church history, but it was only on account of the intellectual efforts of many a religious personality, the endeavors of many a religious movement, and the effects of many a political development that this situation was re-established in Christian Europe.

The formal political tolerance granted at that early time was due to circumstances that are typically transitional. The unity of the pre-Christian state was being threatened by the Christians, and they were therefore ostracized and persecuted. But when the heathen state was displaced by an integrated Christian state, the governing authority revealed the same intolerance as before, prohibiting alien cults and persecuting the adherents of other religions. Now the Constantinian period, in which the state power had not yet associated itself clearly with the Church and with Christianity, lay between these two stages: it was transitional. Only after Constantine did the Church identify with the State. This emperor, however, demanded general tolerance by decree. He acknowledged Christianity not for religious reasons, but rather for purely political ones. The main thing for him was to consolidate the empire's unity with the aid of the ever stronger, growing Church. This motive of unity is always decisive when formal tolerance is granted. The Church itself could only be serviceable to that political goal as a unified body, not as an organization rent apart by different groups. Thus Constantine intervened decidedly in the doctrinal issues of his time. He opted for one party in the dispute about the Arian dogma, for instance, and he imposed a uniform teaching upon the Church in this matter. He also endeavored to suppress minor heretical churches by force. Hence this initial tolerance obviously did not have any spiritual or religious motives but was rather based upon purely political considerations.

The situation effectuated by Constantine where various religions

existed peacefully beside one another did not last long. It clearly
found its end under Constantine's sons, particularly under the most
important one, Constantius, who in 341 prohibited sacrifices and
ordered temples to be destroyed. The command unchained a fanatical
storm of Christian mobs on the pagan temples. A pamphlet written
by a Christian, Firmicus Maternus, and dedicated to the Emperor
in 346, *De errore profanarum religionum* [On the Errors of the
Heathen Religions], was indicative of the situation.

There followed a short intermission in the development toward
an exclusive Christian state at the time of Julian the Apostate
(361–363), whose tolerant tendencies we have already discussed.
But Julian's successors reestablished the privileged position of
Christianity although they refrained from attacking non-Christian
religions. The end of religious freedom was induced by Emperor Theodosius the Great in 380 and by Emperor Gratian. They
both elevated Christianity to the preclusive state religion, at the
same time incriminating "paganism." In the edict of 380 it was
required of every Roman subject that he confess Christianity.
The Theodosian Code, a collection of laws proclaimed by Roman emperors against heretics and those who adhered to "false
religions," is the beginning of the inquisitional practice of religious persecution. Thus the stage was set for the complete political and ecclesiastical intolerance of which we have already
spoken.

One and one-half millenniums passed before the scene started
to change again in the countries of Europe. In the meantime,
many religious struggles took place and many movements had
their effect. Finally, in 1598, in the Edict of Nantes, at the end
of the bloody Huguenot wars (1562–1598) in which the Protestants fought for their recognition by the French state, Henry IV
granted to them freedom of conscience and the right to hold
worship services in all those places where they had been allowed
to do so the year before, Paris and various other major cities being
excluded. The formal tolerance granted here was, of course, very
limited. It pertained only to the Christian Huguenots and even

for them there were restrictions. Later, when Louis XIV attempted to reestablish a uniform Catholic state in France, he realized that the religious liberty given at Nantes was incompatible with absolutism as he conceived it. Hence in 1685 he repealed the Edict, which caused over a half a million Huguenots to flee to other European countries. Whoever failed to escape was executed or died in the galleys.

Similar confessional struggles took place in the Netherlands. Holland's fight for liberty from Spain (1566–1609; 1621–1648) was but partially a religious war. Its outcome, however, was to be decisive for the religious fate of the Netherlands; for the victor, William of Orange, became the main initiator of political and religious freedom in his country.

The terrible Thirty Years' War had evolved out of religious *as well as* political differences. It ended in 1648 with the Peace of Westphalia. The provisions of the Treaty having an effect upon the idea of tolerance were few. In the first place, all stipulations regarding tolerance which the Peace produced pertained only to the Christian denominations; these were the religious parties which were granted equality in the eyes of the law.[200] Only the Reformed (Zwinglians and Calvinists), the Catholics, and those who associated themselves with the Augsburg Confession (the Lutherans) were to enjoy equality and religious liberty according to the provisions of the Peace. As for all other faiths, Article VII, § 2 expressly declared: "Beside the above-mentioned religions no other ones may be introduced into or tolerated within the Holy Roman Empire." It was on this account that Pope Innocent X, in the Bull *Zelo domus dei* of November 20, 1648, protested that dissidents were being allowed to express their heresies freely.[201]

In England, a broad type of tolerance was advocated by liberal thinkers at an early stage. The struggles between various Christian confessions and denominations came to an end when William III of Orange, in agreement with Parliament, issued the Act of Toleration in 1689. The Act legally permitted freedom of conscience, but there were certain restrictions. Here again, Catholics were excluded, not to speak of other religions.

In 1776, the thirteen British colonies in North America broke away from the motherland to form the "Union." Adherents of various Christian confessions and denominations had emigrated to these states in the course of the seventeenth and eighteenth centuries. Various colonies had granted religious freedom to their citizens before 1776; others had denied it to particular religious communities. With the passage of the Bill of Rights, religious liberty was declared one of the basic privileges of every human being. Ever since, state and church are separate in the Union, which, however, bears a general Christian character.

The idea that religious liberty is an inalienable right of man, first officially pronounced by a state in North America, was doubtless an effect of the Enlightenment. It influenced the French National Assembly's famous Declaration on Human Rights of August 26, 1789. The Assembly also demanded freedom of religion and worship as human rights.[202]

The French Revolution established the victory of formal political tolerance in Europe. We do not wish to sketch the path leading to its emergence in the various European countries in detail. Suffice it therefore to make reference to pertinent material available.[203]

We have come to the conclusion of the first part of our study. We have attempted to give a typological description of the forms of tolerance and intolerance appearing in religious history. With this material at hand let us now proceed in the second and third parts to reflect in general upon the underlying motives and reasons involved when intolerance is practiced and tolerance set up as an ideal.

II. *Motives*
for Intolerance

1. The Unity of the Religious Community

In the historical part of our analysis it became clear that intolerance, which has been prevalent in past religious history, can spring from quite different motives. Regarding all the many reasons that do appear, we can make out four basic motives that keep on recurring, although of course they often combine in various ways. Let us consider them separately, for understanding religious intolerance really requires that we analyze this complex phenomenon and look at its elements singly. We shall start by reflecting upon the idea of unity as it is upheld by religious communities.

Contrary to what one might expect, we believe that the basic motive for intolerance in religion is not the truth of religious views; it is not a matter of defending truth rigidly against error and falsehood. Formal factors are always primary—historically as well as in terms of importance—and come before motives regarding the contents of beliefs are brought into play.

We have termed the intolerant preservation of the unity of a religious community "formal intolerance." It is obvious that wherever a religious community rules alone and the truth or ethical value of other religions are left out of the picture, tolerance can prevail as long as these foreign religions do not upset the structure of the ruling community. But formal tolerance is ambivalent.

When it alone determines the scene, it can turn into intolerance or have intolerance at its side.

A formal kind of intolerance can be found even in ethnic religions. Here, firm ties link the community or state to its respective God or gods. These bonds constitute the ethnic-religious community; they guarantee its unity. The intolerance inherent in the situation can be traced throughout the world of ethnic religions. Here, the preservation of the ethnic community's unity is always the dominating element. One may think of the trials against the atheists in ancient Greece. When Alcibiades mutilated the statue of Hermes in Athens in 415 B.C. he was put on trial. Of course this trial had political backgrounds, but it was also motivated by the state's fear that the gods might take vengeance, for their worship places had been damaged and their cult neglected. Legal action was also taken against the philosopher Anaxagoras, who about 432 B.C. gave a natural explanation for sun, moon, and stars, thus degrading the gods of the heavenly bodies to natural phenomena.[1] Protagoras was also put on trial for atheism. In modern terms we would say he was guilty of demythologizing the state religion. Similarly, Socrates, whose case is the most notorious of these trials, died in 399 B.C. after drinking the cup of poison. He, too, had been accused of disloyalty to the state gods. These state deities were the numinous powers to which the sacred state community related. There were, for instance, Zeus, to whom Phidias built a temple in Olympia after the Greeks' victory over the Persians near Salamis, and Athene, the protectress of Athens. As these examples show, religion was an expression of patriotism, and criticism thereof could not be tolerated.

At the time with which we are concerned here, a new development began in Greece. Particular thinkers like Socrates, Xenophanes, and others, in opposing the general state creed, started considering religion as a matter of the individual and of personal inner attitude. There was a clash between the generally accepted belief and the faith of individuals.

In the old state religions, as in the religion of ancient Rome [2] and of other ethnic communities and nations, religion was primarily a matter of the group. In a way, there was no individual here as such. Religion being a public affair, the religious duties of a citizen were part of his civil obligations. Walter Bauer vividly describes how life in all its aspects was determined by religious responsibilities. Talking about life in classical antiquity, he says, ". . . the old cults and customs that had been hallowed by local history found their preeminent position within the setting of public affairs. All of public and private life was most intimately connected with them. They consecrated and transformed every significant moment in both spheres of life, captivating the senses, hearts, and imagination of men in the most varied ways. Everywhere there were temples inviting worshippers to enter; and numerous holidays, festivals, and ceremonies of every kind—sacrifices, rogations, processions, dramas, public singing of hymns —would remind people day after day of the power and might of the gods and of their relationship to men." [3]

The organically integrated state religion thus guarded the formal unity of the community. This is especially obvious in the old state religion of Rome, which tolerated alien cults as long as they were not disturbing, but at the same time distinguished and separated them as "alien" cults (*sacra peregrina*) from the indigenous ones (*sacra Romana*). Not practicing the state cult— that is, the worship prescribed by the state—was regarded as "atheism," and was to be punished. Not observing the cult of the emperor, of which the Christians were mainly guilty, was called "impiety toward the ruler" (*impietas circa principes*). It was mainly for this reason that Christianity became an "unpermitted religion" (*religio non licita*) in Rome.

Let us now turn back to the intolerance of the Israelite religion. The inner structure of this ethnic religion corresponds precisely to that of polytheistic ethnic religions. In Israel, the unity with which we are concerned here appears in the form of a "Covenant" between Yahweh and his chosen people. Yahweh is Israel's

God, Israel is Yahweh's people. This exclusive relationship guarantees well-being, weal, or salvation (*Heil*); it may not be disordered by the acceptance of foreign gods and their cult. In the religious history of Israel, the prophets of all centuries fight against apostasy from the one God, Yahweh, to whom alone the community should relate; and, even in preprophetic times, the thing at stake was not the truth of their own religion or the falseness of other creeds. Elijah's contest with the priests of Baal (1 Kings 18) makes it clear that the *superiority* of the *Israelites'* God over foreign deities is the most that can be said about the relationship between Yahweh and other gods. The fact that other peoples have their own gods which do actually exist, and that other religions do have their own truths, is not at all drawn into question at this time. But that is not the crucial point. The only thing of importance for Israel was the maintenance of the nation's weal, which is so intimately bound up with a close and unshakable relationship with its God. Well-being, or salvation, is innate in this situation of positive contact with Yahweh; weal does not have to be struggled for, as is the case in religions of deliverance.

Preprophetic Israel saw in the Mosaic Covenant with Yahweh the warranty that He would always be on the side of His people, even at times of evil. This view was shattered by the prophets. As regards the self-certainty of the people, Jeremiah for instance says, "Do not trust in these deceptive words: 'This is the temple of the Lord, the temple of the Lord, the temple of the Lord.' For if you truly amend your ways and your doings . . . then I will let you dwell in this place, in the land that I gave of old to your fathers forever" (7:4ff). This means that the unity between God and His people, which is also the main thing for the prophet, has been disturbed by inner disobedience. It has been disturbed in spite of all outward cult activity. This idea of unity which dominates everywhere in ethnic religions lets us understand the formal intolerance displayed in Israel towards foreign cults. Alien beliefs as well as disbelief within the ethnic community jeopardize the nation and the state. It is not in order to *gain* salvation but in order to *maintain* the weal of the community that the foreign religions must be persecuted if they throw the ethnic group into disarray.

Exceedingly important for the maintenance and well-being of ethnic communities is the performance of the traditional cult. Tending to the cult is fostering the relationship obtaining between man and the world of the Divine. Wherever such attendance to the gods is discontinued or carried out incorrectly—that is, in a manner not prescribed by the tradition—disastrous results may ensue for the community. The greater prophets of Israel who proclaimed calamity did so for this reason.[4] The right doctrine is never the main thing. Rather, the preservation of the nation and the state is decisive. These constitute the highest values in ethnic religions.

Here again we can take the religion of Israel as an example. One thought is expressed time and again in the Old Testament. Deuteronomy 5:32, for instance, put it like this: "You shall be careful to do therefore as the Lord your God has commanded you; you shall not turn aside to the right hand or to the left. You shall walk in the way which the Lord your God has commanded you, *that you may live, and that it may go well with you, and that you may live long in the land which you shall possess."* The ethnic group is addressed here. It is to last and live long in the promised land. Its existence and wellbeing is really all that is essential. The salvation of the individual, whose importance lies only within and in relationship to his ethnic community, is insignificant. Not even his fate after death is relevant to Old Testament concerns. All that matters is that the *one* religion should prevail in the land conquered by Yahweh's assistance. Therefore, Deuteronomy 12:2ff commands: "You shall surely destroy all the places where the nations whom you shall dispossess served their gods, upon the high mountains and upon the hills and under every green tree; you shall tear down their altars, and dash in pieces their pillars and burn their Asherim [wooden posts set up as representations of the goddess Ashera] with fire; you shall hew down the graven images of their gods. . . ." A more radical form of intolerance towards foreign religions is hardly conceivable.

Let us now turn to universal religions. As we have indicated, the main thing here is basically not the unity of a firmly consolidated ethnic community. In universal religions, however, which have developed some kind of organization of their own, the idea of unity does soon arise and the preservation of the new religious institution does gain significance beside various other factors which we shall discuss shortly. This fact is intimately connected with the motives that lead to the formation of such universal religious organizations. Let us sum them up briefly.[5]

The experience of a religious master and his disciples that marks the beginning of a universal religion is unconventional in form and often stands in contrast to the prevailing tradition. The expansion of the circle of disciples and the growth of the congregation necessitates a "passing on" (*traditio*) of the initial experience to outsiders and following generations. But such transmission requires the formation of a new doctrinal and constitutional tradition. The self-preservation of the community, which keeps on absorbing more and more heterogeneous elements as it grows larger, demands utmost formal rigidity in teaching, cult, and jurisdiction, which, in turn, implies closure to new insights and experiences. This was the reason why conflicts could arise, for instance between the Christian Church (as an organization) and the great scientists and discoverers—Giordano Bruno, Galileo, etc.

The religious life of the first believers was rooted completely in personal experience granted by grace. The community that was formed on account of that initial experience was a true optional community consisting of members who had decided to join personally. Subsequently, however, those who belonged to the group were often only members by birth or habit. The only way the institution could warrant its general salvational values—that is, contact with the numinous—in view of this situation, was by demanding of its members that they participate outwardly in its rituals, without prerequiring personal experience of grace. This after all, cannot be assessed or determined objectively. Saint Augustine, for instance, says expressly: "The Church gives to all the possibility of participating in God's grace." [6] Thus the mystery of the Divine's presence is no longer a matter of grace but becomes, increasingly, an affair that can be induced in a particular place at a particular time by outward, culto-magic means. This is at least true of the understanding of many, if not even of the masses. Furthermore, the religious organization becomes a salvation-granting institution which bestows and guarantees redemption objectively. E. Troeltsch expresses the matter pertinently: "The Church as traced back to Jesus, his person and his work, becomes a wondrous institution granting salvation and grace and appearing as a ready supplier thereof; it becomes a cultic institution of redemption. . . . All its sanctity and divinity is regarded as being derived from the initial miracle of its foundation, and as being present in its objectively revealed truth, in the independent miraculous power of its sacraments, and finally in the divine consecration of its cult leaders and priests who attribute their charge to Christ and the Apostles, being appointed miraculously again and again. Thus there develops a Church in which holiness is shifted from the person to the institution." [7] This fact again leads to the strict exclusiveness of the organization. As religious life is tied to the outward acts of the priests in the organized Church, its organization has to be maintained strictly as an exclusive institution and has to form an integrated sociological entity remaining intact as long as belief in it is steadfast.

Yet a third motive must be mentioned. In its living core, universal religion is always supra-ethnic. In accordance with the universality of its nature, it strives for geographic universality or global expansion. Not matter how such expansion may take place, it always entails the religious institution's becoming a mass organization and necessarily absorbing heterogeneous elements. Most of the members are of the multitude of those who are religiously uncreative and lack self-sufficiency in faith. The preponderant influence of such

religiously dependent associates, who incline toward an unsophisticated type of religiousness as the only kind to which they can adapt,
has various consequences for the organization, and these consequences bear a remarkable effect upon its attitude to tolerance. The
religious institution, or church, becomes the only authority capable
of controlling the masses in matters of faith, cult, and ethical behavior. Its unity is maintained by uniform norms to which believers
must orient themselves.

So far as the Catholic Church is concerned, Nikolaus Monzel, a
Catholic theologian and sociologist, expresses the matter at stake in
this way: "The only direct sources of Catholic faith are the various
channels the Church employs in its teaching. These are general ex-
positions by bishops, priests, and laymen, and special proclamations
of the Pope, or of the Pope and the Council.[8] Authorities in the
Church see to it that every Catholic orients his religious thinking
toward the ecclesiastic norms of faith. The means utilized are religious education starting at the infant age, sermons, circulars of
popes and bishops, censorship of all religious books written by
Catholics, and the proscription of all writings that could lead to
deviations from the doctrine. As long as the Catholic Christian lives
on earth *in statu viatoris* [as a pilgrim], the main thing for him is
not to understand particular dogmas but to be obedient in faith to
the doctrinal authority of the Church." [9]

Viewing the matter from a sociological perspective, these sentences
enumerate all the elements necessary for a uniform disciplining of
the masses who belong to the worldwide Church as believers: the
denial of the individual's independence of God or the Church,
authoritarian leadership in accordance with uniform Church patterns, censorship of literature that results from independent thinking, condemnation of beliefs and opinions diverging from Church-
set norms by prohibition of such writings through the *Index libro-
rum prohibitorum* [Index of Prohibited Books], and a demand to
relinquish personal insights of faith in favor of religious obedience
to authority. Such obedience alone is required. Monzel similarly
shows how in two other areas of religious life—cult and ethics—

independence has been virtually abolished or at least restricted considerably in the Catholic Church. The individual is allotted certain private spheres of religious life (for example, a sphere of personal revelation, a sphere allowing for particular forms of worship and ethical behavior in the following of Christ, etc.). But every one of these areas is only *relatively* independent and they are only recognized as autonomous so far as they do not give rise to ideas contradicting the uniform norms of the Church.[10] This makes it quite clear that the Catholic Church maintains "a far-reaching claim to control" (Monzel).

Obviously, all these implications serve one ultimate ideal: to preserve the unity of the Church institution, which, according to Catholic belief, was founded by Christ. The unity upheld and defended in an authoritarian manner almost completely abolishes individual freedom. Dostoevski has given a classical picture of the situation in the Grand Inquisitor scene of his ingenious work, *The Brothers Karamazov.* In this tale, Christ returns to earth and is immediately captured by the Grand Inquisitor, who tells him:

> We [the Church] have improved your work and have founded it upon the miracle, the mystery and authority. And men rejoiced that they were being led again like a flock, and that the terrible gift that had caused them so much anguish [i.e., freedom] had finally been taken from them. . . . When we reign, all will be happy, and they shall neither revolt nor destroy each other, as it happens everywhere in your free kingdom. O we will convince them that they shall be free if they give up their liberty for our sake.[11]

When religion is no longer a living expression of personal experience but rather a set of patterns rquired and regulated by an ecclesiastical authority for the sake of the unity of the organization alone, a shift has taken place in respct to what is regarded as essential. Things become relevant that are controllable and can be determined outwardly. Christianity thus largely turns into a religion of rules and regulations, for only observance of such regulations is controllable and can be demanded of everyone. Actually, however, deeply stirring religious experiences, faith, and the personal encounter with grace cannot be commanded or controlled. The only things that can be influenced by an authoritarian organization with uniform patterns are outward acts of obedience and outward adherence to rationally comprehensible dogmas. Even if there is often genuine, living religiousness in such motifs—which is not at all to be doubted—this kind of obedience can *guarantee* only a formal type of devotedness to Church authority. The same is true of compliance with doctrines and morals; for in the ethical sphere, too, the Church can only enforce a minimum of average mass morality.

I think these facts show that the intolerance of the Catholic Church is primarily of a formal type. The ideal of unity determines the Church's exclusive attitude toward everything disorderly. It has been evidenced above that this attitude is accompanied by a far-reaching tolerance with regard to content. The tremendous profusion of forms of religiousness within the Church as an organization is only possible because of a practical type of toleration. But here again, there are limits, and they are marked by the integrity of the organization, which may not be disrupted. If the institution and its authority is attacked in any way whatsoever, the Catholic Church displays utmost intolerance, as its strict action against Luther and the reformers shows.

Modern Catholic theologians like Lortz and J. Hessen are of the opinion that a far-reaching understanding could be reached today with those who represent Luther's religious concerns. But I think that the main thing in Protestant-Catholic differences is not so much a matter of religious opinion as of inner attitudes.[12] According to the Protestant view, man and his conscience have an obligation to God alone, and to His word. But man is quite free in determining his relationship to the visible Church organization. For reasons discussed above, this is unacceptable to the Catholic Church.

The Protestant Church also became an immured organization, however. It had already experienced its consolidation in the post-Lutheran period of Orthodoxy. As L. Fendt points out, it "objectified" its spirituality at that time.[13] Thus an ecclesiastical system developed here that was in structure analogous to the Catholic Church.

Freedom in revolt is no matter for the broad masses. As Protestantism started organizing an independent ecclesiastical system of its own, it also ran the risk of relapsing into a static, uniform Church, preserving its unity with intolerant methods. Luther originally considered establishing an *ecclesiola in ecclesia,* an embryonic church within the Church—that is, a union of those "who seriously desire to be Christians" instead of the broad mass of "everyone" (*Herr Omnes*). In making this distinction, the reformer knew that only very few in the Church, even within the Protestant Church, could truly be "Protestant."

Actually, the Protestant Church did become a mass organization as early Catholicism had done, although it laid emphasis on the spiritual factor and on personal decision. Like every church organization, it became an ecclesiastical system in the second generation, in the lifetimes of the children of those who had first united in peril and distress to form a free confessional group.

At the beginning of the Reformation, the principle *cuius regio eius religio,* "whose region his religion" (according to which the ruler of a state determined the religion of his subjects), was put into practice. The effect was that people entered the Protestant Church who had no inner relationship to the ideas of the Reformation and who were merely following outward compulsion. Thus certain things became common in the Protestant Church which had been characteristic of Catholicism. Emphasis was placed on the outward correctness and truth of the doctrine; outward objects were regarded as sacred; bodily presence in the worship service independent of inner participation became a habit or even a requirement of custom. The living Word of the Scripture turned into a paper pope, and even the Bible was interpreted in an authoritarian way—through the Creeds. The priesthood of all believers was never really practiced; instead, there emerged a ministerial Church oriented toward the Scriptures but directed by preachers. The individual was subject to an ecclesiastical structure merely replacing the Catholic Church with its hierarchic setup and sacramental patterns.[14] The formation of the Lutheran Church was capped by the *Formula concordiae* of 1577; as an orthodox doctrine it was to form the basis for the coercion practiced henceforth in ecclesiastical and dogmatic matters. In Calvinism, too, the same development set in. Unlike Luther, Calvin regarded the organizational form as an essential element of the Church itself. Calvin wanted his church not only to be based on the "right faith" but also to be composed of the ethically pure. Hence not only dogmatic coercion was introduced but also strict moral discipline. The individual was subject to the institution's uniform regulations, and these pertained to matters of faith as well as to general conduct, dress, etc. Here, too, a totalitarian church regime was thus established, and people were subordinate to it in all walks of life. The intolerance of the church organization discussed above is understandable from this background.

In the Protestant Church there was no lack of movements reacting against the development toward an institutionalized ecclesiastical system. Pietism was such a reaction; so was Theological Liberalism.[15] But there were also counter-movements. Under the influence of Karl Barth's theology, for instance, there emerged in post-war Germany, after the Confessing Church had fought against the Third Reich in the *Kirchenkampf* (church struggle) with courage and self-sacrifice, an authoritarian "one party church" in which ecclesiastical unity was often defended against liberal tendencies in an intolerant and exclusive manner.

When we were discussing the primary motive for intolerance, we started by considering ethnic religions. If we now compare the situation there with the endeavor to maintain unity in the Church, a universal-religious community whose main features we have traced above, one thing becomes evident: The Church fosters a kind of religiousness which is to be found in ethnic religion as well. There is certainly no community like a Church independent of the society as a whole in ethnic religions, but we can discern an ecclesiastical type of religiousness here and we can make out trends toward an ecclesiastical form of rulership. Hence an organizational religiousness of an outward type becomes visible, which is always guarded and controlled by institutions in the same way, no matter what the background. In the ethnic setting, the society maintains the cult. Religion is a public affair requiring of all the observance of certain general laws. In the Church, the mass of members form a societal group cultivating a religiosity very similar in structure to that of ethnic religion. They are even encouraged to react religiously in a certain prescribed manner, just as people in ethnic religions are. As the state once protected the unity of the ethnic community or nation and safeguarded the common religion, the Church now takes over this role. In fact, it often does so in connection with the state. This was, for instance, the case in the Middle Ages. Here, the Church even superimposed its own intolerance upon the State. During the Inquisition, and even before that time, heresy was considered a political crime, as we had occasion to see; it was punished by the State on behalf of the Church.

Viewing the matter sociologically again, we can discern an interesting cyclical development here. Religious history teaches us that ethnic-religious communities with their institutional religiousness disintegrate when universal religions appear upon the scene. These, in turn, found free communities of their own, independent of ethnic or national ties. Their congregations comprise those who have been moved personally and who join the new group in free and personal decision. The congregations of universal religions are originally geared to meet the needs of individuals. They proclaim a spiritual message. But when they become "churches" (that is, organizations), they reestablish formally and on a new basis what the universal religion had destroyed: institutionalized religiousness demanding the observance of certain rules and regulations. The level of such religiousness corresponds to that of early ethnic religion, at least so far as the average members, the masses, are concerned. Folk belief (*Volksglaube*) in universal religion is very similar in structure and form to folk belief in ethnic religion.[16] The reason is that the same stratum of society maintains folk belief in both cases; the nature, the inclinations, and the desires of these people remain the same throughout the ages. Furthermore, the institution always seeks to preserve its organizational unity against all upsetting influences, and that can only be achieved by the intolerant exclusion of all disordering factors. Ignatius of Antioch long ago emphasized the necessity for unity, concord, harmony, agreement, and integratedness in the Church and uttered the warning: "Flee from schisms, the source of all evil." [17]

2. RULERSHIP AND POWER

A second basic motive for intolerance is the claim to rulership as it is often raised by religious institutions and organizations, which even form alliances with earthly powers in order to accomplish their goals.

Let us again begin by considering the structure of ethnic religion as we have discussed it above. Our aim is to make the motives visible which have lead repeatedly and in various ways to the claim to rulership in religion.

The forms of rule in ethnic-religious communities correspond to the basic pattern of religion here. The authority to rule issues from certain leaders. As religion is maintained by the ethnic community and weal is guaranteed by contact with the group's numinous powers, religious leaders are tribal or national leaders having numinous significance. Such personalities are, for instance, sacred chiefs and kings.

Three forms of sacred ethnic-religious leadership can be discerned. First there is early charismatic kingship. In primeval times, the power to rule was conceived of as being numinously granted; it was imagined to be a substance-like charisma. Rulership pre-required such charisma, no matter whether it was regarded as being granted by heaven or thought of as being inherent as a mysterious power in particular people. It is not the office that grants the charisma; rather, a person first possesses or receives it, and then he obtains the authority to rule by virtue of that qualification. A sacral ruler can be deprived of his rulership if he loses his charisma. The Teutons, for example, regarded waning luck in war as a sign that the king had lost his charisma, his "weal." The attitude of men to the charismatic king is virtually the same as that to numinous power. The king is *taboo*, and he has to observe *taboo* laws himself. This is why the sacral king was often isolated in nature-religions and why he was treated the way he was. The charismatic king is the power-center of his ethnic-religious community. [Tribal "nature-religion" (*Naturreligion*) and national "culture-religion" (*Kulturreligion*) are the two forms of "ethnic religion" (*Volksreligion*) the author distinguishes.]

Originally, power was considered to be universal; it could be effective in any way whatsoever. The ethnic community is subject to sacral authority in all areas of life. Hence the sacral and charismatic king wields all forms of power. He is the magician and sorcerer, the priest, the judge, the commander-in-chief, the ruler. Later these originally integrated functions of a king are divorced, and magicians and sorcerers gain importance beside the ruler. The office of the priest is maintained by an autonomous personality, and the judicial functions are taken over by an independent judge. Only rulership and command over the army remain in the hands of the king. This process of division of power is part of a secular development affecting the originally sacral community with all its forms and functions.

Beside charismatic kingship there is the kingship ordained by God. The difference lies in the fact that here the office lends the charismatic quality necessary for rulership to the king. The king does not possess charisma before assuming authority. He is appointed to his position by divine vocation, and he is the organ through which the numinous power operates that is bound to the office. Such a king is naturally also a guardian of justice, and he himself is to set a practical example for virtue and morality. Often, the divinely ordained king is regarded as the son of the deity. In the age-old idea of divine kingship, the king is frequently even identified with the god, being regarded as his mortal incarnation and representative. The Japanese emperor, the Tenno, for example, was considered to be the son of the Sun Goddess Amaterasu, and the Babylonian king Hammurabi was called "Sun God of Babylon."

The ancient oriental myth of the Sun God was transmitted by way
of Hellenism to Rome where it was adopted, the Roman Emperor
being regarded as "invincible" (*invictus*) and "eternal" (*aeternus*)
like the God Mithra, who was celebrated as "the invincible sun"
(*sol invictus*).

The idea of divinely ordained kingship can develop to entail
a universality that is political and not specifically religious as in
universal religions. According to the Babylonian account of Creation, sovereignty over the universe is promised and granted to
Marduk, the god of Babylon. But this religious idea is bound up
with a political implication: it leads to the concept of the mortal
ruler of the world, a notion appearing here for the first time.
Marduk is clothed in a celestial cloak adorned with shining stars,
and like him the human king is also considered to be the ruler of
the universe. Thus an Assyrian inscription says of the king, "Thou
art Marduk's likeness." [18]

The concept that a human king representing the God of the
Universe can hold sway over a world empire is, hence, originally
an Oriental one, but it traveled from the Orient to the West.
Here, Alexander the Great, for instance, let himself be declared a
god by the Oracle of Amon. There is a characteristic difference,
however, between the East and the West. Whereas the sanctity and
divinity of the office motivates the glorification of its bearer in the
Orient, the deeds of the king lead to his deification in the Occident.
The powerful personalities that appear upon the scene in Hellenistic times seem to the people as "saviours" (*soteres*). (The roots of
that concept lie, to some extent, in the ancient hero cults.) From
Hellenism, the idea of divine kingship (and regal saviorship) spread
to Rome, where the Roman Emperor was identified with Jupiter.
Thus Dio Cassius (44,6,4) calls Caesar Jupiter.

We are still within the setting of ethnic religion here. The universal rulership of the king and the hope that is often connected
with it pertain not to the religious salvation of individuals but to
the general welfare of the community, the nation, or the empire.
The king is regarded as the bringer of a general time of weal in

the ethnic-religious sense. The expectation that such a messiah-king will arise is, incidentally, not specifically Jewish; we find it among the Persians and Egyptians as well, and it also gained importance in later Rome.[19]

Yet a third type of sacral rulership can be distinguished: theocracy. When we speak of theocracy we mean constitutionally established spiritual governance representing the rule of the deity. The prototype of theocratic constitution is ancient Israel. Moses, who was according to the oldest tradition a Levite, established such a type of rule.

Now it is not the priestly king who exercises theocratic power, but the royal priest. In a genuine theocracy, the worldly power actually lies in the hands of an organized priesthood. Hence a theocracy prerequires the independence of that priesthood. Characteristic of the situation, however, is not the rule of priests itself, but rather the exercise of rulership as divine governance. Over all other forms of dominion, a special sacerdotal relationship must obtain in a theocracy between the priestly ruler and the deity.

We might hold the opinion that the three forms of sacral rule just sketched can only be found in ethnic societies, for only here do the religious and the natural communities overlap. But let us examine this matter more closely.

Rulership is certainly a legitimate form of leadership in a state, nation, or ethnic community. And here it is naturally based upon power. Within a sacral ethnic community, the power a ruler exercises is numinous power, the ruler himself being a numinous personality. In universal religion, however, the natural community (the family, nation, state) loses its sacral character and becomes a profane community ruled by worldly authority. The concern of the universal religion is not the outward wellbeing of the community, as we have pointed out repeatedly, but the salvation of the individual. Hence there is no legitimate place for rulership here. Jesus describes the matter pertinently when he says: "You know that the rulers of the Gentiles lord it over them, and their great men exercise authority over them. It shall not be so among you; but whoever would be great among you must be your servant, and whoever would be first among you must be your slave" (Matthew 20:25f).

In universal religions there are, however, unquestionably institutions—specifically religious institutions—that raise a total claim to rulership. Sociologically they are representative of a development that actually constitutes a reversion to patterns of the ethnic-religious stage. These organizations are universal, but their universality is such that their claim to authority pertains not only to the specifically religious relationship between the individual and his God, but encompasses all areas of life. Theoretically, membership in these institutions prerequires personal decision, but in practice it is largely all a matter of tradition and of being born into the community. Such church organizations often become ruling bodies which are again maintained by an organized priesthood and possess a monarchic leadership, a "hierarchy." They have a form of authority that belongs to the general sphere of universal religion but is ethnic-religious in character.

Let us now trace the inner development by which a religion of personal salvation becomes an established authority. We shall take Christianity as an example, for it alone has really been decisive in our culture. In the New Testament, *ekklesia,* which is usually translated as "church," merely means "congregation." As this congregation is organized increasingly, there emerges a Church. It in turn elaborates its creeds, lays down cult obligations, and trains a priesthood that is distinct from the laity and is hierarchically subdivided in itself. Now the Church develops a certain self-understanding. It is universal and it claims to be the sole salvation-granting institution. (Historically, this claim has been asserted repeatedly ever since Cyprian, being expressed, for instance, in the famous Bull *Unam sanctam* of Pope Boniface VIII [1302] and at various other places.) The implication is that the Church has the obligation to subject all people to its blessings, even if it be against their will, for it is for their own salvation's sake. The religious desire to help others acquire their redemption is soon inextricably connected with the general human urge to wield power and to hold authority. The instrument for attaining such power is, in the first instance, the Church's sacramental authority, which encompasses all areas of life. Furthermore, excommunications and interdicts, practiced ever since the time of Gregory VII, become the weapons of the popes. In the Middle Ages, such excommunications also had civil consequences; namely, being excluded from society and completely outlawed.

Theoretically, Luther and the Reformation wanted to return to a pure community of believers and free confessors. Hence the Church of the Word was to have no organs to enforce doctrine and discipline. It was left to the political ruler to deal with those things which the Church as a community of love could not enact by compulsion. But this was how inquisitional practices reappeared and a church system subscribing to force emerged again.[20]

Another problem in this connection is the relationship of the Church to the State, which has now become wordly. When Christianity was founded and while it was beginning to develop, it was interested only in the individual and in his salvation alone. Jesus and the early congregations were quite indifferent toward the state. In view of the expected end of the world, the state, being pagan, was accepted as something transitional. Paul commended obedience to the governing authorities which, as he said (Romans 13), were instituted by God even though they were heathen. At this time the Christian Church was not in any way a political force in itself. It was just starting to emerge as an institution and hence as a power factor. But it was only recognized as such later, by Constantine. The question was now what relationship should obtain between the State, now Christian, and the Church, now a powerful organization.

At this point we must refer again to our discussion of sacral kingship. When Christianity carried the day in the West, Constantine was proclaimed the Christian Emperor, and Christianity became the privileged state religion. At this time, two phenomena were determining the scene. On the one hand, the ancient idea of sacral kingship continued to hold sway in the Christian state, qualities and epithets stemming from the worship of the sovereign in antiquity now being attached to the Christian emperor. He was called *vi-*

carius Christi, Christ's representative, whereas the pope was termed *vicarius Petri,* Peter's representative. Gradually, however, the ancient ruler cult was eliminated on Christian soil; at the same time, an ecclesiastical hierarchy was established. This second factor led to the development of a complete papal theocracy. The pope now became *vicarius Christi,* as the emperor had been; he was no longer merely *vicarius Petri.*

Let us now interpret these historical developments in sociological terms. The sacral kingship in Christian garb at the beginning of the Christian Era was but a mere preservation of the ethnic-religious form of rulership. Like their subjects, the sovereigns who had become Christian could only conceive of and, indeed, practice rulership in the traditional form of sacral kingship. Only gradually was the non-Christian ruler cult eliminated on Christian grounds when Christianity took the place of the ancient state religion. This development lay in the wake of a secularization of the state and was a consequence of Christian ideas. But at the same time, the Church, now organized, established again a new kind of ethnic-religious community among the mass of its members, thus reinstituting also a new sacerdotal kingship which soon started to raise its claim to power over the state. Saint Augustine's theory of a Christian church state in which state and church are closely connected under the leadership of the church was put into practice from the eleventh to the fourteenth centuries. During this time the Church raised and substantiated the claim that it was a divine universal state for all people. Thomas Aquinas became the ideological propounder of the concept; furthermore, he laid the theoretical foundation for the uniform church culture which was to determine the Middle Ages and is still a postulate of modern Catholicism today. It was in the Middle Ages that the papacy as a form of rulership reached its climax. The Bull *Regnans in excelsis* (1570) states unequivocally that the pope is instituted as a ruler "over all peoples and all regal powers" (*super omnes gentes et omina regna*).[21]

Thus the sacred organization's claim to complete authority is the second motive for intolerance.[22]

3. TRADITION AND RELIGIOUS REVOLUTION

We come now to a third important motive for intolerance: the tendency to preserve the tradition against any infringement or attack upon it. This phenomenon is to be observed in all religions. Tradition (*traditio*) literally means "passing on," and in religion the concept naturally refers to the transmission of religious views, concepts of God, cult practices, and ethical precepts. A tradition can be looked at either from its origin or from its end. If considered in the first way, "tradition" is what was there in the beginning and *was to be handed down*. In this case one will have to ask for the motives leading to its formation. If "tradition," however, is regarded in the second sense, it is what *has been transmitted*—that is, what is the result of a process. The question of origin is not decisive; rather, the integrative power of the tradition strikes us as most noteworthy. This cohesive force brings into focus the tension that develops time and again between fixed traditions and spontaneously new and revolutionary religious messages.

If we consider religious history from this perspective, we will find that ethnic religions possess "tradition" only in the second sense. Their origin lies in the distant past. We cannot study the formation of their traditions; we can merely note the tremendous force and authority of what has been passed on, and observe that here the power of "tradition" remains effective even when its content is hardly understood. Sacred customs, for instance, are handed down from primeval times; they are strictly observed and any deviation from them is severely punished. However, in the religions whose historical beginnings we can grasp through available source material, the characteristic tension between the formation of a new tradition and the adherence to the old fixed patterns does indeed become clearly visible. When religions are founded, they are always established on the soil of some *traditional* faith. Hence such founded religions always engender a more or less vehement conflict between the newly formed and the old "tradition." This tension can be observed in the Mosaic religion, for instance. Moses united the Israelite tribes under the one God Yahweh (who had already been worshipped by various of these groups beforehand) and founded a "tradition" which largely opposed the polytheistic tradition—which, however, is still visible later on in the Old Testament.

The formation of a new "tradition" is an inevitable necessity, since that is the vessel in which religious substance is passed on to following generations. It holds not only what has been set down in Holy Writ and usually dates back to a founder, but obviously also bears and preserves oral and later even literary traditions that serve to complement and interpret Holy Writ. Such secondary traditions are always also regarded as being divinely authorized.

Here, again, the Israelite religion is a case in point. According to rabbinic teaching, there is, beside the revelation set down in the sacred law, another equally binding tradition, which is also traced back to Moses.[23] It was with this tradition that Jesus came into conflict. Here the tensions we are referring to become quite evident. The official guardians of the tradition, the Pharisees and Scribes, ask Jesus, "Why do your disciples transgress the tradition of the elders?" (Matthew 15:2). In Mark, where the same discussion is narrated (Mark 7:2ff), Jesus says to the Pharisees and Scribes, "You leave the commandment of God, and hold fast the tradition of men" (Mark 7:8). Here Jesus makes a very characteristic difference between the "commandment of God" and the "tradition of men." He traces back to human sources the tradition that is so highly esteemed by the Israelite church as divinely inspired. Here we have the typical conflict between the organized church (with its priestly representatives) and one who is spontaneously called by God. The discussion in such cases always revolves around the question of authority. The high priest asks Jesus, "By what authority are you doing these things, and who gave you this authority?" (Matthew 21:23).[24] The same question is put to Peter and John by the Sanhedrin: "By what power or by what name did you do this?" (Acts 4:7). These people thought that only the church, which is founded upon the holy tradition, can grant authority. In their eyes, Jesus and his disciples lack such authority.

Let us now trace this development further. It is apparent that the early Christian Church also formed a tradition of its own. At first it was a tradition in the sense of a transmission of the message proclaimed by Jesus and the Apostles.[25] Gradually, however, the concept of tradition broadened. Irenaeus and Tertullian are the first literary representatives of a more sophisticated idea of tradition. Vincent of Lerins (434) gives the concept a classical formulation. He defines it as "what was believed everywhere, by all and at all times."[26] It is in his theology that the tradition of the Catholic Church gains importance alongside the Holy Scriptures.[27]

At the Council of Trent, not only scriptural but also oral tradition was traced back to Jesus and the Apostles. Hence oral tradition gained the same importance and authority as Holy Writ.[28]

We need not sketch the further development of the concept of tradition in the Catholic or the Protestant Church (where it also gained significance).[29] Suffice it to point out that in the Christian Church on the whole the same conflicts appear again that had marked Jesus' relationship to the tradition of his Church.

The formation of tradition is a phenomenon we can observe in other religions as well. It is especially striking in Islam. Here, the Koran could not answer all questions that would arise at later times. Thus bits of tradition were compiled in a collection of material called *hadīth*. It reports how the Prophet Mohammed would set in particular cases, reference being made to the authorities of the tradition, and these alleged habitual deeds of the Prophet as narrated here thus became important sources of religious cognition alongside the Koran.[30]

The attitude to tradition in the broadest sense gives rise, time and again, to conflicts which break out even on the topmost level of religion. An antithesis develops between religious organizations which are built upon a tradition and men of religious genius who break that tradition. The founders of the three world religions— to speak only of them—all came into conflict with their traditions. We have already referred to Jesus' attitude in this matter. The situation is similar in Buddha's case, too. In one discourse, Buddha tells some tradition-oriented Brahmans (who were having a dispute about the only true way to gain salvation) that none of the men in the long line of doctrinal teachers had an immediate vision and experience of the Divine upon which they could base their religious claims.[31] He compares them to a row of blind men who all depend upon the person ahead. It can be readily shown that Mohammed, too, adopted the same attitude toward tradition. The pre-Mohammedan ethnic religion of Arabia certainly had its fixed traditions. The Prophet, however, departed from the religious patterns of his tribe and thus occasioned a breach with his own tradition; consequently, he had to flee from Mecca to Medina. We have already pointed out how the tension between Mohammed and the representatives of the old belief finds repeated expression in his arguments with his critics.

In summing up, we can lay bare a number of factors that always come into play when men of religious genius protest against tradition and are involved in conflicts with its keepers. Molded traditions which are passed on just because they evoke reverence and are hallowed by being handed down from generation to generation for centuries are often the result of uncontrolled and uncontrollable transmission. In being transmitted, they are obviously altered and often even changed to their very opposite; they adopt new and alien motifs and tendencies. Hence the concern of all religious reformers is understandable. As the word "reformation" (*reformatio*) implies, reformers aspire to "re-form" the religious tradition in accordance with the original form of their creed. They endeavor to go back to a primal stage in their religion which either actually did exist or which they falsely take as having once existed. The prophets of Israel, for instance, reproached the valid religiousness of their times for having departed from the old Mosaic tradition formed in the wilderness.[32] Jesus himself regarded the old Jewish cult patterns as arbitrary human arrangements, unnecessarily burdening men.[33] Luther's Reformation also began with the criticism of the Catholic Church's distortions of the pure Gospel. Similarly, non-Christian reformers like Hōnen Shōnin and Shinran Shōnin in Japan and Tsong-kha-pa in Tibet endeavored to regenerate a traditional form of religion.

A second factor that should be taken into account when we

speak of tradition is the habitual force of religious patterns and ideas. The routine adherence to old forms and concepts and the customary performance of religious practices often leads to lifeless, mechanical religiousness, especially if it is accompanied, as it often is, with a lack of understanding for these ancient forms of religion. Repeatedly, however, individuals who have received a vocation arise and fight against this type of dead piety, being involved in a conflict with its representatives.

Finally, it must be pointed out that the tradition of an organization forms a fixed structure. It often has the function of a kind of religious "shell" or "casing" (*Gehäuse*) within which men live. Karl Jaspers, who coined the term *Gehäuse,* defines it as "an intellectual attitude which gives to man a world view safeguarding him against nihilism and skepticism and relieving him of constantly having to come to terms with life."[34] Now such "shells" also have a tremendous significance for religion. Traditions as we described them above make "shells" out of religious teachings, creeds, and cult systems. Hans Schär, in his excellent book, *Erlösungsvorstellungen und ihre psychologischen Aspekte* [Conceptions of Salvation and their Psychological Aspects] (1950), has given an illuminating description of the phenomenon of obligation to tradition.[35] People who seek such "shells" for the inner support want their doctrines to be firmly established beyond all doubt; they wish to have a cult venerable with age, elaborately developed to the point of perfection and standing above all tides of change. Schär points out that, in the religious sphere, authoritarianism is necessarily an element of the structure of the "shell." There are many who cannot appreciate intellectual freedom and liberty. They would rather submit to an authority that will relieve them of the trying and strenuous task of having to come to terms with the constantly new problems of life. Hence many would rather accept religious authority than enjoy personal religious independence. "Authority wants to be accepted," says Schär, "it does not wish to be analyzed critically and discussed. A person adopts it as a *Gehäuse,* and he reflects upon everything, except the *Gehäuse* itself. Only from within it may he think quite independently about things approaching him." [36] This kind of thinking is not free, however; it is bound to the principles of the system within which a person stands. We can now understand the inquisitors on the basis of this concept of the *Gehäuse*.

Schär explains quite pertinently that in Catholicism the Jesuit Order was largely responsible for transforming the Church into a *Gehäuse*. In Protestantism, says the same author, Karl Barth is accountable for a similar development. "Through his theological principles and through the rigidity with which he seeks to establish them, Karl Barth apparently aspires to achieve what the Jesuits attempted in Catholicism when they employed their subtle means of spiritual guidance and even made use of the outward power of the Church, for it was their aim to eliminate all experiences that could be dangerous to the structure of the *Gehäuse*." [37]

Indeed, many who are incapable of solving the problems of life themselves are inclined to enter into an authoritarian "shell" that will protect them from such problems. This brings us again to the question of tolerance. The mentality of the *Gehäuse* intolerantly excludes and condemns everything that is alien to and different from itself. This makes it quite clear how difficult it is to further a tolerant attitude in this kind of a situation. As there is a widespread tendency to recede into traditional "shells," intolerance is deeply rooted in the thinking of those who, for want of religious independence, seek firm authority.

So far as the conflict between obligation to and opposition against tradition is concerned, there is a deep structural difference pertaining to types of religiosity. On the one hand there is a static and mediated piety affirming the tradition; on the other, a dynamic, immediate religiousness standing against it. The piety of the institution and religious system, formed and preserved as it is by tradition, always bears the stamp of the mediated. A complicated structure of religious media of every type is built up in the course of a long tradition. [38] It threatens to intercalate in the direct relationship between God and man, claiming to be necessary and indispensable. Jesus, for one, clearly perceived this state of affairs. In his great fundamental discussion with the Pharisees and Scribes in Matthew 23:13 he says, "But woe to you, Scribes and Pharisees, hypocrites! because you shut the kingdom of heaven against men; for you neither enter yourselves, nor allow those who would enter to go in." Jesus makes it quite clear that the ecclesiastical organization is pushing itself between man in search for salvation and God; it is acting as an ineluctable intermediary authority. So, opposing this mediative religious institution, here is a man who lives out of the direct relationship with God and therefore rejects every kind of interagency; he discards all human vehicles that claim to be necessary.

The tragedy is that media as such are unavoidable in religion. But they are legitimate if it is realized that they have merely relative significance. In the situation just referred to, religious media and mediative authorities gain absolute importance; there is ascribed to them a self-value that is allegedly willed by God. In fact this is what usually happens when religious media have been hallowed by tradition. And when value is ascribed to religious mediation, any kind of religious liberty and religious immediacy an individual may have will appear unacceptable.

The conflict between immediate and mediated religious apprehension is thus to be found even on the highest level of religion: it determines the relationships of religious leaders and founders of religion. Indeed, their conflict is a model of what keeps on recurring on the plane of simple religiousness among their disciples in following generations.[39]

4. THE STRUGGLE FOR TRUTH AND AGAINST ERROR

The various motives for intolerance mentioned and discussed here are usually connected with a religious claim to absoluteness. All universal religions raise a general claim to absolute truth. In rationalistic apologetics, this factor even becomes decisive.

We have already pointed out the significance of such claims in the historical part of our analysis, and we shall consider and interpret the concept of truth and the claim to absoluteness as general (recurring) phenomena in greater detail in the third part of this study. Yet we want to make reference at this point to various implications.

The claim to absolute truth is to be found, in the first place, in prophetic religions. [In the author's terminology, "prophetic" and "mystic" religions are two basic types of religiousness (rather than religions as such). They appear—beside and beyond other types—on the plane of universal religion. It should be noted that this typological distinction is not of the same kind as the "structural," historical differentiation between "nature-religion" and "culture-religion" in the ethnic-religious setting.] This matter need not be illustrated here. But it certainly also appears in mystical religions. A Buddhist commentary, for example, states, "There is no other way to gain salvation than through his [Buddha's] teaching." [40] And a Hindu scripture says of the Vishnu devotee:

> His outward and inward prayer is directed but to Vishnu. He knows not the service of other gods, vows not to them, calls not upon their name, envisions them not, asks not for their reward; he bears not their signs, wears not their vestments, rejoices not at their festivals, and turns away from their feasts. He makes no pilgrimages to their sacred spots and neither honors nor serves them. He knows not the rituals or sacred customs [relating to the worship] of other deities, save of Narayana alone, the only lord and protector of all the world.[41]

It can be observed everywhere in universal religions that the claim to absoluteness is founded, explicitly or implicitly, upon the conviction that one's own religious community is the sole possessor of truth. In prophetic religions, the battle against those who are steeped in the darkness of religious error or have departed from the truth of their own religion is particularly passionate, being waged in the name of truth. Especially the institutions of these religions are involved in that battle, as well as the representatives of their theologies that have developed out of living initial stages. The actual motives for intolerance which we have discussed are usually not indicated expressly because they are not well reconcilable with the basic teachings of these religions, particularly not with the original messages of their founders. Nevertheless, these motives are there, and they are latently effective. But they can be inferred, as we have seen, from the practices and pronouncements of the respective religious institutions.

One reason given for exclusivist actions in religion is that truth and error exclude each other. It is pointed out that only *one* thing can be true. This is plausible at first sight. Two and two is four, and there are no two ways about it. Yet this does not prove that only *one* thing can be true, or that there can be only *one* truth, about God and his relationship to the world. It does not imply that all statements and teachings deviating from the revelation which one holds to be true oneself must needs be false. According to that view, only *one* religion is true, and all other faiths are false and hence unacceptable. Only one religion is revealed, and hence all other revelations must be erroneous, aye, must even be battled.

Opinions vary as to the way that battle should be waged. We have already mentioned Pope Pius XII's formulation of the Catholic Church's viewpoint. In essence, it is this: error can never be tolerated, but the Church does not have the charge to suppress it by force. Referring to the parable of the tares among the wheat, the Pope points out that Jesus instructed his followers to allow the wheat to grow together with the tares until the time of harvest. So far as religion is concerned, the inference is that error should be tolerated formally, even though resisted innerly. Hence people who go astray should yet be forborne.

The Catholic Church often recommends such an attitude of permissiveness towards those who, in its view, adhere to religious error, and it denotes this attitude as religious tolerance. We must make it quite clear, however, that this is definitely not true tolerance in our sense. Religious tolerance, and respectively intolerance, always pertain and apply to religious views and religious patterns of life. Of course men are also affected by intolerant actions when they represent "false" beliefs in the eyes of the judging religious authorities, but it is quite evident that in this case their person is contingent on the false idea or pattern itself. As for genuine religious tolerance, the same is true here, as well. It, too, applies to patterns and forms of religious faith and practice rather than to people. As soon as a distinction is made, however, between the religious view which is rejected and the person who is forborne, even if he remains in error, the problem of tolerance is deferred to another plane—to the plane of decorum and to the level of what is befitting for a Christian society.[42] When the relationship of men "with right faith" to fellow-men "who err" is placed under the precepts of Christian ethics by a supreme authority, this is a mark of progress. (Obviously, this did not happen during the Inquisition, and regrettably it does not even happen everywhere today, as confessional school education and school politics reveal.) But even then, exhorting people to outward ethical conduct has nothing to do with religious tolerance if the religious views of others are not tolerated in the least but rather rejected radically.[43]

Another result of the claim to absolute truth is missionary activity. The practice of missionizing religions is naturally based upon the conviction that peoples who have not yet come into contact with the "true" faith are error-stricken and therefore await nothing but eternal damnation. Missionizing religions like Christianity regard all people outside their own fold as "pagans," no matter how deep or sublime their religiousness may be. They all uniformly succumb to the intolerant verdict that, as heathens, they are lost without exception. We must of course add that, when we speak of missionary activity, we mean the type characteristic of prophetic religions like Christianity and Islam which proclaim a divine revelation by God's command with the purpose of converting other people to their faith, or of inducing them with a greater or lesser degree of force to embrace that faith. Missionary activity can also be understood as an offer of religious values capable of enriching the lives of others. The Ramakrishna Mission, which was founded by Vivekananda in 1897, is an example. It seeks not to convert people from their inherited religion to a new faith, but desires rather that the Christian be a better Christian, the Hindu a better Hindu, etc. Furthermore, it strives to awaken a sense of unity among religions while they maintain their diversities.

On the whole, Protestant theology reflects greater intrinsic intolerance than Catholicism does; the Catholic Church is more formally intolerant. Protestantism—especially under Karl Barth's fatal influence—considers man in non-Christian religions to be lost without exception. Any attempt to discern any values in non-Christian faith, says Barth, "must be abandoned without reserve. Christendom should advance right into the midst of these 'religions,' whatever their names may be, and, let come what will, deliver her message of the one God and of His compassion for men forlorn, without yielding by a hairbreadth to their 'daemons.' "[44]

The image of non-Christian religions which Catholic theology has is much more latitudinarian. In accordance with Justin Martyr (150 A.D.), Clement of Alexandria, and Saint Augustine, it considers Christianity to be implicit in lofty forms of paganism by assuming that the *logos spermatikos* (the seed of the divine word) is also present outside the Church and outside Christianity. Furthermore, Catholicism has the concept of the invisible Church to which men may belong who stand outside the visible Church. We can only perceive what is visible, say Catholic theologians, and hence we have no right to judge. However, this view, which is occasionally even propounded by top-ranking members of the Catholic Church, does not prevent the Church from engaging in missionary activity and from leading as many as possible into the safe harbor of salvation within the visible Church. A radical view according to which the Catholic mission has often acted in history was voiced by Bernard of Clairvaux (1091–1153). During the Second Crusade (1147–1149), he preached against the unbelievers and demanded the waging of missionary war under the watchword "baptism or death." Peace was to be granted only to those who subjected themselves to "the true peace-bringer," Christ.[45]

It is not our purpose here to discuss the different theories on expansion that various religions may hold. The basic motive for all missionary activity is clear: it is to spread truth for the salvation of one's fellowmen. Missionary activity in the sense of the prophetic religions involves a twofold purpose: the extirpation of paganism and the establishment of the "true" religion in foreign areas.[46] Jesus pointed out the dangers that lie in successful attempts to alienate people from their traditional faiths and to lead them to other religions. In Matthew 23:15 he says to the Scribes and Pharisees, who propound proselytizing, "Woe to you, Scribes and Pharisees, hypocrites! for you traverse sea and land to make a single proselyte, and when he becomes a proselyte, you make him twice as much a child of hell as yourselves." What Jesus apparently had in mind was that the experience of conversion from an inherited religion to a new creed, which may perhaps even be due to some kind of coercion, can entail grave danger for the individual if he embraces the new faith without inner preparation. For centuries, Christian missionary activity was frequently connected with political and economic interests; missionaries often came to foreign lands as representatives of imperialist trends, frequently pursuing and achieving their goals in alliance with political powers. We need not discuss the sad malpractices of some missions here in detail.[47] At any rate, we can understand Mahatma Gandhi's admonition to the missionaries from our perspective when he tells them, "It is not your call, I assure you, to tear up the lives of the people of the East by their roots." [48]

Another danger lies particularly in mass conversions, which have occurred often in the history of the Christian missions. People who are thus converted fail completely to comprehend and appropriate the substance of the new religion in any way whatsoever. The result is often a mere renaming of traditional religious and cult patterns. A great mass of material could be cited to illustrate this fact. It is reported of the Indian Christians of Guatemala, for instance, that they "really hardly know whether they are praying to their god Gucumatz or to Jesus Christ. The ceremonies are half pagan, half Christian, and no Catholic priest would venture during 'Holy Week' to forbid the Indians their masked dances, in honor not of Christ but of Judas." [49] So far as Christianity in India is concerned, missionaries deplore the prevalence of aboriginal practices.[50] And Hughes says of Chinese Christians: ". . . it is certain that the mass of the Chinese people still regard Christianity as essentially a foreign religion, as being indeed the religion of the West: and there are grounds for doubting whether any considerable section of the three millions who make up the Christian community have really come to feel at home in their new faith." [51]

Under these circumstances it is evident that, if one looks at the situation closely, the triumph of the mission is actually a victory for the indigenous religion. Native religious elements carry the day over the outwardly victorious proselytizing faith. In Catholic Mission theology, this process of taking over other religious customs and endowing them with a new Christian meaning is termed "substitution." [52] The phenomenon is a common one. It was on account of such substitution that Buddhism could tolerate ethnic religions in Tibet and East Asia. Sophisticated systems in Indian religion endow primitive belief with a deeper significance by this method. And Catholic missions follow the same principle even now, when they hand out medals with the inscription "To Our Dear Lady" to South American Indians and Negroes to replace native amulets as objects of superstition.[53]

With this fourth motive, the claim to possessing truth, we have now discussed the main reason for intolerance in religion. At the same time we have approached a crucial and most decisive point in the study of our problem; its solution alone can ultimately lead to intrinsic tolerance.

In the final part of our study we shall suggest possibilities of accepting tolerance as an ideal and an obligation. We shall have to begin our consideration with a reflection upon the question of truth in religion, and this will lead us to all the other reasons there are for assenting to that ideal and adopting that obligation.

III. *The Postulate of Tolerance*

In turning now to the idea of tolerance, we wish not only to describe objectively the concept and its motives, but also to establish tolerance as a postulate. Let us start by coming to grips with a charge that is often made, the claim that tolerance springs from religious indifference. Reference is made in this connection to Frederick the Great, who said that "every religion must be tolerated" in in his kingdom, and everyone must have the possibility of gaining salvation "in his own *façon*." Frederick the Great himself was actually religiously indifferent, hence his attitude can doubtlessly be understood on the grounds of his lack of concern for religious matters. Indifference can hence be involved when formal tolerance is granted, especially when granted by a secularized state. But it is quite false simply to equate tolerance with indifference. As we have seen, there is a type of true tolerance, which we have termed intrinsic, that does not in any way stem from an indifferent attitude toward religion. On the contrary, an especially deep religious experience and understanding of what is essential to religion forms the basis of intrinsic tolerance, as we shall show. The theory that tolerance and true interest in religion are incompatible presupposes a particular understanding of "truth" in religion, which we shall now have to disprove.

1. The Idea of Truth in Religion

In order to clarify the concept of truth in religion, we must start by considering the general usage of the term in everyday life. Here it has a twofold meaning. In the first case, it is not something in itself, but rather the quality of a statement about an objective state of affairs; it implies correspondence between the statement and the matter referred to. This is truth in the sense of rational correctness. Its opposite is falseness, which may be either error in the sense of unintentional falsehood, or falsity as deliberate falsification.

The second meaning the term truth can assume in general usage is that of an objective reality of some kind. When a person says, "I have realized the truth," he means in the sense of such a reality, which has become the object of perception.

If we turn now to the world of religions, we will find that both these notions of truth are known and used. We shall have to analyze when and under what circumstances the one or other concept is employed, and how the two concepts relate to one another.

In ethnic-religious texts that contain the word "truth," the term is almost always used in the sense of a numinous Reality. There is never talk of the correctness of a doctrine here, for in genuine ethnic religions there are no doctrines as such. Practices of cultic life affecting the individual more or less deeply dominate here. Contact with the deity is there and it must be continually fostered by the observation of traditional cult practices. Truth in itself is not mentioned, but at times it is applied to the deity. Here are a few examples. Ancient Egypt had the concept of *Maat*.[1] Usually translated as "Truth," the word is closely connected with god, especially with the god Ra. In a cult hymn it says, "Thou wanderest through heaven and leadest the earth while *Maat* is with thee; and when thou resteth in the Underworld, *Maat* is with thee. . . . As long as thou existeth, *Maat* doth exist; as long as *Maat* existeth, thou dost exist. It is united with thy head [as Uraeus[2]]; it is eternally with thee. . . . Thy flesh and thy limbs are *Maat;* the breath of thy body and thy heart are *Maat,* thus annointest thy head with *Maat.*"[3] It is apparent here that the term *Maat* refers to numinous reality. It is in this sense that it says of Amon, the universal God, who is called the "Lord of Truth" that he is a God who "liveth daily by Truth."[4]

The concept of truth is quite clearly used in this same sense in the Indian Upanishads where it says, "In Truth resteth the Universe,"[5] or "The gods are of Truth."[6] The Sanskrit word for "truth," *satyam,* refers to reality, for it contains the word *sat,* being. Hence truth is that which truly exists, it is the primal reality.[7]

The Old Testament, mirroring an ethnic religion with no specific doctrines as such, uses the Hebrew word *emet* for truth.[8] In the first instance, this term means the reality that is directly accessible to religious feeling. Psalm 36:5 is a case in point: "Thy faithfulness [truth] reacheth unto the clouds"; also Psalm 117:2: "For his merciful kindness is great toward us: and the truth of the Lord endureth forever." Evidently the Psalmist does not mean that God's utterances about specific matters are correct epistemologically; rather, he is speaking of divine reality itself when he makes reference to the "truth of the Lord." Psalm 100:5 says of this reality: "His truth endureth to all generations." In the Israelite religion of the Old Testament, God's reality is experienced more specifically as holy Will. The rational element in the Hebrew concept of truth leads us to a second meaning: truth is also God's Law. It is perceived as a source of truth for the legal questions concerning human conduct. Psalm 119:142, for instance, says, "Thy law is the truth," and Psalm 86:11 emphasizes, "I will walk in thy truth." But this meaning amounts to the same as the meaning in the first case, for the Law is the Will of Yahweh moulded into percepts; it is revealed Will, and hence ultimately divine reality.

The matter is quite different in universal religions. As opposed to ethnic faiths, we find here rationally formulated and developed doctrines. One might think that truth in the sense of correctness is applied to these doctrines. This, indeed, is often the case in certain stages of the development, as we shall see, but it is not always so. In fact the usage of the term truth as correctness is not even prevalent in universal religions; it is certainly not to be found in the initial stages of the development when there was direct contact with the numinous. The most common usage of the term "truth" in universal religions is exemplified by a Zen Buddhist text: "Have you never seen a person who is the truth himself? Such an one stands above all knowledge and doctrines, he rises above all actions and effects and is completely free. He seeks no further truth, he condemns no error." [9] This passage actually contains both notions of truth. First, it expresses the idea that the Zen devotee must transcend the subject-object gap in order to be filled with numinous reality himself. He is not to have truth, but to be Truth. According to the text, this is the higher form of truth rather than the seeking for further truth (which obviously has error as its counterpart). Truth in the sense of right teaching has to be transcended and overcome by the higher Truth.

The New Testament uses the word *alētheia* for truth. In order to clarify the meaning of the term here, the *Theologisches Wörterbuch zum Neuen Testament* first examines the Greco-Hellenistic usage of the word. The original signification is "not to keep secret"; that is, to disclose what has been seen, or become apparent. Hence, for the historian, truth here is historical fact (not myth); for the philosopher, *alētheia* refers to that which truly is. Plato, for instance, regarded truth as genuine and actual reality, not the illusions of worldly phenomena. For him, truth was the Divine itself. In Hellenism, the world that shaped early Christianity—especially through Paul and John—there is a dualistic view of the universe. Truth is that in which man must participate in order to be saved from the woe of worldly existence. Truth, light, and life are terms that have essentially the same meaning. [10] All these currents flow together in the New Testament. In the first three books, the Synoptic Gospels, the word truth appears only twice, being used in each case in the general, not specifically religious, sense of "saying the truth." In the Gospel of Saint John, however, truth is a central concept used solely in the sense of divine reality. "And the Word became flesh and dwelt among us, full of grace and truth" (John 1:14). "I am the

way, and the truth, and the life" (John 14:6). "Everyone who is of
the truth hears my voice" (John 18:37). "The Spirit is the truth"
(1 John 5:7). This usage is also to be found in Paul. In 2 Corinthians 11:10 he says, "The truth of Christ is in me." Obviously,
not a correct teaching is meant here, but a divine reality in Christ,
which has been received by faith.

In addition to truth as reality, there is, as we said, also the other
connotation of correctness. Of course this meaning can also be
traced in the universal religions other than Christianity. One may
think of the "Four Noble Truths" that play such an important role
in Buddhism. Let us limit ourselves here, however, to Christianity,
to show that the term truth in its meaning of correctness of teaching
appears relatively late in the early form of this religion, and that it
presupposes or is expressive of a clear shift of emphasis. This shift is
a change of emphasis from living faith to doctrine, for the doctrine
is part of the ecclesiastical structure which is gradually established.
It strikes one that truth as correctness of doctrine is to be found
quite often in the late New Testament writings, in the so-called
pastoral epistles. In 2 Timothy 2:18, Hymenaeus and Philetus are
mentioned, and it says of them that they "have swerved from the
truth" by spreading false teachings about the resurrection. In Titus
we read of certain false teachings being spread in Crete. With regard
to men associated with such heresies, the writer of the letter gives
this advice: "Therefore rebuke them sharply, that they may be
sound in the faith, instead of giving heed to Jewish myths or to
commands of men who reject the truth" (1:13f).[11] The Letter to
Titus incidentally also contains this admonition: "As for a man
who is factitious . . . have nothing more to do with him" (3:10).
According to general opinion in critical scholarship, these pastoral
epistles were written in the first half of the second century A.D.[12];
that is, at a time when the Church was being organized: when it
was establishing ecclesiastical offices and formulating fixed doctrines. Here, the word truth is clearly used in the sense of correctness.

The question with which we shall now have to be concerned is how these two notions of truth originated and how they relate to each other. Let us start by considering the oldest and most original form of religious expression: the myth. Formerly, especially in the so-called "History of Religions School" (*Religionsgeschichtliche Schule*), myth was defined as primitive history of the gods. Gunkel called the myth "a narrative in which the lofty figures of the great gods play the main role." [13] Gressmann characterized it in this way: "Generally, it is characteristic of the myth that it lets deities act and that its arena lies beyond time and space." [14] According to Gressmann, the myth is "in content, primitive science," and "in form, primitive poetry."

Against such rationalistic interpretations, we would propound the thesis that the myth is an account of a timeless numinous event and a representation thereof; in myth, numinous reality is appropriated.[15] The form of the myth is of course conditioned by the thinking of the time; its actualization takes place when elements of a world familiar to man are interwoven, as in dreams, with images unconsciously and symbolically representing an experienced numinous reality. It is quite characteristic of the time of the unshattered myth that man has no concern for the question about the objective possibility and factuality of the events narrated. He does not care about the truth of the myth in the sense of the accuracy of its statements. The notion that a mythical event could be impossible—this is often a stumbling block for modern thinking—presupposes the awareness that there do exist universally valid and unbreakable laws of nature. Men of mythical times, however, did not have such an awareness. For them, everything was possible, and nothing was basically impossible in their realm of experience. They knew what was usual in nature and human life, and with this they reckoned; but the unusual and extraordinary also seemed quite possible to them (even though modern man would consider such things principally impossible). The concept of what is impossible presupposes the notion of what is possible and how far it is possible. The limits of the possible can only be determined, we assert, by knowing the laws of nature. But mythical man had no such notion of the possible. He measured the unusual with the yardstick of the usual, not of the possible. Hence the ususual, the miracle, is the preeminent sphere of divine revelation. Myths are full of miracles. But mythical man's attitude to miracles is basically different from modern man's. Mythical man encounters the holy, the power of the deity, in extraordinary events. That is why the incidents in the New Testament which we usually call miracles are there termed *dynameis*—"acts of power" wrought by divine authority. This word indicates that it is the connection of the miraculous event with numinous reality and not its relationship to the laws of nature that is decisive. Miracles as events that mirror numinous reality are hence essentially part of living myths. The mythical word and its reenactment in cult and drama actualizes sacred reality for the mythical consciousness.

Our interpretation of myth as based on the comparative study of religions is quite in harmony with the understanding set forth by modern ethnology. A. E. Jensen, in his book *Myth and Cult among Primitive Peoples* (English trans. 1964), seeks to prove that in myth and its reenactment in the cultus, reality is realized by primitive man. W. F. Otto, in his *Gesetz, Urbild und Mythos* [Law, Prototype, and Myth] (1951), says something quite similar. In myth, he maintains, genuine perception of reality is expressed. Of course it is done in a manner we can no longer appropriate. The absolutely central role of myth and myth-related ritual in the religious life of "primitive peoples" can only be understood if this immediate connection between myth and reality is realized.

In summing up we can say that the vitality and intactness of the myth is rooted in the fact that it conveys the meaning of an event— to be reenacted in the cult—in which the numinous, and genuine life, are comprehended and appropriated in an immediate and unreflected manner. The myth loses its vitality and starts to die when it gives way to reason; that is, when the *logos* rises out of the *mythos*. At this point, man becomes independent as an individual, and his rationality emerges as a critical factor confronting the world and the religious tradition. At such times—and the period of Greek

Rationalism was such a time—the question of the "truth" of the myth is raised. It is sought, but vainly, in the correctness of the statements and accounts of the myth. It is characteristic of rationalism that it always lacks a sense for the nonrational elements in life; hence it seeks the truth of the myth in all kinds of supposedly latent rational truths. Greek rationalism already strove for a kind of "demythologizing" along these lines; it attempted to eliminate those elements in the myth that contradicted reason and were unbeseeming, and it took great pains to discover hidden wisdom in the mythical accounts. But by doing this, it was missing the myth's living meaning.

The shift from *mythos* to *logos* must be viewed from yet another perspective. The early religions of mankind were all, without exception, of the ethnic type; that is, they were maintained by primal natural communities (families, tribes, nations, states). The inner structure of these communities was such that a simple and elemental connection held together the members and united the community as a whole with the numinous powers of the surrounding world. As we have emphasized above, the myth is the adequate form of expression of primeval religious experience. There are no rational doctrines and teachings here, there are only myths and rituals.

In universal religions—which are, of course, maintained by individuals—the situation is different. They proclaim a message of salvation because their point of departure is the existential plight of the individual. The path to redemption they proffer is either a path man must follow in order to approach the deity, or a way in which God acts to come to man. Originally, the mythical form of expression is still employed by the great founders of religions in order to express their messages of salvation. It is also employed by the early congregations to describe the personalities and lives of their respective founders.

Compared to ethnic religions, universal religions appear relatively late in history. They were proclaimed at a time when the intellectual elite had awakened to a penetrating rational attitude that allowed for an investigation of the factors determining man's life. Hence, soon after their founding, these religions were confronted with the necessity of subjecting their religious statements to conceptual clarification within the framework of their respective systems. Thus religious doctrines about salvation were formulated. The statements of early theologians like Paul about God and salvation, which sound like rational assertions, are oriented toward truth in the sense of numinous reality, if taken in their intrinsic meaning and intention. They are still mythical in that they are based upon mythical events; and, like true myths, their language is figurative. This leads us to the concept of the religious symbol, which we shall discuss later on.

We have already discussed the transition that universal religions undergo when they assume ecclesiastical forms of organization. This transition entails a decisive change so far as the question and notion of truth are concerned. What has been experienced religiously as something generally valid for the individual concerned is soon turned into a universal truth, detached from the individual's experience, and formulated in a manner that makes it *rationally* binding for everyone. Hence there is a shift here from the absoluteness of the religious experience to the absolute validity of the religious assertion. This is how an "Orthodoxy" emerges; it always understands truth as correctness of teaching. Such a development leads to a fatal confusion of the two concepts of truth. It is occasioned, as we have pointed out, by the transition of a universal religion from the stage of a living community maintained by individuals who have had a personal experience of faith and who chose to become members, to the stage where it is an objective institution granting salvation. Of course this process does not necessarily affect all members—it does not concern the religiously creative elite, but it does apply to many. Hence there emerges a religious mass organization, composed mainly of those who are religiously uncreative and who need religious leadership. Such members then make up the majority.

This circumstance makes it necessary that the experiential sphere of the religion be marked off and specified, so that there will be a basis for the further formation of community. The "confession" or "creed," serves this purpose; as a fixed formula it always forms the basis for the organization of the church. The original meaning of the word "confession" is still very clearly discernible in the term itself: the confession springs from an act of confessing that is based upon the experience of being overwhelmed by a religious reality, or truth. It is of this reality, or truth, that the confession or creed, speaks. A decisive shift takes place when this credal word is no longer regarded as a relative form of expression testifying to a living encounter with divine reality, but is rather considered to be a rational, doctrinal statement about objective facts and events. The correctness of the statement is then taken to be "truth." Such an understanding suggests itself especially to those who have no sense for religion and its meaning.

The development of these "rational" sounding confessions of faith is determined by a legitimate need—by the requirement on the part of the community to confess its spiritual life as flowing from one numinous source, and to let this confession become a dynamic power effective among members and outsiders. However, such confessions are only legitimate as expressions of personal experience. In mass religious organizations, the creed does not meet this requirement so far as the majority is concerned. The masses always apprehend the words in their rational sense; they take them to be doctrinal statements that possess the binding force of reason. So truth is, in this case, nothing but true, or correct, doctrine (as opposed to erroneous or false teaching). Man's relationship to the holy is completely disregarded in such a concept of religious truth.

Now a mass religious organization that keeps on growing necessarily has a need to preserve its institutional integrity. Hence the leaders of the organization must, and do, keep watch over its unity. What threatens its unity? One would suppose lack of spiritual life. In sophisticated religious organizations, however, it is not primarily this threat that is taken into account, but rather deviation from the letter of the doctrine—heresy. Thus, here again, there is a shift in the idea of truth, a shift from the sphere of numinous reality to that of rational correctness.

Let us now sum up the difference between the two notions of truth we have discerned in our study of religious history, complementing what we have already stated. In religion, truth is, first of all, the divine reality which men have encountered in experience. Religious concepts of the mythical type attest to that reality and to that experience. Their "truth" lies in the fact that they are expressive of a relationship with that reality; it does not lie in the rational accuracy of statements made about the numinous. The accounts of mythical events are true symbols. (We shall discuss the nature of the religious symbol in particular further on.) The conceptual expressions to be found in religion also have their truth. But this, too, must be seen as lying on the plane of an existential relationship with numinous reality.

The concept of truth and the claim to truth can also be meant in the sense of rational correctness. In this case, "truth" implies that there is correspondence between a statement and the matter to which it refers. In religious assertions, this means that there is correspondence between the rationally understandable content of a mythical or conceptual statement and the numinous object, quality, or deed to which it refers. The lack of distinction between these two forms of truth is baneful.

What we have said does not imply that the term truth cannot be used legitimately in religion in the sense of correctness. The mythical or conceptual assertions that bear witness to an encounter with numinous reality always also involve a certain "perception," and in this sense we do have correctness here. Wherever there is perception, it is true or false, correct or incorrect. The question is what one considers to be correct. As we have noted, mythical statements refer, in form and content, to events. There are two possible ways of understanding the perceptual "correctness" of such mythical assertions. First, the report itself may be correct—the event to which it refers may have actually taken place in time and space in the manner described. This is correctness in the sense of rational correspondence between the statement and the event. In this case, the myth would be history in a direct sense. But that is not right. If we approach the myth in this way, we refer its truth to another level. The second possibility is that the truth of the myth is seen as pertaining to the reality of the numinous. In this case, the myth apprehends that reality and expresses it in a manner that is in itself apprehendable. The correctness of the immanent perception involved here lies not on the plane of historical fact but of divine reality, which cannot be expressed adequately in rational terms. In spite of this fact, we assert that divine reality has been perceived and experienced "correctly." As to the divine reality in itself to which the myth makes reference, its nature is so elusive that science cannot pass judgment on the question of its truth.

Here is an illustration of what we mean: Myths of creation appear again and again all over the world of religions. Two attitudes can be assumed toward such myths. One can maintain that what is narrated corresponds precisely to events that took place when the world began. Then the truth of the myth is seen as outward correctness and it is taken for granted that there is correspondence between the account and the occurrences it speaks of. This would be "outward correctness"; here, truth lies on the plane of phenomena. The other approach is to see the mythical account as referring to a numinous reality in and beyond the empirically perceivable world of which it speaks. Here, too, perception of truth is involved; for in the encounter with reality to which the creation myths testify, man has been confronted with something sublime and numinous, and he has been touched by it in a manner that is expressive of the divinity's creative relationship to the world, its ordering care for the world, etc. There is no way of ascertaining scientifically whether the relationships between the divinity and the world which are sensed and believed here do actually obtain; that is, whether the religio-mythical statements about the divine are, in this sense, "correct" or not. If they are, their correctness cannot be of the outward type, but will rather pertain to the inner symbolic relationship between the mythical expression and the divinity.

The same is true of conceptual expressions. If, for instance, the deity is called love, or if he is referred to as a father, a rational, orthodox opinion will assert the correctness of this statement in terms of its reasonableness. This is what Christian orthodoxy does when it claims that Christ is the Son of God in body. Here we have that shift of the concept of truth from the specifically religious to the rational level of which we have spoken. However, if we take concepts like "Son of God" and similar expressions as terms of analogy referring to experienced encounter with the Divine, they do involve a correctness of perception, but a correctness that can only be affirmed by faith.

We shall now have to examine the religious claim to absoluteness more closely, for intrinsic intolerance rests mainly upon this claim. We have already touched upon the problem without interpreting the issue at stake. In order to do so we shall first have to investigate the meaning of the religious symbol, as it is important for the understanding of religious truth.

2. THE NATURE OF THE RELIGIOUS SYMBOL

The religious symbol can have many different forms; in this respect it corresponds to symbols in general, which we shall therefore first discuss.

Everything can become a symbol that is taken to represent a reality referred to by the object, yet distinct from it. Symbols can be found in the most diverse realms of life. Man obviously must feel a general need for symbolization in his thinking. Now how can the inner structure of this common phenomenon be described? Let us consider the above definition point for point. We said, "Everything can become a symbol." This means that there is basically no limit to symbolization in the objects employed. Fundamentally, every empirical phenomenon and everything conceivable can become a symbol. When Goethe says, in well-known verse in *Faust*, "Everything fleeting *is* but an image," this is pan-symbolism, which does not do justice to the matter. That leads us to the first important thing about symbols: they do not exist by themselves; they are invented. Anything can become a symbol, if particular conditions prevail, the primary one being that the object in question is consciously instated as such.

Our definition goes on to say, "Anything can become a symbol that is taken to represent a reality . . . distinct from the object itself." This expresses the decisive structure of the symbol. We discern a difference here between the symbolic object and the significance to which it points. Every symbol consists of these two elements: the concrete object, and its meaning. A perceived object or even a notion can become a symbol if a meaning is attached to it that is independent of and distinct from it. We call the relationship between the object and its meaning one of "representation," for the significance is represented by the outward phenomenon. Symbols do not exist in themselves but only in relationship to an experiencing and thinking person who establishes this relationship of "representation." It is clear that the validity of the symbol is hence limited to those who are in a position to realize the symbol's relationship in view of concrete symbolic objects. Family souvenirs, for instance, are true symbols, but only for family members who can reestablish the meaning relationship involved here.

We said the symbol represents a meaning distinct from the object. This relationship must be analyzed. How distinct is the meaning from the object? The degree of distinctness can vary and depends upon the meaning rendered to the object. A mathematical sign refers to a rational conception; a flag as a national symbol refers to the complex notion of a country. Hence in a symbol as a given outward phenomenon, a meaningful reality is referred to and somehow comprehended by a person or a number of people.

We called the relationship between the object and its meaning one of "representation." Other relationships are conceivable; instead of a representation there could also be an image or picture of what is meant, or a rationally adequate expression of it. But evidently that is no longer a symbol. The mere expression of an insight is no symbol, neither is a photograph. The (concrete) existing or conceivable object can only become a symbol if a meaning originally distinct from it is associated with it. When we call this relationship "representation," the term is used quite literally, for it means "making present," "actualizing." When a symbol is set up or recognized, its intended meaning is actualized. That can happen in various ways, corresponding to the respective symbolic forms: there can be actualization in thought, experience, etc.

We cannot deal with the whole range of religious symbols here, for that would lead us away from our theme.[16] Suffice it to point out that there are symbols of language (myths, dogmas, creeds), of action (cult), of nature, art, etc. All these religious symbols have exactly the same structure as discussed above, for they all consist of objects representing numinous meaning.

It has become common to associate religious symbols with feelings and ideas that are supposedly less than true and authoritative. "Only a symbol," we say at times, thereby suggesting that there is an imperfect truth or reality involved here. Wherein does the truth of the symbol lie? We come here again to the question of truth discussed in the last chapter. Let us take up the results of our earlier analysis. In accordance with its setup, the truth of the symbol always refers to numinous reality distinct from the symbolic object itself. Here truth is conceived of as reality, yet this is only one side of the matter. Because of the notion of truth involved here, such symbolic objects themselves cannot be regarded as being identical with the numinous, as has often been asserted falsely in some quarters of the scientific study of religions. If we take the notion of truth in the sense of correctness, the truth of the symbol—be it an object, an event, or a concept—lies in the fact that sublime divine reality is actually comprehensible in it. This means that the subtle associations of ideas aroused in a person by a symbol do correspond in some way to divine reality. Symbols must be "pertinent" in what they mean with regard to the numinous, even if they cannot express it adequately.

We must make another distinction between the understanding and the actualizing of symbols. What we have endeavored to do in our analysis serves the understanding of symbols—the rational interpretation of these basic phenomena of religious history. Such an endeavor prerequires detachment from the object; its aim is to comprehend a symbolic process; namely, the live, conscious actualization of the symbol by the believer. A person engaged in such an actualization is not in the detached position of the historian; he is not aware of the different elements we have discerned in our analysis.

To illustrate: Genesis 28 gives an account of how a symbol is set up. Jacob rests his head on a stone and dreams of a ladder reaching up to heaven. Upon awakening, he speaks of the encounter with God in his dream, saying, "How awesome is this place. . . . Surely the Lord is in this place and I did not know it" (16f). On the basis of this experience there follows a genuine symbolic institution. Jacob sets up the stone on which he has slept, pours oil on it, and calls the memorial "Bethel"; that is, "house of an El" (a deity). Thus the visible object becomes a symbol; for Jacob, who has had this ex-experience, takes it to represent the deity.

We can now apply the results of our considerations to the problem of tolerance. It is clear that the kind of intolerance in religion that springs, essentially, from a claim to truth involves the failure to recognize the symbolic character of a religious statement and the failure to discriminate truth as experienced reality from truth as rational correctness.[17]

As we have said, all forms of religious intolerance set up a claim to absoluteness as to what they regard as truth. We must now study this claim more closely, for it contains all forms of intolerance, as it were, in one focal point, and is on the other hand in itself the point from which the idea of intrinsic religious tolerance issues as an allegedly necessary measure. Let us see if our concept of truth allows for an interpretation of the claim to absoluteness that does justice to this claim itself, yet at the same time permits us to maintain the postulate of tolerance.[18]

3. The Interpretation of the Claim to Absoluteness

The claim to absoluteness must be seen in a wider perspective. Let us therefore turn again to the distinction between ethnic and universal religions in this connection, so that we can supplement what we have said about absoluteness and bring it into focus on that basis.

In genuine ethnic religions such as the preprophetic religion of Israel, we can observe a peculiar kind of claim to absoluteness. Here, the relationship between the ethnic community and its god is seen as being absolute. "I am the Lord your God, who brought you out of the land of Egypt, out of the house of bondage. You shall have no other gods before me." [19] There is a covenant relationship between Yahweh and Israel, and it excludes any and all obligation to foreign gods. I call this "intensive absoluteness," for it reflects the religious commitment that a community feels for its own members alone. As we have seen, the gods of other peoples are recognized as truly existing and wielding power in their respective domains. Now there is also "extensive absoluteness," and it is to be found when a religion puts forward a claim to be absolutely valid not only for the circle of its own adherents—in an ethnic religion, for the members of the ethnic community—but for the whole world. In this case, the religion in question regards itself as the only true and authoritative faith. In all pure ethnic religions there is an intensive claim to absoluteness. Turning to other gods is, as we have seen, an infringement upon the principle of ethnic absoluteness.

Many ethnic religions become universal in the course of their development, although they remain ethnically limited in content. The prophetic religion of Israel is an example of such an ethnic religion with universal character. We need not show that intensive absoluteness is maintained and even heightened here. The idea of a universal God arises and gains importance at a certain point for the first time. This notion, as does the prophetic experience of God, expresses itself in a definite claim to extensive absoluteness. "Besides me there is no God," says Isaiah 44:6, and this idea is repeated in many other passages. The new relationship to other religions is expressed in words such as these: "For from the rising of the sun to its setting my name is great among the nations, and in every place incense is offered to my name." [20] "For great is the Lord . . . he is to be feared above all gods. For all the gods of the peoples are idols; but the Lord made the heavens."[21]

In India, the tendency to absolutize one's own relationship to one's deity as an expression of an intensive union with that god can be traced back to Rigveda. In a hymn to Indra, for instance, it says, "Thou alone art the true one."[22] Yes, at times Indra is even absolutized in an extensive sense: "No one is higher or mightier than thou, no one is equal unto thee. All peoples follow in thy train as do the wheels [of a chariot behind the horse]."[23] It is evident that this absolutizing of Indra is only an expression for the intensive union of the devotee with this one god preferred by him; it does not lead to any theoretical conflicts with the claim to absoluteness raised in connection with other gods. Characteristically enough, we can also find within the same world of Indian religions utterances to the effect that Rudra is the absolute God. "Thou art the most glorious of all that is born, the mightiest of the mighty."[24] And even of Agni it says, "Unto thee, Agni, the Lord of all tribes, do we call. Thou art the common Lord of all. . . . Thou, Agni, art the mightiest of all mighty."[25] These and similar passages reveal an extensive absoluteness in rational wording, but this is only an absoluteness as against the deities of the ethnic religion, which was polytheistic. The intensive personal union of the devotee with one god among others finds its conceptual *expression* in the fact that his god is absolute over all others. Of course we do not find here an extensive absoluteness that also takes foreign, non-Indian gods and religions into account; hence these ancient ethnic gods of India lack genuine universality.

The matter becomes quite different as soon as certain great Indian deities rise to assume true universality—as does, for instance, Vishnu. We have already had occasion to quote a Vaishnava text where it says in part, "He [the Vishnu devotee] knows not the service of other gods, vows not to them, calls not upon their name, envisions them not. . . ."[26] Clearly, an extensive absoluteness develops here.

Now it must be noted that in universal religions of the mystical type a particular claim to absoluteness is maintained. I call it "inclusive absoluteness"; here the accepted deity alone is worthy of worship, but the notion of this deity is so inclusive that it encompasses all other gods as well.

An express claim to absoluteness can be found everywhere in the important world religions, and we need not add much to the material we have presented above in our historical part. In Early Buddhism there is no exaction concerning Buddha's uniqueness. According to Buddhist teachings, other Buddhas in past and future ages do exist, but their teaching is always the same. This teaching is the absolute point of orientation; it alone brings salvation. The historical Gautama Buddha merely claims uniqueness for the present age.[27]

In Mahāyāna Buddhism, however, we often find a completely exclusive relationship to Buddha. "Beside him I have no other sure path to salvation," says one text.[28] Mahāyāna Buddhism has often incorporated other gods into its system, regarding them as incarnations of its own universal deity. It, too, is mainly a mystically oriented religion, and its extensive claim to absoluteness appears in inclusive form.

In Christianity as compared to the ancient Israelite religion, the intensive claim to absoluteness is enhanced and deepened with reference to the individual. The rigidly exclusive and intensive union with the divine lies in the believer's fellowship with the Father God of Jesus and in personal discipleship. The union with the "Lord" (kyrios) is marked by intensive absoluteness but is expressed in an extensive claim: "That every tongue confess that Jesus Christ is Lord" (Philippians 2:11). The Church has always advocated this exclusive claim to absoluteness; for, since Christianity is a prophetic religion, inclusiveness is not to be expected of it. The Church has repeatedly declared that all religions outside Christianity are marked by total darkness and enmity to God.

Islam grew out of a nationally restricted faith into a religion possessing universal latitude. Here, too, this inner development shows that the initial intensive union with Allah gradually started to express itself in an extensive and exclusive claim to absoluteness. The Koran says, "Whosoever craves other than Islam for a religion . . . shall, in the next world, be of those who lose." [29]

How can we now interpret the exclusive claim to absoluteness in terms of comparative religion? The various claims that are raised rule each other out. If we consider the disqualifying verdicts about other gods which we have quoted from the ethnic religion of India, where one god is called the mightiest (either Indra, or Rudra, or Agni), these verdicts invalidate each other if taken rationally. Not every god can be the mightiest. But such expressions can be understood on the basis of the sense of absoluteness experienced in each particular case. We would maintain that each one of these verdicts that contradict each other in logical terms are not to be viewed epistemologically but as expressions of such an experience. They are "true" in the sense discussed above; their truth refers to a reality.

We have found that all world religions raise an extensive claim to absoluteness. Every one of them claims to be the only true and valid faith and every one of them demands to be accepted as such. We saw that this claim, which is the basis for intrinsic intolerance, appears in two forms in religious history. In the mystical religions which are essentially tolerant, it appears in inclusive form; in prophetic religions, it is rigidly exclusive. Prophetic religions are therefore intolerant by their very nature. Now as we said, these various claims exclude each other on the level of intellectual insight and logical thinking. Considering them rationally, one would have to point out that they must either all be false, or that just one of them can be "correct." That is, if Christianity is right with its extensive and exclusive claim to absoluteness, then all other such claims should be rejected as unfounded; and if Islam, on the other hand, is right, then again all other religions err. The problem arising here appears in quite a different light if we seek the meaning of these verdicts about the absoluteness of one religion and the lack of truth in others not in the sphere of intellectual insight but of experience. It is a well-known fact that in living religions views are often expressed that are indicative of an experience. Religious men express their inmost assuredness in the conceptual form of statements about an objective state of affairs. Think of the concept of truth as reality; myths, concepts, and actions bear witness to the encounter with this reality. What we have here is the attestation to an experience of absoluteness.

Likewise, the intensive personal encounter with holy reality always bears the mark of absoluteness. It is expressed in the creed which has the form of conceptual absoluteness of an extensive type that is either inclusive or exclusive. The "truth" of such a verdict lies not in its rational correctness, in the fact that an objective state of affairs is represented adequately here, in the sense that one's own religion *is* actually the only true, unique, and in every way incomparable faith. Rather, the truth of an extensive claim to absoluteness lies in the circumstance that there has actually taken place genuine encounter with the divine and that there does exist an intensive union between the devotee and his God. Now a person who expresses his personal bond with and experience of the divine in absolute terms has never studied other religions and their claims to truth, either theoretically or practically. His claim springs from his own experience of faith alone, and issues from the uniqueness that is always involved in such an experience. The experience is always absolute, but its expression is relative.

If something is absolute (*absolutus*), this implies, strictly speaking, that it is completely incomparable in two ways: it would be meaningless to compare it with something else, and it is unique. Every orthodox form of religion reinterprets and represents the original unsophisticated claim to absoluteness in such a rational manner. But then a false claim to absoluteness is upheld, for truth is no longer taken as experienced reality, but as logically perceivable correctness. In their apologetical endeavors, religions, and especially churches, attempt to prove logically the rationally misunderstood claim to absoluteness. Hence they seek truth on the level of soundness of contention and miss the inner truth that lies in the simple and spontaneous immediacy of the statement.

So far as any rationally founded claim to absoluteness is con-

cerned, this is what we must maintain on the grounds of comparative religion: religious history reveals that the claim to absoluteness
springs from a powerful religious experience at an initial stage
where it is expressed in a spontaneous and unsophisticated manner.
If the truth of the claim is interpreted as referring to an experienced
encounter with numinous reality, then the various claims to absoluteness that are raised do not conflict (not even in the case of India,
where all these different claims are maintained within one religious
system). An attempt to prove the absoluteness which historical texts
voice would lead to a misunderstanding of the meaning and truth
of the respective expressions of absoluteness.

Hence the manifold claims to absoluteness that have been raised
in religious history virtually prove that these are typical religious
forms of expression referring to an experience that reflects an intensive and exclusive assuredness and union with the Divine. The
realities of religious history make it most difficult for anyone to
maintain a rational claim to absoluteness. The historical attempts
to prove the "truth" and the absoluteness of one's own religion are
either based upon a wrong image of the other religions or they
compare the sublime elements in one's own faith with the base ones
in others. Another misleading comparison often made is that between
one's own dogmatic concepts and the practices of other religions,
which may often appear quite questionable. It is clear that all these
rational and historical ways of proving the absoluteness of one's own
religion are caught up in a vicious circle: they all uphold the authority of their own holy scriptures to begin with, accepting them as
binding. But they view this "truth" as rational correctness, and this
they hold up against the claims of other religions. Hence they all
start with a rationally unfounded presupposition.

Let us now draw the consequences of these considerations for
the problem of tolerance. We have seen that intrinsic intolerance
springs from a concept of truth that is oriented toward rational
correctness, and from an ensuing claim to absoluteness that is
equally misunderstood in rational terms. We have shown that in
simple, living religiousness truth and absoluteness are always meant

in a completely unsophisticated sense and that they must be interpreted on that basis. This fact points the way towards a feasible intrinsic tolerance. Ernst Troeltsch realized that the claim to absoluteness is emotionally and not rationally founded: "All religions are born absolute because they follow an unreflected compulsion and express a reality that demands recognition and faith, not only for the sake of its existence, but more yet for the sake of its validity." [30]

In addition to the arguments we have just mentioned, there is yet another reason why intrinsic tolerance is possible and necessary: the unity of religions.

4. The Unity of Religions

The most important reason why intrinsic tolerance is essentially justified and therefore necessary is the fact that there is a profound unity of religions. There are various ways of arriving at such a unity. Let us consider them one after another.

Whenever one's own religion is regarded as *the* truth in an intolerant manner, the many other religions appear as a source of annoyance and as something that must be overcome for the sake of one's own faith. If such a unity is striven for, it is attempted to be brought about *in place of* plurality. In this case, unity would be brought about by the victory of one creed over the others and the elimination of all religions but one. We reject such an attempt, for it is based upon views that substantiate intolerance and that we have proven to be essentially unjustified.

A second possibility of bringing about a unity of faiths is to abstract that which is common to all of them and to regard this common core as the true religion. This unity would be an abstraction *out of* the many divergent existing faiths and beliefs. We encounter such an endeavor in the Enlightenment. It believed in a "natural religion" (*religio naturalis*) of reason concealed beahind the garb of "positive" religions. In his *Speeches on Religion to its Cultured Despisers* (1799), Friedrich Schleiermacher, the great thinker who overcame the Enlightenment, characterized such a constructed faith pertinently. In talking about the consequences of such an abstraction out of the wealth of relgious experiences and notions, he says, "The so-called natural religion is usually so much refined away, and has such metaphysical and moral graces, that little of the peculiar character of religion appears." [31] And in the same place he points out, "The essence of natural religion consists entirely in denying everything positive and characteristic in religion and in violent polemics. It is the worthy product of an age, the hobby of which was that wretched generality and vain soberness which in everything was most hostile to true culture." [32]

A rationalistic view, then, fails to recognize the living nature of religion and substitutes a dead, unhistorical and abstract unity of religions for a living plurality. This type of unity is to be rejected, too, for it fails to do justice to the historical reality of religion.

But then there is a third possibility which I would like to call unity *in* plurality. With this term I would like to suggest that the plurality of positive religions is not to be eliminated for the sake of an abstract unity; but that there is, rather, an apparent unity of life in the various religions and their manifold forms of expression. This claim will now have to be substantiated.

Let us start by pointing out again that every religion has its own particular living core which gives it its unmistakable peculiarity.[33] To study this living core is one of the most important tasks of modern history of religions.[34] But over against these specific characteristics there are certain basic features in the life of historical religions that are, ultimately, all identical. These features belong to the very nature of each and every religion; they are often to be found under the garb of the most varying religious manifestations. Let us consider them.

It is obvious that those who truly confess a religion, no matter what it is, especially if it is basically intolerant, are all filled with "the same sincerity, the same uprightness, the same yearning and love, the same obedience, the same preparedness to make sacrifices," [35] be they Hindus or Moslems, Jews or Christians. This fact even struck a man of such intolerant passion as Savonarola, who set the pious outside Christianity before his countrymen as an example, as it were, for true religiousness. He pointed out: "Jews and Turks keep their religion much better than Christians, who should take the reverence Turks attach to the name of God as an example. . . . They [the Turks] would have long been converted if they would not rightly have found a stumbling block in the lives of Christians." [36]

The fact that men everywhere in all religions express the same yearning for the holy and all confess and defend the values that their religion has handed down to them, often sacrificing much, even their very lives—all this can only be explained in one way: without making an allowance for a theological bias, one must assume that such men have actually experienced an encounter with the holy and have shared in fellowship with it. Having this in view, the only attitude that is mandatory is one of respect for the convictions of men of other faith.

In addition to the motives for intolerance we have already discussed, an objectively false view of the nature of other religions is the main reason for religious polemics. In this regard, much credit is due to the scientific study of religions for correcting such historically false opinions. Friedrich Heiler, in the essay quoted above, gives examples for the positive effect of the scientific study of religions on the understanding of other traditions. First, Christian polemics denounced Mohammed as a deceiver for centuries, until finally the incorrectness of this view was proven by historical research.[37] Second, for a long time the opinions about Hinduism were also quite false. Goethe saw in Indian religion nothing but "the maddest idols, fashioned in giant size and worshipped." [38] Now modern research has brought to light that there is not only grotesque polytheism but also sublime mysticism and personal love of God (*bhakti*) in Indian religions.[39] It is in this sense that most of the arguments of Christian apologetics proved untenable in view of the more developed Eastern religions.

In the fight against other religions it was, and still is, common in Christian theology and mission theology to term the adherents of

non-Christian faiths indifferently "heathens." This collective de-
valuation is to be understood on the basis of the Christian claim to
absoluteness, or rather of its rational orthodox interpretation. But
if there were a greater knowledge of the profundity of worship
and greatness of vision of God in wide areas of the world of non-
Christian religions, and if there were an awareness of the truly
determining power of religion in personal and public life there,
the theoreticians of missions would perhaps be more hesitant in expressing such presumptive generalizations and depreciative verdicts
as have been uttered. Luther still acknowledged a "general revelation" (*revelatio generalis*), an idea today's Protestant theology in
the wake of Karl Barth has relinquished. In his *Commentary to
Galatians* (1535), Luther could, with good conscience, make this
distinction between non-Christian religions and Christianity: "There
is a twofold knowledge of God: the general and the particular. All
men have the general knowledge, namely, that God is, that He has
created heaven and earth, that He is just, that He punishes the
wicked, etc. But *what God thinks of us,* what he wants to give and
to do to deliver us from sin and death and to save us—which is the
particular and the true knowledge of God—this men do not know.
Thus it can happen that someone's face may be familiar to me,
but I really do not know him, because I do not know what he has
in mind. . . . Now what good does it do you to know that God
exists if you do not know what His Will is toward you?" [40]

Luther could make this naive distinction between Christianity
with its knowledge of salvation and nonchristian religions with
their mere awareness of God's existence, because he was not familiar
with the high religions in the non-Christian world. But once it is
realized that outside Christianity there is not only a longing for
redemption but also a live, genuine experience and assuredness of
salvation, this distinction cannot be maintained any longer. On the
basis of our present information, there is no scientific reason why the
Christian knowledge about salvation should be "true" and the non-
christian insight—often expressed in quite similar terms—"false."

There is yet another motive for an ultimate unity at the base of all religions: the fact that identical basic religious experiences are to be found in all of them. This has been established by historical research. Religion is experiential encounter with the holy, and the responsive action of man determined by the holy. Rudolf Otto, in his epoch-making work, *The Idea of the Holy*, set forth what the holy is and how it is experienced, taking facts from all of religious history into account. (His book was first published in 1917 and has been translated into almost all important languages; the thirty-first German edition has recently appeared.) Otto maintains that the primal experiences of the *mysterium tremendum* (the mystery that evokes trembling), the *fascinans* (the fascinating), and the *augustum* (the sublime) are present in all religions of the world, though with different emphasis. The ultimate unity comprehended by this insight is of a quite different type from the *religio naturalis* proposed by the Enlightenment, for the "natural religion" was a quite unhistorical product of the mind, constructed by abstracting the ideas common to all religions. That was a theoretical and blood-less religion of reason, and those who propounded it disregarded the living nature of religion and looked upon the historical phenomena as things obscuring its purity. Otto, on the other hand, in his analysis, discerns and describes the experiential encounter with the holy as it affects the religious individual and as it is reflected in the data of religious history. As opposed to Rationalism, he stresses the non-rational character of the holy and the non-rational significance of religious expressions.

Religious research concerned with structural forms, or patterns, has discerned yet another kind of unity among religions. It has realized that the ethnic religions form a unity and have a common structure—we described it above—although there are differences in their respective living cores. This unity is established primarily by the circumstance that natural communities (families, sibs, tribes, nations, and states), not individuals, maintain these religions. The individual is of quite secondary importance here. His membership in the community alone ensures him contact with the divine—weal or salvation. The universal religions, too, form a unity. Here the.

individual, not the community, is the main thing. He has acquired self-awareness, and religiously he realizes that his situation is one of doom. In the mystical forms of universal religion, *self-centeredness* is equated with lack of salvation. This plightful situation is overcome by merging with the Absolute. In the prophetic religions, on the other hand, *selfishness,* alienation from the living God, is the source of woe. Here salvation is acquired by turning to God in faith and trust and by thus entering into communion with Him.[41]

If we take all these facts into account, a subtle unity of all religions will become visible; it will become clear that it is impossible to mark off one faith, like Christianity, from all the rest and to uphold its absoluteness in a rational sense. Modern comparative religion is concerned not only with inner structures but also with outward phenomena of religion. The results of phenomenology[42] justify a phrase of Schleiermacher's, who seemed to sense a crucial issue here when he pointed out: "The more you progress in the understanding of religion, the more the whole religious world will appear to you as an indivisible whole."[43] Phenomenological research has made it evident that there are many common features in the different religions: there are similar manifestations of the holy (holy stones, mountains, trees, animals, places, times, words, scriptures, etc.), similar ways of dealing with the divine (through sacrifices, prayers, mystery cults, sacraments, etc.), and similar ideas (about God, the Otherworld, salvation). Hence by this approach, too, we can discern a unity in the way religions express their inner life.

There is yet another science that makes the unity of religions visible: psychology of religion. This field, and especially depth psychology, has shown us how religious feelings and sentiments are related everywhere in the world and have certain inner principles in common, and how conceptual images in religion are always determined by the same general psychological structures.[44] The danger of such an approach arises when *everything* in religion is explained as a product of psychological factors. That is psychologism. But one does not have to adopt a unilateral attitude that oversteps the boundaries of psychology's competence. Other approaches are possible here, and they can be assumed without endangering the legitimate concerns of research in the field. One can legitimately strive for a discernment of the part which the human mind plays in the process and formation of religious life.[45] Even such studies would reveal that there are typical tendencies and forms of expression of religious experience that are determined by the psyche.

Finally, a comparison of the ethical value systems in the different religions shows that a far-reaching relationship does obtain between them.[46] Many sets of values are recognized by peoples adhering to the most different religions. The five Buddhist commands of ethical discipline, for instance, or the Decalogue in the Old Testament, or basic Islamic laws, all reflect fundamental social concerns, and they order the relationship between the people of a community; furthermore, they determine the relationship of men to worldly possessions and to their respective communities. Although these ethical values appear in different order, they are basically the same in all the different religions of the world. Beside these general values there are also others that are not discovered everywhere but at various points in religious history. Here they are then regarded as binding. The great universal religions especially proclaim particular ethical values, such as love for neighbor and foe, obedience, compassion, etc.

The far-reaching unity of religions on the ethical level allows for a certain cooperation amongst them on this basis, for there is a universal ethical consciousness common to all mankind. It was on account of such considerations that Rudolf Otto founded the "Religious League of Mankind," the goal of which was not to integrate all creeds, but rather to influence the lives of peoples on the basis of their widely common religious ethic. The pursuit of that goal is even more urgent today than it was at Otto's time.

We have endeavored to show in this chapter that, in spite of all central differences between religions—differences that must not be underestimated—an ultimate unity is clearly discernible amongst them, as various different scientific approaches show. This insight does not spring from a preconceived opinion, but arises out of a study of the realities of religious history itself. The fact that there is such a unity provides a feasible basis for intrinsic tolerance. Our academic insight is confirmed by the religious experience of unity made throughout mystical religions. Perhaps it would be better to put it the other way around: the unity of the divine and the relatedness of all ways leading to it, which is experienced everywhere in mysticism, can also be established on academic grounds. Both approaches, then, that of rational insight gained by the scientific study of religions and that of unreflected and immediate mystical experience, lead us to the same conclusion, that there is a unity of religions *in* all historical plurality.

We pointed out that the intolerance of prophetic religions is rooted, primarily, in a spontaneous, personal experience and in the conviction that this experience is absolute and incomparable. As to mysticism, tolerance belongs to its very nature; for mysticism has emotional access to the perception of the unity of religions. That is why even a minimum of formal tolerance had to be struggled for in those parts of the world where prophetic religions prevailed, as in Europe. In the East, however, this was, on the whole, not necessary. The prophetic religions have always revealed greater naiveté and unreflectedness than mysticism;[47] because of their inner structure, they have shown a greater tendency toward the formation of organizations. Hence they have also greatly opposed formal and intrinsic tolerance. Their main concern was always to defend the unity of their respective communities. Their extensive and exclusive claim to absoluteness springs from the experience of an intensive union with one overpowering, universal God, but their sophisticated theologies understand that claim not in the light of its origin but in a rational sense, and they go on to defend it with utmost rigidity.

In order to come to a correct understanding of the claim to absoluteness (which was quite legitimate at an initial stage), a reorientation is necessary in prophetic religions. But such a reorientation and reinterpretation is more difficult here than in mysticism. The theological and ecclesiastical tradition of a prophetic religious organization with its authority and its characteristic tendency to preserve inherited structures always declines basically new readjustments, as the times of reformation in religious history show. Furthermore, though mystic and prophetic religions are both basically maintained by individuals who have made a personal decision for their respective faiths, the masses soon dominate in prophetic religions and their organizations, and largely limit or even abolish the religious independence of the individual. Mysticism, on the other hand, remains what it always is: a religion of the individual. Organized prophetic religions necessarily have to suffer loss of the religious spontaneity and immediacy that marked their founders and early congregations. They can only accept those views and ideas that are in compliance with their fixed forms and teachings. Subsequently, this entails an intolerance that is hard to overcome. Yet the reasons brought forth above make it mandatory that intolerance be overcome.

5. MANIFOLDNESS AS FULLNESS OF LIFE

Present as well as past religious history reveals a manifoldness of faiths encompassing an immense profusion of religious ideas and views. This circumstance is a source of annoyance for those who would accept but *one* "truth" because of the way they conceive it and because they have a rational understanding of the absoluteness of their own faith. We have shown that the plurality of religions does not lead to *contradictions* (in the sense that various solutions of one mathematical problem are contradictory). The historical fact that there is a plurality of religions must be viewed from two perspectives. With regard to God, this plurality manifests the fullness of life espoused by Him. Hebrews 1 asserts that God has spoken to man "in many and various ways." To this effect, too, Pierre Bayle (1647–1706) writes: "As peculiar and basically different as they may be, the many religions correspond to the infinite greatness of the highest and most perfect being which wanted all creatures to praise Him in His infiniteness through their manifoldness." [48] Modern authors can also be cited as attesting to such an attitude. Rilke, in his *Book of Hours,* writes:

> You are the thing's most inmost meaning, hidden deep,
> which keeps its being's final secret close,
> and otherwise itself to others shows:
> to ship as coastline and to land as ship.[49]

With regard to man, the plurality of religions is an expression of his diversity and his limitation in understanding or apprehending other views. Rabindranath Tagore expressed this idea pertinently when he said, "Cannot faiths hold their separate lights in place for the separate worlds of minds that need them?" [50] And Mahatma Gandhi maintained, "All religions are like different roads leading to the same goal." [51]

From this viewpoint, the manifoldness of religions appears as an inexhaustible fullness of life. There would be a deplorable impoverishment if all religions but one were destroyed to make room for this one alone. Such an idea has been expressed by Rabindranath Tagore, too: "If ever such a catastrophe should break in over mankind that one single religion would overflood everything, then God would have to care for a second ark of Noah, in order to save his creatures from spiritual annihilation." [52]

The standpoint of intrinsic tolerance, which this book maintains on the basis of a comparative study of the nature of religion and its phenomena, and which it seeks to establish as feasible and necessary, does not, in any way, require the severing of bonds with one's own religion. Gandhi did not relinquish his inherited faith, although he preached and practiced tolerance and even paid for it with his life.[53] Likewise, we urge no one to give up the religion appropriate for himself as a result of accepting our findings. Religion is possible and real in concrete historical faiths alone. When Schiller said that he confessed none of the religions named him, because of religion, he expressed only a partial truth; it is justified in criticizing the limitations and many deficiencies of historical religions, but it overlooks the fact that religion in itself, as a pure idea, is impossible in a world determined historically by men with different intellectual and experiental capabilities and varying degrees of spiritual and religious independence and maturity. Because of this fact, there can be no uniform universal religion for all of mankind which everybody would confess in the same way. Even if one religion should be victorious over all others—an idea Tagore rejected and a circumstance that is, in fact, very unlikely to occur, judging by the course of religious history—men's differences in religious thinking and feeling would not be abolished. One can point to the many differences that exist already within Christianity alone. The author of this book confesses Christianity in its Protestant form, being quite aware of the inevitable limitations of its historical garb [54] and of the possibilities of encounter with God—"Truth"—outside Christianity. But why then confess Christianity? Because *for me* access to the holy is most immediate in this historical form of religion. For other men, other historical forms will be more appropriate. This has to be acknowledged.

What are the consequence of this view with regard to missions? We are of the opinion that mission work has a right if it wants to do nothing but present a religious possibility of encounter with and personal experience of God. This means that the mission should refrain from endeavoring to convert men. A word of Goethe's can be applied directly to religion. He wrote: "Why did I seek the path so yearningly, if I should not it to my brothers show?" This was precisely Mahatma Gandhi's view. In an essay entitled *Why I am a Hindu,* written in 1927, he said: "I took the liberty of telling English and American missionaries at various mission conferences that India would have appreciated their life and work and would even have profited from their presence if they would stop telling India stories about Christ and would rather have only lived a life in the spirit of the Sermon on the Mount. . . . I do not believe people who tell others something about their faith, especially if they have intentions of converting them. Faith does not need any explaining and narrating. It must be lived, and then it becomes self-propagating." [55] In another essay, he expounds the same opinion: "I do not believe that there is such a thing as a conversion from one faith to another in the general sense of the word. A conversion is a most personal matter between the individual and his God. . . . I certainly regard all great religions of the world as true for those who confess them, just as I regard my own as true for myself. After reverently studying the holy books of the world, it will not be hard for me to comprehend the beauty of all of them. It is impossible for me to conceive of summoning a Christian, or Muslim, or a Parsee, or a Jew to change his religion, just as I can't imagine changing my own." [56]

In a world that is growing smaller, the religions of the world are coming into closer contact with each other than ever before. In this situation, genuine mission work could be most serviceable to a living and fruitful but tolerant encounter. Rudolf Otto once expressed it this way: "The mission as a free self-presentation and advancement of the living spirit of one's own religion, not of its crusts and shells, is a necessity in itself if it is connected with a deepened insight into the nature of religion as such and is carried out in recognition of and understanding for every genuine expression of the religious urge, as well as with ethical maturity, intellectual refinement, and a cultured world view. However, it is not only necessary in itself, but also to be desired for the establishment of contact between religions for competitive, mutually enlivening stimulation, purification, and self-enhancement and for the solving of common problems in the lives of peoples and nations." [57]

6. THE LIMITS OF TOLERANCE

Let us now sum up our findings. We saw that at an initial stage of a religion, intrinsic tolerance manifests an intensive and exclusive union with the divine. It is to be found in a legitimate form when it is connected with a religious experience that appears absolute—as it always does—and reflects naive immediacy. In universal religions, this union is expressed in an exclusive claim to absoluteness. Formal intolerance is rooted in a tendency to preserve the unity of the religious organization.

The comparative study of religions lets us realize that intolerance is a typical phenomenon, having similar religious premises everywhere, no matter what the religion. But it also lets us see the profound unity at the base of all religions, of every kind of religious life and thinking. Such a unity is there in spite of all differences with regard to the living cores of the particular religions. We cannot pass judgment on the "truth" and on the correctness of this truth in religion on academic grounds, because the numinous in itself is no object of scientific study, being only accessible to faith, through religious experience. But an academic inquiry into the structure of what the various religions regard as truth is quite possible and has been attempted in this book. On account of this study, and on account of the discernment of similar assertions, tendencies, and structures in all religions, one thing has become visible: the basically homogeneous stream of religious life, in all its historically varied forms, that calls for tolerance in the intrinsic and formal senses.

Religious man who has grown out of the stage of naive unreflectedness and has become familiar with the objective historical facts should consequently accept tolerance for the sake of "truth" in religion, without giving up his own religious standpoint. He should not only realize the life in religions other than his own but also be convinced about the "truth" of the statements made by other creeds concerning God and salvation. This he should do if he conceives of truth not as something rationally comprehensible, but as the abundance of symbolic-mythical aspects of the holy, and eternal, that appears differently to different men in their different stages of maturity.

Religious views should adapt themselves to what scientific study has disclosed; for all historical religions have their historically determined form, and the portion that is determined, or fashioned by man, is academically discernible and should not be ignored, for the sake of scientific truth and veracity. On the basis of our present deepened insight into the formative laws of religious history, tolerance as an acknowledgment of the different genuine possibilities of living encounter and relationship with the divine is an indispensable postulate. Today, intolerant claims of absoluteness and fanatic persecutions of other beliefs and believers—even if they be most subtle—are always signs of a lack of insight. This must be maintained in spite of the fact that claims to absoluteness in early stages of prophetic religions were typical, symptomatic expressions of an immediate experience of and personal union with God.

The limits of tolerance, however, are intolerance. This does not mean that intolerance is called for in view of other religious views that are self-asserting in their expressions. The religious intolerance we oppose negates other convictions. When we advocate intolerance, we do not mean intolerance toward other religious convictions as such, but toward religion's intolerant activities. We do not wish to attack other religious beliefs because we feel they are false; we oppose intolerance in every form, and we do so on the basis of an awareness of an ultimate unity of all living religions. This awareness of unity has found pertinent expression in a beautiful parable in Zen Buddhism. It speaks of the "Moon of Truth," which is reflected in different waters, although it is but one moon:

> One and the same moon is reflected
> in all waters.
> All moons in the water
> are one in the one and only moon.[58]

Notes

ABBREVIATIONS

ERE *Encyclopaedia of Religion and Ethics,* ed. James Hastings, New York, 1908–27, repr. 1955.
RGG *Religion in Geschichte und Gegenwart,* 3rd ed., ed K. Galling *et al.,* Tübingen, 1957–62.
RGL *Religionsgeschichtliches Lesebuch,* 2nd ed., 7 vols., ed. A. Bertholet, 1926–34.
SBE *Sacred Books of the East,* 50 vols., ed. F. M. Müller, Oxford, 1879–1910, repr. Delhi, 1965–66.
WA Luther's Works (German), Weimar Edition.
WE Luther's Works (German), Erlangen Edition.

INTRODUCTION

1. Cf. H. Wulf, S.J., "Religiöse Toleranz: ja oder nein?" *Welt am Sonntag,* Aug. 30, 1953.
2. *Die Lage der Protestanten in katholischen Ländern* (Zurich, 1953), p. 87. Similar views were expressed by theologians in San Sebastian in 1949, as the *Herder-Korrespondenz "Orbis catholicus,"* 1950 (vol. 7), reports. Article 1 of the Concordat of 1851, valid still today, also states: "The Roman Catholic Apostolic Religion which continues to be the sole religion of the Spanish nation, *to the exclusion* of any other, will always be maintained in the dominions of Her Catholic Majesty with all the rights and privileges which it should have in accordance with God's law and the prescriptions of the sacred canons."
3. Article 3 of the "Law Concerning Elementary Education" says, ". . . Acknowledgment is also made of the Church's right to supervise and inspect all of education at this level in the public and private institutions, in all things that pertain to faith and customs. . . ." In

Article 5 we read: "Borne by the Catholic spirit which is adapted to the Spanish educational tradition, elementary education must conform to the principles of Catholic dogma and Catholic ethics as well as to the prescriptions of valid canonical law."

4. A pamphlet which Catholic students at Madrid distributed before raiding an Anglican chapel says, "We Spanish intellectuals of 1947 consider ourselves the heirs to the spirit of the Inquisition in the true sense of the word. We hurl this statement at the broadcasting networks and the press abroad. . . ." In another pamphlet one reads: "We would prefer the pyre of the Inquisition to liberal tolerance! No step further in heresy!" Cf. *Die Lage der Protestanten in katholischen Ländern,* pp. 120, 124ff. A Spanish police order in 1940 decreed that, "through a generous tolerance of religious opinion of foreigners who reside in our country, so far as they are not opposed to Christian morality or infringe upon police and health regulations," foreigners may continue to gather "in chapels in which rites and ceremonies dissident from the Catholic religion are celebrated." This formal tolerance, granted exceptionally to foreigners, is, however, immediately restricted again, for in the same order it says that foreigners "must withdraw from the walls, entrances, doors, and other visible places any lettering, emblem, flag, or other sign which might lead to confusion of the said chapels with churches of the Roman Catholic religion." M. S. Bates, *Religious Liberty* (1945), pp. 19f. Persecution of Protestants is also reported from Mexico and especially Colombia. Cf. Bates, pp. 62ff, 73ff.

5. It says here: "Atque ex hoc putidissimo indifferentismi fonte absurda illa fluit ac erronea sententia seu potius deliramentum, asserandam esse ac vindicandam cuiuslibet libertatem conscientiae." Mirbt, *Quellen zur Geschichte des Papsttums und des römischen Katholizismus* (4th ed., 1924), pp. 30–32, 439.

6. Ibid., p. 450. Cf. also the Concordat with Spain (1851), ibid., p. 446.

7. The text formulates that error in this way: "Liberum cuique homini est eam amplecti ac profitere religionem quam rationis lumine quis ductus veram putaverit." Ibid., pp. 33f, 451.

8. According to a report of the *Frankfurter Allgemeine,* Jan. 19, 1954.

9. Cf. also J. Witte, *Die Christusbotschaft und die Religionen,* 1936. Many Catholic writers concerned with history of religions reveal a broadminded understanding of non-Christian faiths. I refer only to F. von Hügel, *Eternal Life,* 1912, and *Essays and Addresses on the Philosophy of Religion,* 2nd ed., 1930–31; Otto Karrer, *Das Religiöse in der Menschheit und das Christentum,* 3rd ed., 1936; Thomas Ohm, *Die Liebe zu Gott in den nichtchristlichen Religionen,* 2nd ed., 1957.

10. *Freies Christentum* (Frankfurt), Jan. 1, 1955.

11. See, for instance, the bimonthly periodical *Yana,* which is edited by the Altbuddhistische Gemeinde [Old Buddhist Congregation] in Utting am Ammersee (Germany).

12. Cf. S. Radhakrishnan, *Eastern Religions and Western Thought*, 1959; *Religion and Society*, 1956.

13. The Ahmadiyya mission edits the periodical *Der Islam* in Germany and has recently brought out a German translation of the Koran.

14. Cf. G. van der Leeuw, *Religion in Essence and Manifestation*, 2 vols. (trans. J. E. Turner), 1963; G. Mensching, *Vergleichende Religionswissenschaft*, 2nd ed., 1949, and *Die Religion*, 1959.

I. TOLERANCE AND INTOLERANCE IN RELIGIOUS HISTORY

1. On this sociological problem, see N. Monzel's essay "Abhängigkeit und Selbständigkeit im Katholizismus" and G. Mensching's article "Abhängigkeit und Selbständigkeit im Protestantismus," in Leopold von Wiese's essay collection *Abhängigkeit und Selbständigkeit im sozialen Leben*, 1951.

2. We can refrain from giving a detailed explication of that structural difference at this point, since we have already said what is necessary concerning the matter in various previous works, first in *Volksreligion und Weltreligion*, 1838; then in *Soziologie der Religion*, 2nd ed., 1968. Cf. also *Die Religion*, 1959.

3. Ethnic religions of the past are all similar in their *structure* but quite dissimilar in their "living cores." Every religion has its own unmistakable living core. This term implies that religions are forms of life and not strange products of the mind, composed of all kinds of odd notions and customs. Religions are, in a certain sense, organisms that exist out of a center of life, and can only be understood from that point of view.

4. The words of the incantation used when Carthage was being besieged were these: "May a god or a goddess protect the people and the state of Carthage, and especially you (the guardian spirit of the city), who have taken this city and this people into your care; I pray and beseech and entreat you for the grace of relinquishing the people and state of Carthage. Leave its soil, its temples, its sacred shrines, and the city itself. Depart from here, bestow upon this people fear, terror, forgetfulness (of all religious duties), and having thus abandoned everything, come to Rome, to me and mine own. May our soil, our temples, our sanctuaries, and our city be more acceptable and pleasing to you. To us, the Roman people and its soldiers, be gracious, so that we may know and perceive thy grace. If you do accordingly, we pledge you temples and games" (Macrob. Sat. III, 9, quoted in *Religionsgeschichtliches Lesebuch*, V, p. 10).

5. 2 Kings 17:24ff.

6. *The Laws*, X, 910 (Jowett's English translation in *The Dialogues of Plato*, 3rd ed., V, 297f.). Similarly it says in the Roman Twelve Table Law: "Nemo privatim habessit deos neve novos sive advenas nisis publico adscitos privatim colunto." In *The Laws*, X, 907-10, Plato refers to three

types of heresies that should be punished with the death penalty: denial of the existence of the gods, of their providential activity, and of their incorruptibility. Everyone who does not accept and practice the state religion is impious, for he is dangerous to others. Hence, clearly, it is the concern for the community that dominates here.

7. Cf. Pliny, *ep.* 10.97. Pliny the Younger, in 112 A.D., came across the Christian propaganda and had those Christians arrested who refrained from offering to the state gods. He asked Trajan if the steps he took were correct, and the Emperor gave him this answer: "The procedure which you, my Secundus, have observed in connection with those who have been reported to you as Christians, was as it should be. . . . They are not to be sought out, but they must be punished when they are reported and referred to you." Whoever denied being a Christian and sacrificed (to the state gods) was freed. Tortures were permitted as a means of determining the truth (Pliny, *ep.* 10, 96, 8).

8. As a further illustration for the exclusive relationship entailing intolerance toward those in the community, see Joshua 24:25ff. Another example is Exodus 22:20, "Whoever sacrifices to any god, save to the Lord only, shall be utterly destroyed." The practical effect of this law can be seen in Numbers 25:1ff, "While Israel dwelt in Shittim the people began to play the harlot with the daughters of Moab. These invited the people to the sacrifices of their gods, and the people ate, and bowed down to their gods. So Israel yoked himself to Baal of Peor. And the anger of the Lord was kindled against Israel . . . And Moses said to the judges of Israel, 'Every one of you slay his men who have yoked themselves to Baal of Peor.'" As late as in the 17th century (1656), the Jewish community dealt with Baruch Spinoza (1631-1677), who had turned away from the Jewish faith, in the intolerant manner prescribed by the Law. It placed him under the ban, using these words: "According to the resolution of the angels, according to the verdict of the saints, we ban and expel, curse and condemn, Baruch de Espinoza with the consent of the Holy God and His whole *kehilla kadosha* [holy community]. We do so before the holy books of the Law and the 613 ordinances they contain. We ban him with the ban with which Joshua banned Jericho, we curse him with the curse with which Elisha cursed the boys, and we condemn him with all execrations found in the Law. Be he cursed when he lies down and be he cursed when he arises. Be he cursed when he goes out and be he cursed when he returns. May the Lord not pardon him. The wrath and the fury of the Lord will be kindled against this man, and will let all curses come upon him that are written in the Book of the Law. The Lord will wipe out his name under heaven, and the Lord will exclude him from all tribes of Israel, rejecting him with all curses of heaven that are written in the Book of the Law, leaving him to the Evil One. But all you who adhere to the Lord your God will live today. We decree that no one should associate with him, neither by word of mouth nor in writing; that no one should do him

any favor; that no one should stay under one roof or within four yards of him; and that no one should read any of his works." Quoted in H. J. Schoeps, *Jüdische Geisteswelt*, pp. 208f.

9. Thule 23,169. In W. Baetke, *Die Religion der Germanen in Quellenzeugnissen* (1937), p. 50.

10. In the saga of Bard Snaefellsas, ch. 11 (Baetke, p. 50), we read, "In the next night, after Gest was baptized, he dreamed his father Bard came to him and said, 'You have done evil in giving up the faith of your forefathers and letting yourself be forced into a change of custom; you have become the greatest shame of this stock.'"

11. We shall not discuss here the question how this basic change came about. It strikes one that this type of religion appears relatively late in human history, viz. since about 800 B.C. Apparently, this matter is connected with man's development toward an awareness of his own individuality and personality, a development that can be reexperienced by every person today. It is in a late stage of human existence that man awakes to an individuality of his own. This process brings in its wake peculiar new metaphysical problems which the ethnic religions with their collectivistic attitudes could not answer. That is why ethnic religions were displaced by universal religions, at least in those classes that have awoken to true individuality.

12. Cf. the pertinent literature, e.g., H. Beck, *Buddhismus*, 3rd ed., 1926; E. Frauwallner, *Geschichte der indischen Philosophie*, vol. I, 1953; H. von Glasenapp, *Der Buddhismus in Indien und im Fernen Osten*, 1936; G. Mensching, *Buddhistische Geisteswelt* (Texts), 1955.

13. Cf. Fr. Heiler, "Prophetische und mystische Frömmigkeit," in *Das Gebet* (4th ed., 1921), pp. 248ff (English title: *Prayer*, trans. S. McComb and J. E. Park, 1958).

14. Udāna VI, 4. Oldenberg, *Reden des Buddha* (1922), p. 134.

15. Majjhima-Nikāya 72. Ibid.

16. Udāna VI, 4. Seidenstücker, *Pali-Buddhismus in Übersetzungen*, 1923, p. 162.

17. Majjhima-Nikāya 22. Glasenapp, *Gedanken von Buddha* (1942), p. 9.

18. RGL II, p. 150. (English trans. quoted from Bates, pp. 267f.)

19. H. von Glasenapp, *Die Weisheit des Buddha* (1946), p. 180.

20. Mādhyamika-karika. Ibid.

21. H. von Glasenapp, *Der Buddhismus*, p. 82.

21a. See H. Bechert, *Buddhismus, Staat und Gesellschaft in den Ländern des Theravāda-Buddhismus*, Vol. I (1966), p. 109.

21b. Ibid.

21c. *Frankfurter Rundschau*, Apr. 27, 1966.

22. Cf. Matthew 9:11, Luke 7:34, 11:40; Matthew 23:4.

23. Luke 9:62. For a more detailed proof see: M. Dibelius, *Jesus* (trans. C. B. Hedrick and F. C. Grant), 1949; R. Bultmann, *Jesus and the Word* (trans. L. P. Smith and E. H. Lantero), 1960.

24. Surah 3:58–63.

25. Surahs (chapters of the Koran) revealed to Mohammed at Medina after his flight from Mecca (622).

26. According to Mohammed, a messenger was sent to every nation by Allah: "We have sent in every nation an apostle [to say], 'Serve ye God, and avoid *Taghut* [the evil]!' and amongst them are some whom God has guided and amongst them are some for whom error is due . . ." (16:38). "Verily, whether it be of those who believe, or those who are Jews or Christians or Sabaeans, whosoever believe in God and the last day and act aright, they have their reward at their Lord's hand, and there is no fear for them, or shall they grieve" (2:59) (trans. E. H. Palmer, in SBE VI).

27. "We gave Moses the Book and we followed him up with other apostles, and we gave Jesus the son of Mary manifest signs and aided him with the Holy Spirit" (2:81) (SBE VI).

28. The unbelievers may not approach the sacred mosque at Mecca (Surah 9:28). A believing handmaid is better than an idolatrous woman (Surah 2:220).

29. "Prescribed for you is fighting, but it is hateful to you. Yet peradventure that ye hate a thing while it is good for you, and peradventure that ye love a thing while it is bad for you; God knows, and ye—ye do not know!" (2:212).

30. One could speak here, in a sense, of a certain inner tolerance, because of the admittance of particular sects. Five different legal schools (*madhhab*) are accepted, and according to the tradition, the prophet himself foresaw that the congregation would be divided into 73 sects. ERE XII, 366.

31. Cited in Bates, *Religious Liberty*, 1945, p. 258.

32. Ibid. For examples of persecution see ERE IX, 766.

33. Cf. ERE IX, 767. Bates, pp. 9ff, points out that in Islamic countries there is no religious liberty. In many countries, converts to Christianity lose their right of bequest. In Iran, religious propaganda is prohibited in general. No literature may be distributed which could be of religious influence on Moslems. In Egypt, where Islam is the state religion, it is the duty of the state to defend the faith against every kind of heresy or alien religious influence. The constitution guarantees religious freedom, but in practice that freedom does not exist. An Egyptian court decision says, "Seeing that the apostate has, by Muslim law, no religion . . . if he repents his repentance is accepted, and, if not, he is killed . . ." (Bates, p. 11). A circular of the Ministry of Education, issued in 1940, contains these sentences: "Without question, to teach a pupil a religion other than his own, while he is a minor and incapable of true discernment, is an offence against public order and morals. No State which recognizes its duties toward its subjects for the protection of their religious beliefs approves it." In India, the great Moslem Emperor Akbar (ca. 1600) was outspokenly tolerant, but his son Shāh Jehān ordered Hindu temples to be destroyed in 1633, and Aurangzeb added persecutions.

34. Bates, pp. 260ff.

35. *Pensées II*, Article 13.

36. Jesus, too, belongs to the type of the prophet, and his message lays claim to an exclusive absoluteness, but it is kept from becoming practical intolerance by the postulate of love. However, Jesus' nature and significance is not fully covered by the term 'prophet,' for he was also a prophetic savior whose essential function was not to demand observance of juridically formulated principles of behavior, but to establish salvation through his own being and activity.

37. For the beliefs of Mazdaism, see especially: C. Bartholomae, *Zarathustra, Leben und Lehre*, 1924; H. Lommel, *Die Religion Zarathustras nach dem Avesta dargestellt*, 1930; R. Pettazzoni, *La religione di Zarathustra*, 1920; O. G. von Wesendonk, *Das Wesen der Lehre Zarathustras*, 1927, and *Das Weltbild der Iranier*, 1933; H. S. Nyberg, *Die Religion des alten Iran*, 1938.

38. Yasna 28,4.

39. Yasna 31,18; 33,2.

40. Darius I, too, represented polytheistic Mazdaism. As a ruler, he showed consideration for the peoples he governed. As king of Egypt, for instance, he adopted Egyptian names, sacrificed to the goddess Neith as well as to the other great gods of Sais, and was regarded as son of the Sun God in Egypt. He rebuilt the Jewish temple, thus winning over the Jewish priesthood and preventing Jewish attempts to reinstate a Jewish kingship. This, then, is politically motivated tolerance.

41. It was probably Bahram I who took measures against Māni. The resistance his teaching received from the state religion and its representatives is understandable if one considers that, besides Christianity, Manichaeism —which had incorporated the religious forces of Hellenistic mystery religions and gnosticism—was a serious competitor to Mazdaism. Cf. O. G. von Wesendonk, *Das Weltbild der Iranier* (1933), p. 277.

42. Cf. Amos 5:18ff; Hosea 13:7-10; Isaiah 28:1ff; Jeremiah 4:23ff; Isaiah 30:15; Hosea 14:2ff, 5-9; Isaiah 9:1-6; 11:1-8; Jeremiah 31:31-34.

43. Cf. A. Deissmann, *Paul* (trans. W. E. Wilson), 1957; R. Bultmann, *Theology of the New Testament* (trans. K. Grobel), 2 vols., 1951-55; E. Stauffer, *Neutestamentliche Theologie*, 3rd. ed., 1945; M. Werner, *The Formation of Christian Dogma* (trans. S. G. Brandon), 1957.

44. Dibelius, *Jesus* (rev. ed. by Kümmel), p. 17. (English title of the unrevised version: *Jesus* [trans. C. B. Hedrick and F. C. Grant], 1949.)

45. Numbers 25:6ff tells us, for example, that an Israelite man brought home a Midianite woman. When another Israelite saw it, "he rose and left the congregation, and took a spear in his hand and went after the man of Israel into the inner room, and pierced both of them, the man of Israel and the woman, through the body."

46. The shift of accent from the preaching of Jesus to the preaching on Jesus, how it is to be comprehended, and how the sources are to be

understood, is discussed by R. Bultmann in his *Primitive Christianity in its Contemporary Setting* (trans. R. H. Fuller), 5th impr. 1960.

47. Similarly at other places, for example, 1 Corinthians 16:33; Philippians 3:18f; 2 Corinthians 11:15.

48. De Wette, *Wilhelm Martin Lebrecht, Briefe, Sendschreiben und Bedenken Luthers,* 1825–28, III, 89.

49. WA 1,391.

50. WA 1,655.

51. See W. Köhler, *Reformation und Ketzerprozess* (1901), p. 5.

52. WE 22,88. At another place (WE 22,67.87) it says, "God can not and will not let anyone else save Himself rule over the soul. . . . It is impossible that the worldly sword and law should have their way among Christians."

53. *Deutsche Messe* [German Mass], 1526: "In this order [of the congregation] those who do not behave in a Christian way can be made out, punished, urged to better themselves, expelled or banned, according to the law of Christ, Matthew 18." (WA 19,75).

54. De Wette, II, 359.

55. WE 39,226.

56. De Wette, III, 88f.

57. WA 18,299.

58. WA 33,3, p. 552f.

59. De Wette, III, 498. Similarly it says in a decree issued by the Prince of Saxony in 1553, "No one should be permitted to stop common church-going, and everyone should seriously be urged to join." E. Schling, *Die Evangelischen Kirchenordnungen des 16. Jahrhunderts* (1902), vol. I., p. 195.

60. WA 18, 36. In the *Table Talks* (III, 175), we also find most intolerant words, which, however, like many forceful expressions of Luther's, are not to be taken literally. "Heretics are not to be disputed with, but to be condemned unheard, and whilst they perish by fire, the faithful ought to pursue the evil to its source and bathe their hands in the blood of the Catholic Bishops, and of the Pope, who is a devil in disguise" (trans. Acton). At another point, Luther says, "If we punish thieves with the yoke, highwaymen with the sword, and heretics with fire, why do we not rather assault these monsters of perdition, these cardinals, these popes, and the whole swarm of Roman Sodom who corrupted without end the church of God; why do we not rather assault them with all arms and wash our hands in their blood?" (WA 6,347, trans. Acton).

61. WE 37,233.

62. Cf. W. Köhler, p. 27.

63. Deuteronomy 13:6ff says, "If your brother, the son of your mother, or your son, or your daughter, or the wife of your bosom, or your friend who is as your own soul, entices you secretly, saying, 'Let us go and serve other gods,' which neither you nor your fathers have known,

some of the gods of the peoples that are round about you . . . you shall not yield to him or listen to him . . . but you shall kill him; your hand shall be first against him to put him to death, and afterwards the hand of all the people."

64. "Therefore my opinion with regard to those who advocate articles that are not yet seditious but are evidently blasphemous is that the authorities should put them to death. For they have the responsibility of punishing other notorious crimes, like obvious blasphemies. The precedent is set in the Law of Moses." (*Corpus Reformatorum*, II, 17f). According to Melanchthon's view (ibid., XXI, 553), the state is responsible not only for the enactment of the Second Table of the Mosaic Law but also for that of the First Table which has to do with faith.

65. *Corpus Reformatorum*, IX, 133.

66. The same attitude is visible everywhere in the Protestant churches being organized at the time of the Reformation. Justus Menius, the reformer of Thuringia, demanded the punishment of heretics, and in his *Vom Geist der Wiedertäufer* [On the Spirit of the Anabaptists] (1544), declared tolerance to be directly opposed to God's will. Urbanus Rhegius, in his *Handbüchlein eines christlichen Fürsten* [Little Manual of a Christian Prince] (1535), expressed the opinion that a person who errs should be forced to accept truth. Johannes Brenz, who, like Luther, first opposed the use of force in matters of faith, later adopted the view of the other reformers. He emphasized that the state should counter godlessness "with external and legitimate punishments" [*per externa et legitima supplicia*] (*Brentii Opera* I, 569). Capita, reformer at Strassburg, wrote *Responsio de missa, matrimonio et iure magistratus in religionem* in 1537. In it (36a) he advises the rulers "to use force against obdurate persons" (*vis est duris affectibus facienda*), so that "having been intimidated by fear" (*metu pavefacti*), they will accept the teaching. Butzer, too, spoke out against tolerance. He also wrote *Dialogue, or Discourse on Common Articles and Church Practices of the Christians, and What all Authorities Must Observe and Better through the Power of their Office, and by Divine Order* in 1535.

67. WA 30,1, p. 192.

68. See K. Florenz, "Die Japaner," in: Chantepie de la Saussaye, *Lehrbuch der Religionsgeschichte*, Vol. I (1925), p. 402f.

69. Quoted in Florenz, p. 403.

70. Ibid., p. 404.

71. *De civitate dei* XX, 9: "ecclesia regnum eius regnumque coelorum." Mirbt, *Quellen zur Geschichte des Papsttums und des römischen Katholizismus* (4th ed., 1924), p. 71.

72. Cyprian (d. 158), *ep.* 73 to Jubaianus. Ibid., p. 32.

73. "Unam sanctam ecclesiam catholicam et ipsam apostolicam urgente fide credere cogimur et tenere . . . extra quam nec salus est nec remissio peccatorum." Ibid., p. 210.

74. Cat. Rom. I, 10, 16: "ecclesia errare non potest, in fidei ac morum

disciplina tradenda, quum a spiritu sanctu gubernetur, ita ceteras omnes, quae sibi ecclesiae nomen arrogant, ut quae diaboli spiritu ducantur, in doctrinae et morum perniciosissimis erroribus versari necesse est." Ibid., p. 344. J. Locke, whose rationalistic idea of tolerance we shall discuss later, writes in his *Letter on Toleration* (ed. J. Ebbinghaus, trans. W. Popple, 1957), p. 32, "For every church is orthodox to itself; to others, erroneous or heretical. Whatsoever any church believes, it believes to be true; and the contrary thereunto it pronounces to be error."

75. Gustav Krüger, "Imperium Romanum," RGG (2nd ed., 1929), III, 2037. J. Geffken, *Das Christentum im Kampf und Ausgleich mit der griechisch-römischen Welt*, 1920.

76. Cf. Lactantius, *De mortibus persecutorum*, 48: "ut daremus et Christianis et omnibus *liberam potestatem sequendi religionem, quam quisque voluisset."*

77. *Codex Theodosianus* XVI, 1, 2: "Cunctos populos, quos clementiae nostrae regit temperamentum, in tali volumus religione versari . . . ut secundum apostolicam disciplinam evangelicamque doctrinam Patris et Filii et Spiritus sancti unam deitatem sub parili majestate et sub pia trinitate credamus." Mirbt, p. 56.

78. Bates, p. 134.

79. *Codex Theodosianus* (De haereticis) 16,5. c. 40: "volumus esse publicum crimen, quia quod in religione divina committitur, in omnium fertur iniuriam." Mirbt, pp. 81f.

80. For further details on what we have said about Julian see: Bidez, *Julian Apostata,* pp. 265ff. Instructive with regard to the organization Julian had in mind and the spirit in which he planned it is a letter written by the Emperor, probably to the Head Priest of the Province of Asia. See Latte, "Die Religion der Römer," RGL V (1927), p. 86f.

81. Symmachus, 3. rel. pp. 28off; Latte, p. 91.

82. Ad Scapulam 2. Migne, *Patr. Lat.* I, 699.

83. Divina Instituta 54. Migne, *Patr. Lat.* VI, 1061.

84. Concerning these and the following facts, cf. the material in Bates, pp. 136ff.

85. *Divina Instituta* 1,5c 20. Migne, *Patr. Lat.* VI, 516.

86. Hom 46 in Matthew 1:52.

87. Ep. 185, n. 32. Migne, *Patr. Lat.* XXXIII, 807.

88. Decretale "Per venerabilem" 1202. Mirbt, p. 175.

89. Epist. lib. I, 401. Mirbt, p. 178. The relationship between state and Church is compared here to that between sun and moon. As the moon receives light from the sun, regal power is derived from pontifical authority.

90. Book II, art. 13, § 7. Mirbt, p. 188.

91. S. th. 2, 2q. II, art. 4,c, et ad 1.

92. See documentation in P. Flade, *Das römische Inquisitionsverfahren in Deutschland bis zu den Hexenprozessen.* 1902, p. 60.

93. *Directorium inquisitorum* III, 582.
94. Documented in Flade, p. 99. See also: Eymericus, *Directorium inquisitorum*, III, 550: "Cum ecclesia non habet ultra quid faciat . . . de foro nostro ecclesiastico te proicimus et relinquimus sue brachio saeculari tradimus: Rogamus tamen et efficaciter dictam curiam saecularem quod circa te citra sanguinis effusionem et mortis periculum sententiam suam moderetur." A. Vermeersch, in his book *Die Toleranz* (1941), affirms again and again that the Church never executed the death penalty, as that contradicts its principles. To prove this, he points out (p. 75) that Pope Pius V, in the ordinance *Cum primum* of 1556, turned against blasphemers, threatening them with penalization. The most serious punishment, he says, was the piercing of the tongue, not the death sentence. This leads the author to conclude (p. 76), "in later centuries, ecclesiastical law did not renounce the old tradition and always avoided utmost severity." But Vermeersch also adds that when very stern punishment was necessary, the Church took avail of the aid of the state, whereby, of course, the "utmost severity" which the Church allegedly always shunned was, indeed, ensured in a most effective manner. In spite of his statement about the execution of the death penalty, Vermeersch does not hesitate to add (p. 76), that "the Church thus showed that the spirit of Christ was really reigning within her." In view of the Church's inquisitional practices (the most significant stages of which we have sketched above), the author nevertheless admits (p. 109) that the Church's opposition to severe persecution of heretics waned at the end of the 12th century; the reason he gives is this: "The bishops yielded to the public opinion which was held by the people and the Princes and which can be explained by the antisocial tendencies of the false doctrines that were being disseminated at that time."
95. Flade, p. 121.
96. Bates, p. 241.
97. Ibid., p. 243.
98. Quoted in ibid., p. 247.
99. Cf. Völker, *Toleranz und Intoleranz im Zeitalter der Reformation*, 1912.
100. H. Hermelink, *Der Toleranzgedanke im Reformationsjahrhundert.* (Schriften des Vereins für Reformationsgeschichte. 26. Jahrg.), pp. 42f.
101. Cf. Hermelink, pp. 43f; G. Mensching, *Soziologie der Religion* (2nd ed., 1968), pp. 150f, 156ff; E. Troeltsch, *Die Soziallehren der christlichen Kirchen und Gruppen* (1912), pp. 338ff; Troeltsch, *Werke*, IV, 160; "In all worldly matters, laymen and clerics are to obey the Emperor, but in all spiritual things, in questions of dogma, ecclesiastical law, Church property, and Church jurisdiction, the law of God is to be observed. Aye, the worldly power of the Emperor has divine authority only so far as it absolves and hallows itself by serving and being submissive to the Church."
102. F. Heiler, *Der Katholizismus* (1923), p. 108.

103. Quotes are from the Church-authorized German translation: *Zweites Vatikanisches Konzil. Konzilsdokumente. Dekret über den Ökumenismus. Erklärung über die Religionsfreiheit. Erklärung über das Verhältnis der Kirche zu den nichtchristlichen Religionen* (Lucerne/Munich: Rex Verlag, 1966).

104. Cf. the words of Tertullian, Lactantius, and Athanasius that express the right of religious freedom over against the nonchristian Roman state (see pp. 57f).

105. As late as in 1932, the Protestant theologian G. Simon, author of the critical book, *Die Welt des Islam* [The World of Islam] (1948), wrote these words in an essay on Mohammed (published in *Evangelische Pastoraltheologie*): "Are not actually Satanic powers set free in the work of this man [Mohammed] . . . ?"

106. J. Meinhold, *Einführung in das Alte Testament* (2nd ed., 1926), p. 292.

107. Cf. F. Heiler, p. 25f.

108. For this and the following material see Bates, *Religious Liberty*, pp. 274ff.

109. Ibid., p. 276.

110. Ibid.

111. Ibid., p. 277.

112. W. Gundert, *Japanische Religionsgeschichte* (1935), p. 118.

113. Ibid., p. 147.

114. For details, see ibid., pp. 148ff.

115. H. Zimmer, *Ewiges Indien* (1930), p. 48f.

116. We need not discuss here the differentiations within the caste order nor the motives for its hierarchical set-up. See: A. Geiger, *Die indoarische Gesellschaftsordnung, 1935.*

117. *Bhagavadgītā* I, 40–44, in SBE VIII, 41f (trans. K. T. Telang).

118. *Bhagavadgītā* III, 35, in SBE VIII, 56. The caste order is traced back to a divine origin. In *The Laws of Manu* (I, 31) it says, "But for the sake of the prosperity of the worlds, he caused the Brāhmaṇa, the Kshatriya, the Vaiśya, and the Śūdra to proceed from his mouth, his arms, his thighs, and his feet" (SBE XXV, 13f, trans. G. Bühler). And in the Bhagavadgītā (IV, 13). Vishnu says, "The fourfold division of castes was created by me according to the apportionment of qualities and duties." (SBE VIII, 59).

119. See: S. Radhakrishnan, *The Hindu View of Life* (1927; reprint, 1954), pp. 93ff; Same, *Eastern Religions and Western Thought* (2nd ed., 1940; reprint, 1959).

120. Quoted in J. N. Farquhar, *The Crown of Hinduism* (1913, 1930), p. 175.

121. The term "Hinduism" does not refer to a specific religion but rather to a way of life within the caste order. A "Hindu" is a person who has been born into a caste and accepts his caste duties as well as the authority of the Veda.

122. "At that time" means "in the beginning," in "non-time" (*akāla*), when mythical events took place and time and space were not really existent.
123. Rigveda 1, 164, 46.
124. It is interesting to note that the Stoic Maximus of Madaura expresses a view quite similar to this Indian idea of unity: "There is one supreme God," he writes, ". . . who is, as it were, the God and Mighty Father of all. The powers of this Deity, diffused through the universe which he has made, we worship under many names, as we are all ignorant of his true name. Thus it happens that while in diverse supplications we approach separated, as it were, certain parts of the Divine Being, we are seen in reality to be the worshippers of him in whom all these parts are one." Quoted in E. Carpenter, *Comparative Religion* (1916), p. 35.
125. In the Veda, the Ādityas are a group of numinous beings.
126. F. O. Schrader, *Der Hinduismus,* 1930. RGL 14, p. 75.
127. Ibid., p. 73. English trans. (in part) in C. E. Grover, *The Folksongs of South India,* 1871 (reprint 1959), p. 266.
128. See his *Eastern Religions and Western Thought,* 1959, and his *Religion and Society,* 1956.
129. S. Radhakrishnan, *Eastern Religions and Western Thought* (English citations from 2nd ed., 1940), pp. 326f.
130. S. Radhakrishnan. *The Hindu View of Life* (1954), p. 31. *Bhagavan* means "the Lord," and is the name given to Vishnu most of the time in the *Bhagavadgītā* [The Song of the Lord].
131. S. Radhakrishnan, *The Hindu View of Life,* p. 15.
132. S. Radhakrishnan, *Eastern Religions and Western Thought,* p. 314. T. Ohm, in his book *Asia Looks at Western Christianity* (trans. I. Marinoff, 1959), has also pointed out that Asian criticism of Western religion pertains mainly to the West's overestimation of the doctrine as against religious life.
133. S. Radhakrishnan, *Eastern Religions . . . ,* p. 313. We would like to refer here to another representative of mystical tolerance in Hinduism, Ramakrishna (1834–1866), the last great religious teacher of the Hindus. Cf. RGL 14, pp. 82, 236.
134. Jalālu-d-Dīn Rūmi (1207–1273) writes: "Simple are the Koran's words, but only a deeper and more concealed meaning leads beyond the gate of insight to their inner content. This significance, however, is not the ultimate one either, that will quench the thirst for knowledge. The sentences of the Koran embody a third, and also a fourth meaning which only God reveals. Aye, even a seven-fold sense lies concealed in His exalted word. One meaning rests upon the other, and each leads further, right up to the final one. Hence, although the outward sense of the Koran is apparent, its true signification is hidden from human understanding." M. Meyerhof, *Persisch-Türkische Mystik* (1921), p. 10.
135. Jalālu-d-Dīn Rūmi, in ibid., p. 11.

136. The circumambulation of the Kaaba, the central Islamic shrine at Mecca, is a cult obligation for all believers who pilgrimage to that city.
137. Meyerhof, p. 25. English version quoted from J. E. Turner's translation of G. van der Leeuw, *Religion in Essence and Manifestation* (1963), Vol. II, p. 504.
138. Ibn al-'Arabī; quoted in I. Goldziher, *Vorlesungen über den Islam* (1925), p. 170: See also A. Schimmel, "Ich folge der Religion der Liebe," in *Oekumenische Einheit,* Heft 1, 2. Jahrgang.
139. Quoted in F. Ruffini, *Religious Liberty* (1912), p. 24.
140. Augustin, *Retr.* I, 13,3.
141. *Ep.* 93,17.
142. See, for instance, R. Otto's analysis *Mysticism East and West* (trans. B. L. Bracey and R. C. Payne, 1932; reprint, 1962), a work in which Otto compares Meister Eckhart with the Indian mystic Shankara. See also H. W. Schomerus, *Meister Eckhart und Manikka Vāśaga,* 1936.
143. *Meister Eckhart: A Modern Translation,* by R. B. Blackney (1941), p. 23f.
144. Jakob Boehme, *Myst. mag.,* 33, 10.
145. *Von der Wiedergeburt* [On Rebirth], 7, 6.
146. Traktat *Warnung* [Treatise "Warning"], 294.
147. *De triplici vita hominis,* 7. Reference can be made here to a parallel phenomenon in Buddhism. Buddha, too, spoke out against "the way of opinions," "the wilderness of opinions," "the thicket of opinions," "the drama of opinions," "the fit of opinions," "the bond of opinions, full of sorrow, full of perdition, full of irritation, full of torment" (Majjhima Nikāya 485). And in Udāna IV, 4 we read: "The opinion to which one adheres as the best is praised in the world above all else. Whosoever does not teach the same is decried as a fool. Thus there is no end to strife." (H. Oldenberg, *Reden des Buddha* [1922], p. 134.) Similarly, it says in Majjhima Nikāya 72: "Therefore I say that the perfect one is redeemed beyond desire . . . by the elimination, rejection, and disavowment of all self-centeredness, vanity, and conceit." Here too emphasis is placed upon the subjective character of all "opinions."
148. *De incarnatione Verbi,* III, 1, 3.
149. Boehme edition by Schiebler, II, 229.
150. *Vom dreifachen Leben* [Of Threefold Life], 11, 82.
151. *De incarnatione Verbi,* I, 8, 12.
152. *Warnung,* 197f.
153. "Wouldst thou speak out God's name and utter it in time? / Ne'er canst thou voice it here, it is far too sublime." II, 51.
154. Cf. H. Naumann, *Der staufische Ritter* (1936), p. 92ff (Ch.: "Der Mohr im Dom").
155. Walther von der Vogelweide, 22, 3–17. Cf. also: S. Stein, "Der Ungläubige in der mittelhochdeutschen Literatur von 1050–1250" (thesis, 1933); E. Schenkheld, "Religiöse Gespräche in der deutschen epischen

Dichtung bis zum Ausgang des 13. Jahrhunderts" (thesis, 1930); Grimmelshausen, *Der abenteuerliche Simplizissimus*, Book 3, Ch. 5.

156. Cf. E. Troeltsch, *Protestantism and Progress; a historical study of the relation of Protestantism to the modern world* (trans. W. Montgomery), 1958.

157. For more details about the thought of these men cf.: S. Franck, *Chronika, Zeitbuch und Geschichtsbibel*, 1531 (see here the "Ketzerchronik") and *Paradoxa*, 1534; O. Borngräber, *Das Erwachen der philosophischen Spekulation der Reformationszeit in ihrem stufenweisen Fortschritt, beleuchtet an Schwenckfeld, Thamer und Sebastian Franck*, 1909; A. Reimann, *Sebastian Franck als Geschichtsphilosoph*, 1922; R. M. Jones, *Spiritual Reformers in the 16th and 17th Centuries*, 1914.

158. Since 1564, the Calvinistic opponents of the Anglican Church wanting to reform the Church of England along Calvinistic lines were called Puritans. They were severely repressed by Queen Elizabeth.

159. We cannot deal with the history of this movement here. Robert Brown, a Puritan preacher, was its first leader. In Holland it was John Robinson who developed Brown's views towards Congregationalism. Its principles can be summed up: The whole Church is a "congregation of predestined" forming an invisible community. Only the single congregations that are composed of actual believers are visible. They are to be independent of the state and are to be completely autonomous. No difference is to be made between priests and laymen. Anyone who is moved by the spirit may speak at the meetings; fixed creeds are rejected. At the base, there is a mystical element here.

160. Cf. R. W. Dale, *History of English Congregationalism*, 1907; W. B. Selbie, *Congregationalism*. 1927.

161. This tendency shows that we have here a hybrid form of religiousness. Pure mysticism never aspires for a uniform religious, or cultural congregational, pattern—necessarily entailing intolerance and coercion. Hence particular religious motifs like the idea of illumination and indifference toward dogma as well as historical forms of Christianity, but only these, are mystical. The enthusiasm that accompanies the endeavors to materialize certain social and religious ideals within the society is typically prophetic in style.

162. At this time a radical group called the "Levellers" was also founded. It taught that the people should have sovereign rights and that all citizens should enjoy the same political privileges. So far as religion was concerned, it maintained, on the basis of such principles, that the state should be non-religious and that every religious creed, including atheism, but excluding Catholicism, should enjoy liberty. It also taught that revelation occurs within man himself.

163. Quoted from L. Hodgkin, *Silent Worship* (2nd ed., 1919), p. 46f.

164. Cf. G. Mensching, *Das heilige Schweigen* (1926), pp. 91ff.

165. According to Suso, for instance, Christ says, "You must go beyond my suffering humanity, would you truly reach my pure divinity." *Leben* c. 13. ed. Bihlmeyer, p. 34.

166. W. Alberti, *Aufrichtige Nachricht von der Religion, Sitten und Gebraüchen der Quäker* (1750), p. 122.

167. Quoted in E. Grubb, *What is Quakerism?* (2nd ed., 1919), p. 36.

168. The British colonization of North America began with the founding of the colony of Virginia in 1607. Due to political unrest in England, the establishment of such colonies progressed well, for many adherents of persecuted religious groups emigrated to North America where they enjoyed religious freedom in the colonies they founded. In 1620, the "Pilgrim Fathers" founded Massachusetts; in 1632, Maryland was founded by Lord Baltimore. The Puritans in Massachusetts, New Hampshire, and Connecticut were rigidly intolerant in allowing only fellow-believers to settle in their areas. Roger Williams, who was expelled from Massachusetts by the Puritans, founded Rhode Island in 1636; here everybody was to enjoy religious liberty.

169. Fragment 11. Nestle, *Griechische Geistesgeschichte* (1944), p. 63.

170. "They purify themselves in vain by staining themselves with blood, like someone who has stepped into mud trying to cleanse himself with mire . . . And to these idols they pray as if talking to houses, not knowing anything about the nature of the gods and the heroes." Fragment 5. Nestle, pp. 71f.

171. In Augustine, *De civitate Dei*, VI, 10.

172. Fragment 32. Nestle, p. 73.

173. Plutarch already expressed this modern idea in *De superstitione* 6. 167 D: "One must be satisfied with the fact that not these things [i.e., the stone images] are worshipped; rather, through them the deity is venerated."

174. For details cf. G. Mensching, *Geschichte der Religionswissenschaft* (1948), pp. 24ff.

175. *Religion der Klassiker III. Petrarca* (ed. Hefele), p. 70.

176. *Opera* I, 913.

177. In spite of all criticism of dogma and Church in the Renaissance, the full idea of tolerance did not originate here. What is aspired for at this time is what the English literature on tolerance calls "comprehension" within the Church (M. Freund, *Die Idee der Toleranz im England der grossen Revolution* [1927], p. 10). The thinkers of the Renaissance were not seldom intolerant, for in the midst of a crumbling intellectual world, they supported the state as a new sustentative authority. It was at this time that the teachings about the sovereignty and omnipotence of the state were formulated (Freund, p. 8). Whatever endangered the state from religious quarters had to be barred. We find here the phenomenon of formal intolerance connected with intrinsic tolerance.

178. Cf. Mirbt, *Quellen*, p. 264.
179. *Utopia*, pp. 117f (Ch.: "Of the Religions in Utopia").
180. Ibid., p. 127.
181. "They are two things: 'unity' and 'uniformity'" ("Of Unity in Religion" *Essays*. *Works* II, 263).
182. Freund, p. 27.
183. Wm. Chillingworth, *The Religion of Protestants*, 4th ed., 1674 (Ch.: "The Answer to the Preface"), p. 18. In that book we also find these furthergoing statements on the same subject, "If, instead of being zealous Papists, earnest Calvinists, rigid Lutherans, they would become themselves, and be content that others should be plain and honest Christians, if all men would believe the Scripture, and freeing themselves from prejudice and passion, would sincerely endeavour to find the true sense of it, and live according to it, and require no more of others, but to do so; nor denying their Communion to any that do so, would so order their publique service of God, that all which do so may without scruple, or hypocrisie, or protestation against any part of it, joyn with them in it: who doth not see that seeing . . . all *necessary truths* are plainly and evidently set down in Scripture, there would of necessity be among all men, in all things necessary, Unity of Opinion?" ("The Answer to the Third Chapter"), p. 138.
184. For more details see Freund, pp. 46ff. Freund also discusses a number of other thinkers beside those we have mentioned. All of them start out with the same intellectual presuppositions; for instance, Stillingfleet (1635–1699) and I. Seldon (1584–1654). The latter called for a critical study of the Bible and denied the supernatural authority attached to any worldly institution. Harrington (1611–1677) stressed the historical relativity of the Bible; apart from that, his ideas are mainly determined by political considerations. Thus he equates the British Empire with the Kingdom of Christ.
185. Though its methods and aims have beeen modified, both tendencies still determine the two main disciplines of the study of religions today, respectively; there is a historical and a systematic comparative study of religions. See G. Mensching, *Vergleichende Religionswissenschaft*, 2nd ed., 1949.
186. Dilthey, *Schriften* II (1914), p. 248.
187. C. von Brockdorff, *Die englische Aufklärungsphilosophie* (1924), p. 13.
188. Locke, *Works* IV, 19, § 4 ("An Essay Concerning Human Understanding").
189. Locke, *Letter on Toleration*, ed. J. Ebbinghaus (English and German) (Engl. trans. W. Popple), 1957, p. 24. Furthermore, it says here, "No force is here to be made use of, upon any occasion whatsoever: for force belongs wholly to the civil magistrate, and the procession of all outward goods is subject to his jurisdiction" (p. 26).
190. Ibid., p. 2.

191. Ibid., p. 18.
192. Ibid., p. 14. Cf. also p. 54: "This at least is certain, that no religion, which I believe not to be true, can be either true or profitable unto me. In vain, therefore, do princes compel their subjects to come into their Church communion, under pretence of saving their souls."
193. Ibid., p. 94.
194. Cf. his main work, *Essai sur les Moeurs et l'esprit des nations.* 1754–1758. See also *Examen important de Milord Bolingbroke ou le Tombeau du fanatisme,* 1736.
195. Cf. G. Mensching, "Das Problem der Entwicklung in der Religionsgeschichte," in *Studium Generale* (1954), Vol. 3.
196. RGL 11, p. 150. English version (from Luzzatti) quoted in Bates, pp. 26ff.
197. W. Gundert, *Japanische Religionsgeschichte* (1935), p. 30.
198. Ibid., pp. 31ff.
199. Lactantius, *De mortibus persecutorum* 48; Mirbt, *Quellen,* p. 39.
200. Art. V, § 1 ". . . sit aequalitas exacta mutuaque . . . ita ut, quod uni parti iustum est, alteri quoque sit iustum," ibid., p. 378.
201. Ibid., p. 382.
202. RGG, 2nd ed., V (1931), 1220.
203. Cf. H. Fürstenau, *Das Grundrecht der Religionsfreiheit nach seiner geschichtlichen Entwicklung und heutigen Geltung in Deutschland.* 1891; G. Bonet-Maury, *La liberté de conscience en France, depuis l'Edit de Nantes jusqu'à la séparation, 1598–1905,* 2nd ed., 1909; L. Ulbach, *La Hollande et la liberté de penser au 17e et 18e siècle,* 1884; H. M. Gwatkin, *Religious Toleration in England* (in *The Cambridge Modern History* V, 1908), pp. 324ff.

II. MOTIVES FOR INTOLERANCE

1. Cf. details in Derenne, *Les Procès d'Impiété* (Brussels, 1930).
2. The Twelve Table Law tolerated no private cults that were not publicly admitted.
3. W. Bauer, *Der Wortgottesdienst der ältesten Christen* (1930), pp. 11ff.
4. Amos 8:1f; 5:18ff; Hosea 13:7-10; Isaiah 28:1-4; Jeremiah 4:23-26.
5. For details see G. Mensching, *Soziologie de Religion* (2nd ed., 1968), pp. 255ff.
6. Augustin, *De vera religione,* 10; "Ecclesia omnibus gratiae Dei participandae dat potestatem."
7. E. Troeltsch, *Werke* IV, 126f.
8. The Bible is not named as a source. In the course of history, it has been interpreted in many different ways, by individuals as well as by churches and sects termed heretical by the Catholic Church. So the unity of the Church could not be maintained in this manner (that is, by pointing to the unity of the Scripture). That is why the Bible was made accessible

to the laity through the mediation of the Church alone—through its interpretation. Consequently, it is not a direct source of faith.

9. N. Monzel, "Abhängigkeit und Selbständigkeit im Katholizismus," in L. von Wiese, *Abhängigkeit und Selbständigkeit im sozialen Leben.* Vol. I (1951), p. 190.

10. N. Monzel, p. 195: "The independence of faith that is established by private revelation and its consequences is restricted, especially by two elements. The first is the control wrought through the Church's authority in matters of teaching which demands that there necessarily be compatibility in content between the private revelation and the general revealed Apostolic doctrine. The second fatcor is an element that is to be observed again and again, viz. that the outward manifestation of supernatural phenomena as envisioned or experienced in such private revelations usually corresponds to the common representations of the deity and the saints." Concerning cult forms that develop independently, Monzel says, "Here again, the measure of independence is restricted by two elements: first by the control exercised on the part of the central Church authority which prohibits cult forms that seem questionable, and second by the fact that new forms of religiousness almost always have some connection with earlier traditional patterns" (p. 196). As far as autonomy on the ethical level, Monzel points out, "It, too, is limited by the central authority of the Church which watches over the compatibility of all specific religio-ethical tendencies with the general norms of the Church" (Ibid.).

11. This last sentence which is a reinterpretation of the concept of truth is very reminiscent of the understanding of freedom in totalitarian states, especially of the Soviet idea of utmost freedom lying in the individual's being totally bound.

12. For details see G. Mensching, "Abhängigkeit und Selbständigkeit im Protestantismus," in L. v. Wiese, Vol. I, pp. 200ff, and *Katholische Kultprobleme,* 1927; H. Frick, *Vergleichende Religionswissenschaft* (1928), pp. 86ff.

13. L. Fendt, *Der lutherische Gottesdienst des 16. Jahrhunderts,* 1923.

14. E. Troeltsch, *Die Soziallehren der christlichen Kirchen und Gruppen* (1912), p. 449.

15. J. Rathje, *Die Welt des freien Protestantismus,* 1952.

16. Cf. G. Mensching, *Soziologie der Religion* (2nd ed., 1968), pp. 180ff.

17. Smyrn, 7, 2. H. von Campenhausen writes (in *Kirchliches Amt und geistliche Vollmacht in den ersten drei Jahrhunderten* [1953], p. 108: "For Ignatius, unity is the encompassing cosmic and ecclesiastical principle."

18. A. Jeremias, *Handbuch der altorientalischen Geisteskultur* (1913), p. 173.

19. Cf. the famous 4th Eclogue of Vergil. For details see H. Lietzmann, *Der Weltheiland,* 1909.

20. E. Troeltsch, p. 517.

21. Mirbt, *Quellen.* p. 348.
22. It is obvious that the methods of intolerance employed by a sacral totalitarian institution are very similar to those of modern totalitarian and authoritarian states. Institutional totalitarianism as a form of rule is evidently independent of the respective ideology connected with it. The forms are the same, and even the inner problematic involved is similar in each case, for according to the Soviet theory, a permanent revolution is, ultimately, to bring about the eschatological situation of a classless society. But under the impression of the failure of the world revolution—that is, the expected final eschatological event—to take place, this revolutionary attitude has been replaced largely by organizational and bureaucratic institutionalism. Something dynamic has now become something static. On the whole, these are phenomena which are very similar to the process that the Christian congregation underwent after waiting for the end of the world and the return of Christ, when it started to make itself at home in the world and to establish a static church organization replacing the live "dynamism" of early Christian faith.
23. Cf. Elbogen, "Jüdische Tradition," in RGG, 2nd ed. V (1951), 1247f.
24. The two other Synoptic Gospels also narrate this discussion: Mark 11:28; Luke 20:2.
25. Letter I of Clement 7:2; 40–42; Letter of Polycarp 7:2; Jud. 3.
26. "Quod ubique, quod semper, quod ab omnibus creditum est." Vincent of Lerins, *Commonitorium pro catholicae fidei antiquitate et universitate,* II, 3. Mirbt, *Quellen,* p. 73.
27. Ibid., II, 1: "Dublici modo munire fidem suam domino adiuvante deberet, primum scilicet divinae legis auctoritate, tum deinde ecclesiae catholicae traditione." Mirbt, *Quellen,* p. 73.
28. Tridentinum Sessio IV (8 April 1546). Mirbt, *Quellen,* p. 291.
29. Cf. G. Krüger, "Tradition," in RGG, 3rd ed., V, 1249; M. Werner, *Die Entstehung des christlichen Dogmas.* 2nd ed. (n.d.), pp. 171ff.
30. Cf. R. Hartmann, *Die Religion des Islam* (1944), p. 57; A. Guillaume, *The Traditions of Islam,* 1924.
31. Digha Nikāya XII, 8ff. Seidenstücker, *Pāli-Buddhismus* (1923), pp. 228f. It says here: " 'But then, Vāseṭṭha, is there a single one of the Brāhmans versed in the Three Vedas who has ever seen Brahmā face to face?' 'No, indeed, Gotama.' 'But is there then, Vāseṭṭha, a single one of the teachers of the Brāhmans versed in the Three Vedas who has seen Brahmā face to face?' 'No, indeed, Gotama!' . . . 'Well then, Vāseṭṭha, those ancient Rsis of the Brāhmans versed in the Three Vedas, the authors of the verses, whose ancient form of words so chaunted, uttered, or composed, the Brāhmans of today chaunt over again or repeat; intoning or reciting exactly as has been intoned or recited . . . did even they speak thus, saying: 'We know it, we have seen it, where Brahmā is, whence Brahmā is, whither Brahmā is?' 'Not so, Gotama!' . . . 'So that [says Buddha] the Brāhmans versed in the three Vedas have forsooth

said thus: 'What we know not, what we have not seen, to a state of union with that we can show the way, and can say: 'This is the straight path, this is the direct way which leads him, who acts according to it, into a state of union with Brahmā!' " (SBE XI, 172, trans. T. W. Rhys Davids).

32. Cf., for instance, Jeremiah 7:22ff: "For in the day that I brought them out of the land of Egypt, I did not speak to your fathers or command them concerning burnt offerings and sacrifices. But this command I gave them, 'Obey my voice, and I will be your God. . . .' "

33. E.g., Matthew 23:4, "They [the Scribes and Pharisees] bind heavy burdens, hard to bear, and lay them on men's shoulders."

34. K. Jaspers, *Psychologie der Weltanschauungen*, 1925.

35. This is how Hans Schär sums up the views of Jaspers. H. Schär, *Erlösungsvorstellungen und ihre psychologischen Aspekte* (1950), p. 285.

36. H. Schär, p. 296.

37. Ibid., p. 316.

38. We have to think here of specific cult forms, sacred objects and persons, as well as of all kinds of conceptual expressions—creeds, holy scriptures, dogmatic formulations, and ethical norms.

39. Think also of the antithesis between those who are pious by profession and those who are called, between church officers and men with spiritual authority. Cf. H. v. Campenhausen, *Kirchliches Amt und geistliche Vollmacht in den ersten drei Jahrhunderten* (1953), 2nd ed, 1963.

40. Yashomitra, *Commentary to Vasubhandu's Abhidharma-Kosha*. Quoted in H. von Glasenapp, *Die fünf grossen Religionen* (1951), p. 451.

41. *Brihad Brahma Samhita* 4, 8. Quoted in R. Otto, *Vishnu Nārāyana* (1923), p. 42.

42. This is also to be said about the book of the Jesuit Albert Hartmann, *Toleranz und christlicher Glaube* [Tolerance and Christian Faith], 1955. The author understands tolerance as the attitude of love toward fellowmen, or rather fellow-Christians, as demanded by the Christian idea of love. At the same time he maintains the exclusiveness of Christianity and rejects what he calls "the relativizing concept of tolerance." On p. 141 he says, "The tolerance that Christians should practice amongst themselves has its source, at depth, in their love of the common Lord. The truth for which they struggle together is His word and His charge. The opponent (in this case) is not an enemy who must be fought, but a disciple of Christ who is following his Lord to the best of his insight." This idea of tolerance implies but a general attitude of Christian neighborly love which does not acknowledge the truth-value of the other person's religious views.

43. Cf., for instance, the book of Ernst G. Rüsch, *Toleranz, eine theologische Untersuchung und eine aktuelle Auseinandersetzung* [Tolerance: a theological analysis and a discussion of a matter of current relevance] (Zollikon-Zurich, 1955). This theologian, bent upon maintaining an

exclusive monopoly to truth, strictly rejects every kind of religious relativity, for in his eyes, it is an especially reprehensible attitude. He even claims, "When there is no religious intolerance, there is no faith at all in the sense of the New Testament, for that faith would not be faith in the Biblical, the one and only, holy God" (p. 31).

44. Quoted in N. Macnicol, *Is Christianity Unique?* (1936), pp. 168f.

45. Bernard of Clairvaux, *ep.* 457. Migne, *Patr. Lat.* 182, 651.

46. The bishopric of Bamberg was established in 1007, so that, among other things, "the paganism of the Slavs there would be destroyed and the memory of the Christian name celebrated." *Monumenta Germaniae historica, Diplomata Heinr.*, II, n. 143, p. 170, 40f.

47. Cf., for instance, Devaranne, *Der gegenwärtige Geisteskampf um Ostasien,* 1928. On pp. 24ff the close connection betwen religion and politics is discussed; the notorious Treaty of Peking (1860) is a classical example of imperialistic missionary practices.

48. Quoted in C. F. Andrews, *Mahatma Gandhi's Ideas* (1929), 3rd imp., 1949, p. 96. A similar view is expressed by the anthropologist Pitt-Rivers in *The Clash of Cultures and Contact of Races,* p. 240. (Quoted in S. Radhakrishnan, *Eastern Religions and Western Thought* [2nd ed., 1940], p. 329.) Pitt-Rivers thinks that "Christian proselytism has done irretrievable harm to native races by disintegrating their culture."

49. Julius E. Lips, *The Savage Hits Back* (1937), p. 22. (Quoted in Radhakrishnan, p. 333.)

50. *Baptist Missionary Review,* April 1937.

51. Hughes, *The Invasion of China by the Western World* (1937), p. 54f.

52. The Catholic Church has reinterpreted non-Christian cults in a Christian sense for centuries. In 601, for instance, Pope Gregory the Great wrote to the Abbot Mellitus, telling him to save the pagan temples and to turn them into Christian churches, "for if the temples are built well, it is necessary to change them from spots where demons are venerated to places where the true God is worshipped, so that the people, upon seeing that their temples are not destroyed, may give up their error and turn to and worship the true God, assembling at their familiar places all the more confidently." (Mirbt, *Quellen.* p. 100.)

53. Cf. H. Frick, *Vergleichende Religionswissenschaft* (1928), p. 53f; H. Fischer, *Jesu letzter Wille* (4th ed., 1912), p. 92.

III. THE POSTULATE OF TOLERANCE

1. Cf. H. Bonnet, *Reallexikon der ägyptischen Religionsgeschichte* (1952), pp. 430ff.

2. Uraeus is the golden snake adorning the forehead with which the Egyptians embellished their gods.

3. A. Moret, *Le rituel du culte divin journalier en Egypte* (1902), p. 139.

4. Hymn Book of Amon, dating from the time of Amenophis III. RGL 10, p. 6.
5. Mahānārāyana-Upanishad 63,2.
6. Aitreya Brahmana 1,6,7.
7. In the Brihadāranyaka-Upanishad (2,1,20), the divine Brahman is termed the *satyasya satyam,* which can mean "reality of reality" or "truth of truth," both implications being the same. In Taitt.-Up., it says, "The Brahman is truth [*satyam*]."
8. *Theologisches Wörterbuch* (ed. G. Kittel), 1,236. (English trans. and ed. J. R. Coates, 1949–61.)
9. Joka (ca. 700 A.D.). From Ohasama-Faust, *Zen Der lebendige Buddhismus in Japan* (1925), p. 71.
10. *Theologisches Wörterbuch* 1, 239ff.
11. The pastoral epistles talk repeatedly of the right teaching, for example, 2 Timothy 4:3f, Titus 1:9 and various other places speak of the "sound doctrine."
12. Cf. H. von Campenhausen, *Kirchliches Amt und geistliche Vollmacht in den ersten drei Jahrhunderten,* 1953.
13. H. Gunkel, *Das Märchen im Alten Testament* (1917), p. 6. Cf. H. Gunkel, *The Legends of Genesis; the Biblical saga and history* (trans. W. H. Carruth), 1964.
14. RGG, 1st ed., IV, 618.
15. Cf. G. Mensching, *Das heilige Wort* (1937), pp. 37ff.
16. Cf. my essay, "Religiöse Ursymbole der Menschheit," in *Studium Generale* (1955), Fasc. 6.
17. Some time ago, a book was published by Henry L. Miéville, *Toleranz und Wahrheit, ein philosophisches und politisches Problem* [Tolerance and Truth, a Philosophical and Political problem] (Bern, 1955). As the subtitle indicates, this study does not deal with religious tolerance alone, or even primarily. Yet it has a relationship to our analysis, as the main title signifies, which happens to be the same as ours. Miéville also starts out from the concept of truth, seeking to establish tolerance on that basis. With regard to content, however, there are great differences between that study and this one. Miéville also differentiates between two concepts of truth, a static and a functional one. According to his view, truth is, first, something given, something "that exists as we find it, independent of all our doing. This kind of truth we discover one fine day like the Prince who discovers Sleeping Beauty in the forest" (p. 14). Looking at the matter closely, says Miéville, it becomes obvious, however, that this concept is inadequate. Truth is hence, second, not something ready and given, but something in the becoming, the cognitive human mind being always involved in its genesis. "Truth is based upon something that exists or is valid, but it is not something existing or valid in itself. It is always also the effect of the perceiving subject, that is, it is to be understood as a particular expression of a subject–object relation-

ship" (p. 14). Hence Miéville accepts only one concept of truth as valid, the functional one. It can readily be seen that the two concepts of truth differentiated here do not correspond to the two concepts of truth we have distinguished. We saw that truth is, in the first place, reality. But this is not the static truth meant by Miéville who has only rational truth in mind when he speaks of religious truth. He rejects the static concept of truth in religion, because truth, according to him, is the best possible expression of the subject–object relationship, which is always limited "on every level in the development of human thinking" (p. 20). Furthermore, he is of the opinion that the thinkers concerned with tolerance always base their postulate of tolerance on the "static, absolutistic concept of truth" (p. 21). This truth, he says, always springs either from the objective revelation of God occurring without active human involvement, or is based upon the decree of the Church. Of such truth, man has only to take cognizance; he is not involved in its establishment, or becoming. "This is how a totalitarian state acts, and this is how an ecclesiastical authority (not only the Christian Church) behaves when it claims to maintain strict orthodoxy. In this setting, deviating opinions or religious teachings are reprimanded and condemned, for they constitute rebellion against God; disobedience against the revealed word and its mediators; heresy" (p. 23f). I completely agree with this criticism, but not only because free personal insight is excluded in that situation, as the author implies when he points out, "The human mind does not really grasp truth if it cannot form an opinion in complete freedom" (p. 26). The author is quite right in condemning every kind of coercion in religion. But he fails to inquire whether rational insight is at all decisive in religion. Hence the question is not whether this authoritarian idea of truth is to be rejected because it excludes man's free insight, but whether the rational concept of truth upon which the author bases his study is at all legitimate in the sphere of religion. The attitude Miéville postulates as tolerance is, in our terminology, formal tolerance allowing for free intellectual development. "True tolerance wants to promote the development of the intellect; and this can only happen in a harmonious situation through freely gained and deepened insight, but not if a fixed system of truths is imposed upon a person as a guiding principle" (p. 28). On the basis of Comparative Religion, we would certainly admit that general freedom of insight is absolutely necessary and that the demand for such liberty must doubtless be voiced. But Miéville does not see that "truth" can also pertain to a nonrational reality and that the demand for religious tolerance should not only be of the formal but also of the intrinsic type in the sense that the possibility of true encounter with the Divine in the faith of another person is acknowledged.

18. I take up this interpretation of the claim to absoluteness from my study *Volksreligion und Weltreligion* [Ethnic Religion and World Religion"], which appeared in 1938 and is now no longer available.

19. Exodus 20:2.
20. Malachi 1:11.
21. Psalm 96:3ff
22. Rigveda 2,12,15.
23. Ibid, 4,30,1.
24. Ibid., 2,33,3.
25. Ibid., 1, 127, 8.
26. R. Otto, *Vishnu Narāyāna*. p. 42
27. Buddha says, "Having acquired enlightenment by myself, whom could I call my teacher? I have no teacher, one like unto me is not found. In the world with its *devas* (gods) there is no one equal to me" (Majjh. Nik. 26).
28. Quoted from Rāmacandra. R. Otto, *Siddhānta des Rāmānuja* (1923), p. 147.
29. Surah 3:79.
30. E. Troeltsch, *Die Absolutheit des Christentums und die Religionsgeschichte* (3rd ed., 1929), p. 96. At another point, Troeltsch writes, "It [one's own religion] is the countenance of God as revealed to us. It is the way in which we, according to our own manner, receive God's revelation and react to it . . . We regard it as final and absolute because we have nothing else, and because we discern the sound of God's voice in what we have. But this does not exclude the fact that other peoples living under quite different conditions experience their contact with divine life in quite a different way, and can therefore also have a religion which has developed as they have, and from which they cannot disassociate themselves so long as they remain what they are. And therefore they can regard it, quite honestly, as being absolutely valid for themselves, and can lend expression to this absolute validity according to the demands of their own religious feelings." E. Troeltsch, *Der Historismus und seine Überwindung* [Historism and its Overcoming] (1924), p. 78.
31. F. Scheiermacher, *On Religion: Speeches to its Cultured Despisers* (trans. J. Oman) (1958), p. 214.
32. Ibid., p. 233.
33. Cf. my description of the living core of religions in *Die Religion,* 1959.
34. Schleiermacher in his *Speeches* apparently had something similar in mind when he said: ". . . the only remaining way for a truly individual religion to arise is to select some one of the great relations of mankind in the world to the Highest Being, and, in a definite way, make it the center and refer to it all others . . . Hereby a distinctive spirit and a common character enter the whole at the same time" (pp. 222f).
35. F. Heiler, "Die Religionsgeschichte als Wegbereiterin für die Zusammenarbeit der Religionen," *Theologische Literaturzeitung* (1953), No. 12, p. 730. (English trans. in *The History of Religions: Essays in Methodology,* ed. M. Eliade and J. M. Kitagawa, 1959.)
36. Joseph Schnitzer, *Savonarola* (1923), Vol. I, p. 258.

37. Cf. the important work of the Swedish bishop Tor Andrae, *Mohammed, the Man and His Faith* (1935, trans. by T. Menzil, 1960).

38. Goethe, *Noten und Abhandlungen zum West-östlichen Divan* (Ch. "Ältere Perser" [Ancient Persians]).

39. In addition to various scholars like H. von Glasenapp, K. Geldner, O. Schrader, and others, I refer especially to my teacher R. Otto, who promoted the understanding of Indian religiousness by translating Indian texts and publishing comparative studies on that subject.

40. *Commentary to Galatians*, 1535. (WE 1843, *Opera Exegetica*, Vol. VII, 2, p. 196.) English trans. quoted from *Luther's Works*, ed. and trans. by J. Pelikan, Vol. 26 (1963), pp. 399f.

41. Cf. my book *Die Idee der Sünde, ihre Entwicklung in den Hochreligionen des Orients und Okzidents.* [The Idea of Sin; its development in the high religions of the Orient and Occident], 1931; see also my *Zur Metaphysik des Ich* [On the Metaphysics of the Self], 1934.

42. G. van der Leeuw, *Religion in Essence and Manifestation* (trans. J. E. Turner), 1938, reprint in 2 vols., 1963; G. Mensching, *Die Religion*, 1959; M. Eliade, *Patterns in Comparative Religion* (trans. R. Sheed), 1958, 1963.

43. F. Schleiermacher, *On Religion: Speeches* . . . p. 154.

44. Cf. W. Hellpach, *Grundriß der Religionspsychologie*, 1951; H. Schär, *Erlösungsvorstellungen und ihre psychologischen Aspekte*, 1950.

45. H. Schär, p. 9f.

46. For more details see G. Mensching, *Gut und Böse im Glauben der Völker* [Good and Evil in the Belief of Peoples], 2nd ed., 1950.

47. Cf. F. Heiler, "Mystische und Prophetische Frömmigkeit" ["Mystic and Prophetic Religiosity"], in that author's *Das Gebet* (4th ed., 1921), pp. 248ff. (English title: *Prayer*, trans. S. McComb and J. E. Park, 1960.)

48. P. Bayle, *Commentaire philosophique sur les paroles de Jésus-Christ: Contrains les d'entrer*, Part 2, Ch. 6, p. 418.

49. Quoted here from Rainer Maria Rilke, *The Book of Hours* (trans. A. L. Peck, London, 1961), p. 104.

50. From R. Tagore, "Drama Malini," Act 2, in that author's *Collected Poems and Plays* (1936), p. 499.

51. Quoted in Romain Rolland, *Mahatma Gandhi* (1924), reprint 1968, p. 19.

52. Quoted from R. Tagore's German Works (*Gesammelte Werke*, ed. H. Meyer-Franck, Vol. 8, "Flüstern de Seele," § 69, pp. 282f) (retranslated).

53. ". . . the feeling of an indissoluble bond is there [with his own wife]. Even so I feel about Hinduism with all its faults and limitations. Nothing elates me so much as the music of the Gita or the Ramayana . . . I know that vice is going on today in all the great Hindu shrines, but I love them in spite of their failings." In R. Rolland, p. 19.

54. As Paul saw it when he said, "For now we see in a mirror dimly, but then face to face. Now I know in part; then I shall understand fully, even as I have been fully understood" (1 Corinthians 13:12f).

55. *Young India,* Oct. 20, 1927 (retranslated).
56. *Harrijan,* Sept. 28, 1935 (retranslated).
57. R. Otto, *Vishnu Nārāyana. Texte zur indischen Gottesmystik,* 1923. In the appendix there is an essay entitled "Universal religion?" Quotes from pp. 227f.
58. Joka (ca. 700 A.D.) In Ohasama-Faust, *Zen. Der lebendige Buddhismus in Japan* (1925), p. 82.

Bibliography

(Revised and Adapted)

Adeney, W. F. "Toleration," *Hastings' Encyclopaedia of Religion and Ethics*, XII, 360ff.

Alberti, W. *Aufrichte Nachricht von der Religion, Sitten und Gebräuche der Quäker*, 1750.

Anshen, R. N., ed. *Freedom: Its Meaning*, 1940.

Arnold, T. W. "Persecution. Muhammadan," *Hastings' Encyclopaedia of Religion and Ethics*, IX, 765ff.

Bainton, R. H. "The Struggle for Religious Liberty," *Church History*, X (1941), 95ff.

Basagne, H. *Tolérance des religions*, 1684.

Bates, M. S. *Religious Liberty*, 1945.

Benz, E. *Die Ostkirche*, 1952.

———. *Geist und Leben der Ostkirche*, 1957. English title: *The Eastern Orthodox Church* (trans. R. and C. Winston), 1963.

Binchy, D. A. *Church and State in Fascist Italy*, 1941.

Binyon, L. *Akbar*, 1932.

Boehme, Jakob. *Jakob Böhmes sämtliche Werke*, ed. K. W. Schiebler, 1832–1860. English ed.: William Law, *The Works of Jacob Behmen* . . . , 4 vols., 1764–1781.

Bolshakoff, S. *The Christian Church and the Soviet State*, 1942.

Bonet-Maury, G. *La liberté de conscience en France, depuis l'Édit de Nantes jusqu'à la séparation, 1598–1905*, 2nd ed., 1909.

Borngräber, O. *Das Erwachen der philosophischen Spekulation der Reformationszeit in ihrem stufenweisen Fortschritt, beleuchtet an Schwenkfeld, Thamer und Sebastian Franck*, 1909.

Bouché-Leclerq. *L'intolerance religieuse et de la politique*, 1911.

Brockdorf, C. von. *Die englische Aufklärungsphilosophie*, 1924.

Bull *Ad Extirpanda*, 1252.

Bull *Unam Sanctam*, 1302.

Cadoux, C. J. *Roman Catholicism and Freedom*, 4th ed., 1947.

Campenhausen, H. von. *Kirchliches Amt und geistliche Vollmacht in den ersten drei Jahrhunderten*, 1953. 2nd ed., 1963.

———, and H. Chadwick. *Jerusalem and Rome; the Problem of Authority in the Early Church*, 1966.

Carpenter, J. E. *Comparative Religion*, 1913.

Castellio, S. *De haereticis, an sint persequendi*, 1554. English title: *Concerning Heretics* (trans. and ed. R. H. Bainton), 1935.

Codex Theodosianus [Theodosian Code].

Coulton, G. G. *Inquisition and Liberty*, 1938. Reprint, 1959.

Dale, R. W. *History of English Congregationalism*, 2nd ed., 1907.

Dargaud, J.-M. *Histoire de la liberté religieuse en France et de ses fondateurs*, 1859.

Davis, H. C. (Miller). *Some Aspects of Religious Liberty of Nationals in the Near East: A Collection of Documents*, 1938.

Donais. *L'Inquisition. Ses origines, sa procédure*, 1906.

Eliade, M. *Traité d'histoire des Religions*, 1949. English title: *Patterns in Comparative Religion* (trans. R. Sheed), 1958. Reprint, 1963.

Eymericus, V. O. P. *Directorium Inquisitorum*, 1585.

Fawkes, A. "Persecution. Roman Catholic," *Hastings' Encyclopaedia of Religion and Ethics*, IX, 749ff.

Febronius, J. N. (von Hontheim). *De statu Ecclesiae et legitima potestate Romani Pontificus liber singularis, ad reuniendos dissidentes in Religione Christianos compositus*, 2nd ed., 1765–1774.

Finkelstein, L. *The Pharisees: The Sociological Background of their Faith*, 4 vols., 1938. 3rd ed., 1962.

Firth, C. H. *Oliver Cromwell and the Rule of the Puritans in England*, 1900. Reprint, 1961.

Flade, P. *Das römische Inquisitionsverfahren in Deutschland bis zu den Hexenprozessen*, 1902.

Franck, S. *Chronika, Zeitbuch und Geschichtsbibel*, 1531.

———. *Paradoxa*, 1534.

Freund, M. *Die Idee der Toleranz im England der grossen Revolution*, 1927.

Frick, H. *Vergleichende Religionswissenschaft*, 1928.

Fürstenau, H. *Das Grundrecht der Religionsfreiheit nach seiner geschichtlichen Entwicklung und heutigen Geltung in Deutschland*, 1891.

Fuhrmann, C. H. *De tolerantiae religiosae affectibus civilibus*.

Garbe, R. von. *Kaiser Akbar von Indien*, 1909. English title: *Akbar, Emperor of India . . .* (trans. L. G. Robinson), 1909.

Geiger, A. *Die indoarische Gesellschaftsordnung*, 1935.

Gerhard, J. *An diversae religiones in bene constituta republica tolerandae*, 1604.

Glasenapp, H. von. *Der Hinduismus*, 1922.

———. *Die fünf grossen Religionen*, 1951.

———. *Die fünf Weltreligionen*, 1963.

Goldziher, I. *Vorlesungen über den Islam,* 3rd ed., 1963.
———. *Mohammed and Islam* (trans. K. C. Seeley), 1917.
Groot, J. J. M. De. *Sectarianism and Religious Persecution in China,* 2 vols., 1903–1904. Reprint (2 vols. in one), 1917.
Grubb, E. *What is Quakerism?* 4th ed., 1940.
Gundert, W. *Japanische Religionsgeschichte,* 1935. Reprint, 1943.
Gwatkin, H. M. *Religious Toleration in England* (in *The Cambridge Modern History,* V, 1908).
Haas, J. A. W. *The Problem of the Christian State,* 1928.
Hardemann, J. "Relation between Government and Religions in the Netherlands East Indies," *International Review of Missions,* XXXI (1942), 315ff.
Hartmann, A. *Toleranz und christlicher Glaube,* 1955.
Hauck, A. *Der Kampf um die Gewissensfreiheit,* 1889.
Hauer, J. W. *Toleranz und Intoleranz in den nichtchristlichen Religionen,* 1961.
Heiler, F. "Die Religionsgeschichte als Wegbereiterin für die Zusammenarbeit der Religionen," *Theol. Literaturzeitung,* 12 (1953), 730ff. English trans. in *The History of Religions: Essays in Methodology* (ed. M. Eliade and J. Kitagawa), 2nd ed., 1962.
———. *Der Katholizismus,* 1923.
Hermelink, H. *Der Toleranzgedanke im Reformationsjahrhundert,* 1908.
Holtom, D. C. *Modern Japan and Shinto Nationalism,* 1943. Rev. ed., 1963.
Howard, G. P. *Religious Liberty in Latin America?* 1944.
Hügel, F. von. *Eternal Life,* 1912.
———. *Essays and Addresses on the Philosophy of Religion,* 1921. Reprint, 1930–1931.
Jones, Rufus M. *Spiritual Reformers in the 16th and 17th Centuries,* 1914. Reprint, 1959.
Jordan, W. K. *The Development of Religious Toleration in England,* 4 vols., 1932–1940 (Reformation to 1660). Reprint 1965.
Karrer, O. *Das Religiöse in der Menschheit und das Christentum,* 3rd ed., 1936.
———. *Religions of Mankind* (trans. E. I. Watkin), 1945.
Köhler, W. *Reformation und Ketzerprozess,* 1901.
Lactantius, L. C. F. *Divinae institutiones.* English title: *The Divine Institutes* (trans. M. F. McDonald), Books I–VII, 1964.
Die Lage der Protestanten in katholischen Ländern (ed. Evangelischer Verlag, Zollikon–Zürich), 1953.
Lea, H. C. *A History of the Inquisition of Spain,* 4 vols., 1906–1907. Reprint, 1966.
Leeuw, G. van der. *Phaenomenologie der Religion,* 2nd ed., 1955. English title: *Religion in Essence and Manifestation: A Study in Phenomenology* (trans. J. E. Turner), 2 vols., 1963. Reprint, 1964.
Locke, J. *Epistolae de tolerantia,* 1689. English title: *A Letter Concerning Toleration* (Latin and English texts rev. and ed. M. Montuori), 1963.

Luther, M. *Von weltlicher Obrigkeit*, 1523. Volume eleven of *D. Martin Luthers Werke* (Weimar Edition), 1883–1919. English translation in part: *Luther's Works* (ed. J. Pelikan and H. T. Lehman), 1955–

Luzzatti, L. *God in Freedom: Studies in the Relations between Church and State*, 1930.

Marsilius of Padua. *Defensor pacis*, 1326. English title: *Marsilius of Padua, the Defender of Peace* (trans. A. Gewirth), vol. 2, 1956.

Matagrin, A. *Histoire de la tolérance religieuse*, 1905.

Mensching, G. *Vergleichende Religionswissenschaft*, 2nd ed., 1949.

————. "Abhängigkeit und Selbständigkeit im Protestantismus," in L. von Wiese, ed., *Abhängigkeit und Selbständigkeit im sozialen Leben*, 1951.

————. *Volksreligion und Weltreligion*, 1938.

————. *Soziologie der Religion*, 1947. (French trans., 1951.) 2nd ed., 1968.

————. *Die Religion*, 1959. (English trans. forthcoming, title: *Patterns and Structures of Religion*.)

————. *Soziologie der grossen Religionen*, 1966.

————. *Der Irrtum in der Religion*, 1969.

Meyerhof, M. *Persisch-türkische Mystik*, 1921.

Miéveille, H.-L. *Tolérance et vérité; suivi de liberté et démocratie*, 1949.

Mill, John Stuart. *On Liberty*, 1859. (New ed. by C. V. Shields, 1956.)

Milton, John. *Thoughts on True Religion, Schism and Toleration* (ed. B. Flower), 1881. (For a new ed., see D. M. Wolfe, ed., Milton's *Complete Prose Works*, 1953.)

————. *The Ready-and-Easy Way to Establish a Free Commonwealth*, 1915.

Mirbt, C. *Quellen zur Geschichte des Papstums und des römischen Katholizismus*, 4th ed., 1924. (6th ed., 1967.)

Montesquieu, C. L. de. *De l'esprit des lois*, 1759. (New French ed. by G. Truc, 1962.) English title: *The Spirit of the Laws* (trans. T. Nugent, 1962).

Monzel, N. "Abhängigkeit und Selbständigkeit im Katholizismus," in L. von Wiese, ed., *Abhängigkeit und Selbständigkeit im sozialen Leben*, 1951.

Mookerji, R. *Asoka*, 1928.

More, Thomas. *Utopia*, 1516. (New edition by E. Surtz and J. H. Hexter, 1965.) English ed., trans. P. Turner and P. K. Marshall, 1965.

Moreland, W. H. *From Akbar to Aurangzeb*, 1923.

Müller, Karl. *Über religiöse Toleranz*, 1912.

Naumann, H. *Der staufische Ritter*, 1936.

Nestle, W. *Grierchische Geistesgeschichte*, 1944. Reprint, 1956.

Ohm, T. *Die Liebe zu Gott in den nichtchristlichen Religionen*, 1950. 2nd ed., 1957.

————. *Asiens Kritik am abendländischen Christentum*, 1948. English title: *Asia Looks at Western Christianity* (trans. I. Marinoff), 1959.

Otto, R. *West-östliche Mystik*, 1926. English title: *Mysticism East and West* (trans. B. L. Bracey and R. C. Payne), 1932. Reprint, 1962.

Paulus, N. *Protestantismus und Toleranz im 16. Jahrhundert*, 1911.

Radhakrishnan, S. *Eastern Religions and Western Thought*, 2nd ed., 1951. Reprint, 1959.

——. *The Hindu View of Life*, 1927. Reprint, 1962.

——. *Religion and Society*, 1947. Reprint, 1956.

Rathje, J. *Die Welt des freien Protestantismus*, 1952.

Reimann, A. *Sebastian Franck als Geschichtsphilosoph*, 1921.

Reischauer, A. K. "The Development of Religious Liberty of Modern Japan," *Chinese Recorder*, LVIII (1927), 751ff.

Religionsgeschichtliches Lesebuch (ed. A. Bertholet), 2nd ed., 1926.

"Religious Persecution," *Report of Conditions in Occupied Territories*, No. 3 (London: Inter Allied Information Committee), 1943.

Rüsch, E. G. *Toleranz*, 1955.

Schenkheld, E. "Religiöse Gespräche in der deutschen epischen Dichtung bis zum Ausgang des 13. Jahrhunderts" (unpublished thesis), 1930.

Schomerus, H. W. *Meister Eckhart und Mannikka Vāśāga*, 1936.

Seaton. *The Theory of Toleration*, 1911.

Selbis, W. B. *Congregationalism*, 1927.

Simon, J. *La liberté de conscience*, 4th ed., 1867.

Smith, V. A. *Akbar, The Great Mogul, 1542–1605*, 1917. 2nd ed., 1958.

Tertullian, Q. S. F. *Ad Scapulam* (ed. A. Quacquarelli), 1957. For an English translation, see: Tertullian. *Disciplinary, Moral, and Ascetical Works* (trans. R. Arbesmann, E. J. Daly, and E. A. Quain), 1959.

Troeltsch, E. *Die Soziallehren der christlichen Kirchen und Gruppen*, I 12. English title: *The Social Teachings of the Christian Churches* (trans. O. Wyon), 1931. Reprint 1960.

——. *Die Bedeutung des Protestantismus für die Entstehung der modernen Welt*, 1906. English title: *Protestantism and Progress* (trans. W. Montgomery), 1912. Reprint, 1958.

——. *Die Absolutheit des Christentums und die Religionsgeschichte*, 3rd ed., 1929.

——. *Der Historismus und seine Übersindung*, 1924.

Ulbach, L. *La Holande et la liberté de penser au 17e et 18e siècle*, 1884.

Vermeersch, A. *Tolerance*, 1913.

Völker, K. *Toleranz und Intoleranz im Zeitalter der Reformation*, 1912.

Voltaire, F. M. A. de. *Traité sur la tolerance*, 1763. For an English translation, see: *The Works of Voltaire* (ed. J. Morley), 1927.

Witte, J. *Die Christusbetschaft und die Religionen*, 1936.

Workman, H. B. *Persecution in the Early Church*, 3rd ed., 1911. Reprint, 1960.

Index